D1565362

Introduction to
Pagan Studies

THE PAGAN STUDIES SERIES

SERIES EDITORS
Wendy Griffin (California State University, Long Beach)
and Chas S. Clifton (University of Southern Colorado)

The label "Pagan studies" marks the movement of scholarly inquiry into a diversity of religious expressions formerly considered new religious movements. The definition of paganism advocated by sociologist of religion Michael York—"an affirmation of interactive and polymorphic sacred relationships by individual or community with the tangible, sentient, and nonempirical"—emphasizes what these spiritual traditions have in common: a feeling for "the sacred" that is non-monotheistic, based on relationship rather than revelation and scripture, and often includes an immanent dimension for landforms, plants, and animals.

The traditional approach to the study of religions assumes that formal religious traditions are normative, and so misses religious sects that are inherently more fluid and more ambiguous. The approach taken by Pagan studies permits examination of highly dynamic and mutable religious communities within a hypermodern society, and demonstrates the increasing religious pluralism of our times. This shift in perspective will be a welcome addition to the intellectual endeavor to understand and give meaning to a wide variety of religious experience.

The Pagan Studies Series is interdisciplinary in nature and aims to include both junior scholars who seek to turn strong dissertations into publishable monographs and senior scholars who are looking for the kind of attention a small academic press can give their work. The most exciting feature of the series is that it will take the lead in building Pagan studies into a legitimate field by focusing research on this unexplored topic.

BOOKS IN THE SERIES

Researching Paganisms, edited by Jenny Blain, Douglas Ezzy, and Graham Harvey

Her Hidden Children: The Rise of Wicca and Paganism in America, by Chas S. Clifton

Introduction to Pagan Studies, by Barbara Jane Davy

Introduction to Pagan Studies

Barbara Jane Davy

ALTAMIRA
PRESS

A Division of
ROWMAN & LITTLEFIELD PUBLISHERS, INC.
Lanham • New York • Toronto • Plymouth, UK

Figures 1, 11, 13 are from *Rebirth of Witchcraft* by Doreen Valiente, copyright Phoenix Publishing; figure 8 is from *A Witches' Bible* by Janet and Stewart Farrar, copyright Phoenix Publishing; 14 is from *What Witches Do* by Stewart Farrar, copyright Phoenix Publishing; 15 is from *Eight Sabbats* for Witches, copyright Phoenix Publishing, used with permission.

ALTAMIRA PRESS

A division of Rowman & Littlefield Publishers, Inc.
A wholly owned subsidiary of The Rowman & Littlefield Publishing Group, Inc.
4501 Forbes Boulevard, Suite 200
Lanham, MD 20706
www.altamirapress.com

Estover Road
Plymouth PL6 7PY
United Kingdom

Copyright © 2007 by AltaMira Press

British Library Cataloguing in Publication Information Available

Library of Congress Cataloging-in-Publication Data

Davy, Barbara Jane, 1972–
 Introduction to pagan studies / Barbara Jane Davy.
   p. cm. — (The pagan studies series)
 Includes bibliographical references and index.
 ISBN-13: 978-0-7591-0818-9 (cloth : alk. paper)
 ISBN-10: 0-7591-0818-8 (cloth : alk. paper)
 ISBN-13: 978-0-7591-0819-6 (pbk. : alk. paper)
 ISBN-10: 0-7591-0819-6 (pbk. : alk. paper)
 1. Neopaganism. I. Title. II. Series.

 BP605.N46D38 2006
 299'.94—dc22   2006010885

Printed in the United States of America

™ The paper used in this publication meets the minimum requirements of American National Standard for Information Sciences—Permanence of Paper for Printed Library Materials, ANSI/NISO Z39.48-1992.

Contents

Figures

Introduction

A middle-aged bookstore owner is firmly "in the broom closet" and reveals himself as Pagan only to his most trusted coreligionists. A thirty-something lesbian **polyamorist*** is selectively out as gay and/or Pagan to people she trusts in different contexts. A college professor near retirement seems to be "sitting on the fence," appearing to be Pagan to other Pagans, but to be someone who studies Pagans rather than a practitioner when delivering conference papers. A conservative civil servant is openly Pagan and exchanges working Christmas Day for taking the winter solstice as a religious holiday. An internationally known **anarchist** political activist self-identifies as a Pagan, a Witch, and a practitioner of feminist spirituality, depending on the context in which she finds herself. An exhibitionist couple of twenty-year-olds who like to display their **BDSM** fantasies at public festivals, which they see as a safe place for experimentation, are Pagan. An eight-month-old baby, newly welcomed to the **Craft** through a **Wiccaning** ceremony, is being raised Pagan.

Contemporary Pagans are found in all walks of life and are of all political persuasions. Many Pagans are average people, but some are markedly **countercultural**, preferring lifestyles alternative to the mainstream. Some practitioners are attracted to Paganism because of its perceived participation in the countercultural movements that began in the 1960s. Being Pagan can mean living a modern hippy lifestyle, smoking up and communing with the faeries, and participating in outdoor rituals in the nude, but it can also mean sitting through long boring meetings in

---

*Terms that appear in bold are explained in the glossary.

urban community centers. Most Pagans have a middle-class background.¹ Although they tend to have higher levels of education than the general population, many choose lifestyles that put them at or below a middle-class standard of living.² Some early studies of Paganism emphasized its appeal to "outsiders" or social misfits because of the secrecy of the teachings of some traditions, and because of its status as a marginal religion. More recently, in part because of the Internet-based growth of Paganism, the profile of an average Pagan practitioner has become more mainstream, and younger, and there are more **solitaries**, which are practitioners who are not affiliated with Pagan groups.³ Pagans are becoming "successful, educated, and involved."⁴ They tend to be liberal middle-class college-educated Caucasians, some of whom choose to live quite comfortably. Women outnumber men in the religion by about two to one. Pagans are more politically active than average Americans, particularly when it comes to environmental issues, and Pagans support a number of countercultural attitudes and practices, such as **polyamory**, even if they do not enact such practices in their daily lives.⁵

The term "pagan" comes from the Latin *paganus*, plural *paganii*, which originally referred to rural peoples who did not accept the dominance of Roman culture, preferring their local government or *pagus*. The original pagans were people who had not joined the Christian movement and become Roman citizens.⁶ For a long time, "pagan" signified nonbeliever in Western culture and was used as a term for those who did not embrace Christianity or any of the other monotheistic faiths. More recently, people have adopted the term to describe the revived religious traditions of contemporary Paganism, sometimes called Neo-Paganism. Practitioners generally call themselves "Pagan," capitalizing the *P* to affirm that their religion is just as legitimate as any other faith. Some practitioners emphasize their links to pre-Christian traditions, calling their faith "the Old Religion," while others embrace it as a revivalist creation of modern times.

Pagan studies is the study of Paganism as a distinct religious tradition in the context of **world religions**. Some scholars prefer to discuss "paganism" (preferring to use a lowercase *p*) as a global and historical world religion including indigenous religions,⁷ but this text is restricted to commentary on the study of contemporary self-identified Pagans and their traditions. With a lowercase *p*, "paganism" usually refers to all religions that have resisted conversion to monotheistic traditions, including historical and contemporary peoples, while contemporary "Paganism" more often describes people who were raised in monotheistic traditions but have rejected them in favor of revivals and recreations of pre-Christian traditions. Contemporary Paganism does not have a missionary stance or project to convert everyone to its beliefs, so it does not strive to be a world religion by spreading throughout the world, but Pagans are found across the globe.

Some might suppose that Paganism is not a large enough religion to merit study as a world religion. There are two complications in determining who counts as "Pagan." First, Paganism is not organized into groups, like churches that keep membership rolls, and most countries, including the United States, do not include "Pagan," or a comparable alternative, as an option on their census forms, so compiling global numbers of self-identified Pagans is difficult. In addition, some people feel a need to hide their identification as Pagan from governmental authorities, due to fears of religious persecution. Second, there is debate about what is meant by "Pagan." With the inclusion of indigenous religions, between 5 and 6 percent of the world's population is small-*p* pagan, which is a statistically significant portion of the world's population. By comparison, this gives paganism more adherents than Judaism, Sikhism, Jainism, and Bahai, which together constitute less than 1 percent of the world's population and yet are routinely studied as world religions (perhaps with the exception of Sikhism).[8] Without the inclusion of indigenous religions, the global numbers of contemporary Pagan adherents are far fewer, totaling less than one million.

Pagan populations are concentrated in Britain, North America, Australia, and New Zealand, but they can also be found in smaller numbers throughout Europe and scattered through other parts of the world. Paganism became an official religion in Iceland in 1973 as Ásatrú. Ásatrúarfélagidr, the Ásatrú Society of Iceland, had 500 members in 2000, out of a population of 275,000, which amounts to about 0.2 percent. The 2001 census of New Zealand recorded 5,862 people as Pagan, out of a population of 3.7 million, which amounts to 0.158 percent. This appears to be somewhat above the percentages for Canada and Australia, which also publish census data on Pagans. The Canadian census of 2001 found 21,080 Pagans out of a population of 29,639,030, which amounts to 0.071 percent.[9] There may actually be more Canadians who are Pagan. In a study of Paganism in Canada, when respondents were asked how they would record their religion on the census, 25 percent indicated that they would choose something other than Pagan, despite the fact that they self-identify as practitioners of a Pagan denomination.[10]

As in Canada, the Australian Bureau of Statistics does not include "Paganism" as a choice on the census forms, but it does allow people to write in a choice, and it tabulates the results rather than simply classing them all as "other." The Australian census of 2001 recorded 24,156 adherents to "nature religion," a category in which they include Pagans, Wiccans, Druids, and **pantheists** (those who regard the Earth as a living being and/or who wholly identify the Earth with **divinity**) as well as **animists** (those who believe that all things are living and are possibly ensouled beings). According to these numbers, 0.13 percent of the Australian population was Pagan as of 2001.[11]

Estimates of the number of Pagans in the United States in the last few decades have varied from 50,000 to more than 750,000. In 1985, there were an estimated 50,000 to 100,000 self-identified Pagans in the United States, according to a practitioner-authored survey.[12] Within ten years, practitioner estimates had risen to 300,000.[13] Scholars began producing survey data in 1999, estimating between 150,000 and 200,000 practitioners, with some researchers indicating that there may be twice that many practitioners.[14] A practitioner-run Internet poll conducted in 1999–2000 estimated the American Pagan population to be 768,400. This disparity is not necessarily due to the difference between conservative academic estimates and those of enthusiastic practitioners, but also reflects the explosive growth of Paganism in the latter half of the 1990s, fueled by the Internet.[15] If there are 200,000 Pagans in the United States out of a population of 290 million, that makes 0.069 percent. If there are 750,000 Pagans, that would be 0.259 percent of the American population, which seems a bit high in comparison with actual statistics from the New Zealand, Australian, and Canadian censuses.

Estimates also vary on the number of Pagans in the United Kingdom. In 1996, 30,000 to 50,000 was a common estimate for the number of Pagans in the United Kingdom.[16] A 1997 study indicated that there are approximately 100,000 Pagans in the United Kingdom.[17] As of 1998, scholars estimated that there are between 110,000 and 120,000 practitioners of Goddess spirituality in the United Kingdom,[18] which would include some people who do not self-identify as practitioners of Paganism. A Pagan organization recently paid to have Pagan statistics tabulated from the 2001 census in Scotland, and they report that 1,930 people identified themselves as Pagan in the "other" category.[19]

Although contemporary Paganism is not statistically as significant as other world religions, whether a tradition or group of traditions is considered as a world religion is not purely a matter of number of adherents. It is also a matter of differentiation regarding things like theology, **cosmology**, social organization, ritual practices, and historical origins—the type of categories in which this book discusses Paganism. It is not important here to prove that Paganism is a world religion, but rather to note that Pagan studies looks at Paganism as though it is. Paganism is currently undergoing a process of **routinization**, creating institutions and organizational structures. Some practitioners actively work against this formal institutionalization of their religion, rejecting the formation of creedal statements, the adoption of codes of practice, and the development of structures that claim to represent all Pagans. However, it is possible to distinguish Paganism as a distinct religious tradition in the twentieth and twenty-first centuries without distorting it into a more homogeneous appearance than is supported by Pagan texts and sociological and ethnographic data. The fact that Pagans resist formal structures of organization, systematization, **dogma**, and orthodoxy is, in fact, a marker of a unique family of religious traditions.

Paganism must be discussed as a family of religious traditions rather than as a homogenous religion, but this is true of other world religions. Paganism includes Wicca, the largest denomination within Paganism, as well as other Witchcraft traditions; **reconstructionist** denominations including revivals of Greek, Egyptian, Latvian, Druidic, and **Heathen** traditions; and a variety of other contemporary and **eclectic** denominations. Eclectic Pagans draw on a variety of sources in creating their own practices, rather than exclusively following a preexisting tradition. Pagans can be eclectic in their religious practices even within a denomination. Many Wiccans, for example, are eclectic in their practices, being inspired not only by British **folklore** and mythology, but also by traditions from other lands.

Largely due to the marketing choices of a number of popular book publishers, Wicca is much more readily identified as a religious tradition than Paganism is. However, Wicca is more properly a denomination within Paganism than a distinct religion. Referring to Wicca in place of Paganism is like taking Protestantism for Christianity as a whole. This usage of the terms has begun to occur among practitioners in a fairly analogous way to how it does with Protestants who understand their denomination as what Christianity is: if one is part of the mainstream of a tradition, then one's own denomination is often taken to be representative of, if not congruent with, the religion as a whole. Recent media and publishing influences have lead to larger numbers of generic Pagans referring to themselves as Wiccan, that is, as practitioners of Wicca. Historically, "Wicca" refers to Pagans who are **bitheistic**, revering divinity in the forms of a Goddess and a God. Pagans more generally are **polytheistic**, acknowledging the existence of many goddesses and gods. Individuals often have special relationships with one or more of these, or a particular pantheon, such as the Greek gods and goddesses of Olympus, or the deities of Norse mythology. Wiccan traditions are traceable to the tradition popularized by Gerald Gardner beginning in the 1940s and 1950s in Britain, while Paganism more broadly has more diverse roots.

Gerald Gardner was the first popularizer of modern Witchcraft as a religion. He called this religion Wicca (or "Wica"—his spelling was inconsistent), and it has come to be known more specifically as **Gardnerian** Wicca. For more information on Gardner and other important figures in the development of contemporary Paganism, see chapter 7.

Figure 1.   Gerald Gardner (from Doreen Valiente's *Rebirth of Witchcraft*)

Historically, "pagan" has referred to the peoples of the land, as opposed to the peoples of the book, meaning the Bible or the Koran. The term "pagan" has referred to "nonbelievers" in the God of the monotheistic traditions of Christianity, Judaism, and Islam. Generally, contemporary Pagans support the association of their religion with ancient traditions that are historically referred to as "pagan." Pagans like to think of themselves as people of the land, since their religion has a this-worldly focus, celebrating the natural world as sacred and as the home of the goddesses and gods, or of the Goddess and the God. Additionally, Pagans feel a sense of solidarity with people who have been persecuted for holding to their indigenous faith against colonization by monotheistic cultures. However, Pagan religion is different from ancient pagan traditions, in that it is contemporary, becoming a publicly practiced religion in the second half of the twentieth century. Reconstructionist denominations within Paganism stress the connections between their practices and those of the traditions from which they draw their inspiration, but they are revivals and reimaginings of these traditions rather than continuous outgrowths of them.

The twentieth-century origins of Paganism are disputed by some practitioners, notably a minority of Wiccans who believe that Gerald Gardner was initiated into an established group of witches in the New Forest area of Britain that was descended directly from witches persecuted in the medieval witch hunts. Gardner said that he had found a **coven** that was a remnant of the religion of those who were persecuted. However, it is generally agreed by scholars of Pagan studies that the people persecuted during the witch hunts were "witches" only in the anthropological sense of someone accused of practicing malevolent magic. These "witches" are properly understood as alleged Christian heretics rather than as members of an organized religion. Some Pagans identify as "Witches" in solidarity with those who were falsely accused of malevolent acts and were killed during the witch hunts. These Witches use the term for themselves as a way of reclaiming the word. Connecting their contemporary practices with the past can create a powerful sense of identity for modern Witches.

Some Pagans would like to distance themselves from any association with those accused of practicing "witchcraft," in order to differentiate themselves from Satanists who parody and subvert the Christian religion. Not even all Wiccans identify as "Witches." Some Pagans identify themselves as "Witches" without identifying with the label "Wiccan," calling themselves non-Wiccan Witches. This is particularly true of feminist Witches in the Reclaiming tradition. A recent development is practitioners preferring to call themselves "Wiccan" and their religion "Wicca," as a less inflammatory alternative to calling oneself a "Witch" and saying that one practices Witchcraft. Others celebrate their tradition's **occult** connections as a way of challenging mainstream opinions.

Scholars of Pagan studies examine Paganism in relation to nature religion, Goddess spirituality, and the New Age, each of which shares some commonalities with Paganism but is a distinct area of study. Paganism is, in Pagan studies scholar Michael York's respected definition, "an affirmation of interactive and polymorphic sacred relationship by the individual or community with the tangible, sentient, and nonempirical."[20] This means that Pagans recognize and interact with the sacred in a variety of forms, as material beings and personalities with less substantial or quantifiable material forms. Paganism is a polytheistic this-worldly religion. As such, it overlaps with, but is not identical with, nature religion, Goddess spirituality, and New Age traditions. Nature religion is religion in which nature is the location of the sacred, where **transcendence** of nature is not necessary for divinity to appear.[21] Some Pagans affirm a transcendence of nature that does not fit this description of nature religion, believing in a sort of divinity that is not of this world. Goddess spirituality overlaps extensively with Paganism but is goddess focused, sometimes in a monotheistic manner. New Age spirituality is a broad-based phenomenon that cannot be restricted to any one religion. Some Pagan activities can be understood as part of the New Age, but other aspects of the New Age, such as a belief in angels, fit better into a Christian or Jewish view of the world. Pagan studies is the study of Paganism as a distinct religion with diverse denominations that can be discussed in relation to a variety of types of religion and other religious movements, but which is nonetheless an identifiable world religion.

This book introduces the study of Paganism as a world religion and explores how Pagan studies researches the intellectual, religious, and social spheres of Paganism. It examines Paganism in terms of some common categories in the study of religion, including beliefs, practices, theology, ritual, history, and the role of texts and scriptures. Chapter 1 discusses what Pagans believe. Although belief is not an important feature of their religion for many Pagan practitioners, it is a relevant category for the study of Pagans and their religion. There are certain commonalities across denominational borders in Pagan cosmology concerning what they believe about the structure and nature of the universe and the place of humans and divinity within it. This chapter explains a number of relevant concepts in Pagan theology and **thealogy**, the studies of divinity in its male (theo) and female (thea) forms. The meanings of thealogy, cosmology, **immanence**, **polytheism**, **animism**, and **shamanism** are discussed in relation to Pagan beliefs. Other common beliefs of Pagans about magic, the creation of sacred space, and healing are also examined.

Chapter 2 looks at the social organization of Paganism. Paganism is not institutionalized in the same ways that other world religions are. Pagans resist formal structures governing their religion, but from a sociological point of view, the social organization of Pagans is visible as a form of organization that tends to deconstruct itself: as structures form, they are criticized, and they begin to lose their legitimacy as soon as people feel constrained by them. This chapter looks at trends toward and against routinization, examining the fluid nature of the social organization of Paganism in small groups, as well as the larger federated organizations that develop as some Pagans seek to create more formal structures. Additionally, this chapter looks at authority and leadership in Pagan groups and compares Pagan understandings of **clergy** with what has been referred to as "democratized shamanism," participatory religion in which any practitioner can become an expert and act as shaman or priest/ess. Finally, this chapter also comments on the public/private split of Pagan groups into inner and outer "courts," or closed and public groups.

Chapters 3 and 4 discuss what Pagans do, beginning with individual and family practices in chapter 3, and extending into group practices in chapter 4. Chapter 3 focuses on Pagan religious practices and rituals in the home and with their families. It explores Pagan **lifeways**, the things Pagans do that make them identifiable as Pagans, such as keeping home **altars** and **shrines**, as well as the sometimes more formal ritual activities of giving offerings, casting spells, pursuing **divination**, meditating, and doing **trance work**. The tools, accoutrements, and techniques used with these activities are also discussed. Chapter 4 discusses the activities that Pagans tend to conduct in groups. Many of the activities that Pagans engage in individually also come into play in groups, but they tend to be more structured. This chapter discusses the Pagan festival cycle and moon rituals that structure the Pagan year, as well as rites of passage, including birth, coming of age, initiations, **handfastings** and weddings, **croning**, and death.

Chapter 5 explores the role of myth in Paganism and its relationship with history. There are a number of myths associated with Paganism, and Pagans use these myths variously for legitimation, inspiration, and political ends. Those who use them for a sense of legitimation tend to feel threatened by questions of historical accuracy, but others prefer to regard the myths primarily as stories that teach and inspire. This chapter looks at the various meanings of "the Old Religion" in Paganism, the theory of pagan "survivals" once popular in British folklore studies, interpretations of the medieval witch hunts as the "Burning Times," and feminist reinterpretations of history, including what is sometimes called the myth of the matriarchies. It also notes some prominent mythological stories in Paganism that have less controversial relationships with history, such as the Wild Hunt, Ceridwen's cauldron, and Odin's hanging on Yggdrasil, the world tree.

Chapter 6 introduces the major literary origins and influences on the development of Paganism. These literary sources include works from anthropologists, folklorists, poets, and novelists, as well as early prefigurations of Paganism in related religious movements such as **spiritualism** and **ceremonial magic**. This chapter discusses how diverse figures such James Frazer, Charles Leland, Aleister Crowley, Rudyard Kipling, Kenneth Grahame, Dion Fortune, Margaret Murray, Robert Graves, Robert Heinlein, and Marion Zimmer Bradley came to influence the development of Paganism.

Chapter 7 continues to introduce figures of interest in the development of Paganism, but with a focus on social and charismatic influences rather than literary sources. Thus, this chapter focuses on contemporary individuals, social movements, and cultural trends. Beginning with Gerald Gardner, the first popularizer of a Pagan tradition in Britain, this chapter introduces influential authors and charismatic leaders in Pagan revivals, including Starhawk, Z. Budapest, Doreen Valiente, Raymond Buckland, and Scott Cunningham. The impact of social movements such as feminism on Paganism, and cultural trends such as the romantic fascination with Celtic icons and imagery, are also discussed in this chapter.

Chapter 8 introduces the major denominations of Paganism and gives a short description and history of each. Specific denominations covered include Greek, Egyptian, Druidic, Heathen, and Eastern European reconstructionist traditions, as well as other groups involving some degree of reconstruction such as Wicca, Odinism, and **Asatru**, and groups such as Reclaiming and the Church of All Worlds, which have other origins. In addition, eclectic and solitary traditions of Paganism are differentiated, and the overlaps between Paganism and the New Age and goddess spirituality are explored.

Chapter 9 discusses the roles of ethics and politics in Paganism. Pagan ethics are most fully developed in relation to the practice of magic but have also been articulated in relation to feminism, environmental problems, and, to a degree, issues of **cultural appropriation**. In addition, social norms regarding sexuality, social justice, and pluralism are discussed. While virtually all political orientations are evident in the Pagan spectrum, certain trends are more pronounced than others.

Chapter 10 speaks to a number of current issues in Paganism and Pagan studies. Within Paganism, the existence of the New Forest coven and its possible historical antecedents continues to be debated. More recently, the public display of lifestyle choices such as BDSM and other sexual choices, as well as the use of illegal drugs, have become topics of debate within Pagan communities, particularly in relation to the display of these activities at public festivals. The growth of Paganism on the Internet and the influence of popular media on the growth of Paganism are important contemporary issues for scholars of Pagan studies, and to a certain extent for practitioners. The increasing availability of information on Paganism and access to Pagan discussion groups has made Paganism much more accessible outside large cities than previously. Television programs, juvenile fiction, and movies featuring Pagan characters have contributed to a popular fascination with Wicca, which some practitioners feel commercializes and trivializes Paganism as a religion.

Chapter 11 gives a brief history of Pagan studies, discusses current methods of study, and delves into future directions of development for the field. Many scholars of Pagan studies are also practitioners, and this has forced them to become somewhat innovative in their methods of study. **Participant observation**, the favored method of anthropologists and **ethnographers**, has been found to be inadequate to describe the worldviews and religious experiences of contemporary Pagans. Ethnographers in particular are pioneering new ways of accounting for how Pagans see the world, ways that are fair to Pagans and are true to their actual experiences, rather than dismissing them as fraudulent, fanciful, or escapist fantasy.

NOTES

1. Because this is an introductory text, it inevitably makes a number of generalizations. Pagan traditions and practitioners are quite diverse, and counterexamples can undoubtedly be found for any generalization made about Pagans or Paganism. This does not negate the accuracy of the general comments I make. It should be noted, however, that the general comments I make about Pagans and Paganism apply primarily to Paganism in the English-

speaking world. Paganism has developed somewhat differently in places such as Eastern Europe. See, for example, Adrian Ivakhiv, "In Search of Deeper Identities: Neopaganism and 'Native Faith' in Contemporary Ukraine," *Nova Religio: The Journal of Alternative and Emergent Religions* 8, no. 3 (March 2005): 7–38.

2. Helen Berger, Evan A. Leach, and Leigh S. Shaffer, *Voices from the Pagan Census: A National Survey of Witches and Neo-Pagans in the United States* (Columbia: University of South Carolina Press, 2003), 31; Sabina Magliocco, *Witching Culture: Folklore and Neo-Paganism in America* (Philadelphia: University of Pennsylvania Press, 2004), 62.

3. James R. Lewis, "Appendix: Numbering Neo-Pagans," in *The Encyclopedia of Modern Witchcraft and Neo-Paganism*, ed. Shelly Rabinovitch and James Lewis, 303–5 (New York: Citadel, 2002).

4. Lewis, "Appendix," 303.

5. See Berger, Leach, and Shaffer, *Voices from the Pagan Census*.

6. Ronald Hutton, *The Triumph of the Moon: A History of Modern Pagan Witchcraft* (Oxford: Oxford University Press, 1999), 4.

7. See, for example, Michael York, *Pagan Theology: Paganism as a World Religion* (New York: New York University Press, 2003).

8. See York, *Pagan Theology*, 10.

9. For Iceland statistics, see Michael Strmiska, "Asatru in Iceland: Ásatrúarfélagid," in *The Encyclopedia of Modern Witchcraft and Neo-Paganism*, ed. Shelley Rabinovitch and James Lewis, 16 (New York: Citadel, 2002). For New Zealand, see Kathryn Rountree, *Embracing the Witch and the Goddess: Feminist Ritual-Makers in New Zealand* (London: Routledge, 2004), 7–8. For Canadian statistics, see Statistics Canada, *2001 Census*, Statistics Canada website, http://www12.statcan.ca/english/census01/products/highlight/Religion/PR_Menu1.cfm?Lang=E (accessed March 1, 2004).

10. Síân Lee MacDonald Reid, *Disorganized Religion: An Exploration of the Neopagan Craft in Canada* (Doctoral thesis, Carleton University, Ottawa, 2001), 71.

11. Hughes Philip and Sharon Bond, "The status and increased following of Nature Religions in Australia," *On Line Opinion: Australia's E-Journal of Social and Political Debate*, September 29, 2003, www.onlineopinion.com.au/view.asp?article=756 (accessed March 1, 2004), edited version of an article first published in the Christian Research Association bulletin, *Pointers* 13, no. 2 (June 2003). These numbers do not include indigenous animism, which has a distinct category on the census. On the 2001 census form, 10,632 self-identified as Pagan, and 8,755 as Wiccan or Witch. Hughes and Bond did not provide numbers for Druids and pantheists. Thanks to Mandy Furney for referring this article to me.

12. Margot Adler's follow-up survey for the revised edition of her *Drawing Down the Moon: Witches, Druids, Goddess-Worshippers, and Other Pagans in America Today*, revised and expanded ed. (Boston: Beacon Press, 1986).

13. Aiden Kelly, cited in James R. Lewis, *Magical Religion and Modern Witchcraft* (Albany: State University of New York Press, 1996), 2.

14. Helen Berger, *A Community of Witches* (Columbia: University of South Carolina Press, 1999), 9; Sarah Pike, *Earthly Bodies, Magical Selves: Contemporary Pagans and the Search for Community* (Berkeley: University of California Press, 2001); Danny Jorgensen, Lin Jorgensen, and Scott Russell, "American Neopaganism: The Participants' Social Identities," *Journal for the Scientific Study of Religion* 38 (1999): 325–38. The latter researchers indicate that there may be twice as many practitioners as the 200,000 they estimate.

15. Lewis, "Appendix," 304.

16. Charlotte Hardman and Graham Harvey, eds., *Paganism Today* (London: Thorsons [HarperCollins], 1996), ix.

17. *BBC Online Network*, "UK Pagans Celebrate as Numbers Soar," *BBC Online Network*, October 31, 1999, 16:06 GMT, http://news.bbc.co.uk/1/hi/uk/500484.stm (accessed March 1,

2004). Unfortunately the news report does not cite the study by name or author, and I have been unable to identify it. Thanks to Cat McEarchern for drawing this article to my attention.

18. Ronald Hutton, cited in Wendy Griffin, ed., *Daughters of the Goddess: Studies of Healing, Identity, and Empowerment* (Walnut Creek, CA: AltaMira, 2000), 14.

19. *BBC Online Network*, "UK Pagans Celebrate."

20. York, *Pagan Theology*, 157.

21. Barbara Jane Davy, "Nature Religion," in *The Encyclopedia of Religion and Nature*, ed. Bron Taylor, 2:1173–75 (London: Continuum International, 2005).

1

Beliefs

Paganism has no standard **creed** or official system of doctrines, and Pagans tend to eschew dogma. Consequently, Pagans believe widely divergent things about the world. In part, this diversity is caused by the lack of any single authoritative text or revelation founding the religion. Instead of a single holy book, there are hundreds of how-to books available for Pagan practitioners, some making claims to legitimacy or authority in terms of the author's **Craft lineage**, family teaching, or revelatory experience. However, although Pagan beliefs vary from one individual to another, and across denominations, there are general trends in their basic cosmology, or worldview, concerning their beliefs about the universe and the place of humans and others within it. Probably the most common feature of Pagan belief is its plurality: Pagans believe a variety of things about divinity, what forms it can take, and how humans should relate with it, and they are tolerant of a diversity of opinion about these things among their coreligionists. Many practitioners feel that what they believe is not as important as what they do as Pagans, but it is useful to examine beliefs in studying Paganism and its practitioners.

In general, Pagans tend to be polytheists, meaning that they believe divinity to take multiple forms. They believe in a variety of goddesses and gods and other divine beings. They also tend to think of divinity as **immanent**, dwelling within rather than being transcendent of—that is, outside of or apart from—the natural world. Although Paganism has a tendency toward a romantic view of nature, Pagan worldviews have a number of features in common with late modernity, particularly evident in their eclecticism and sense of play, but also in their values of democracy, feminist empowerment, ethnic diversity, and equality. Most Pagans exhibit a belief in **reincarnation** and conceive of death as a necessary aspect of the cycles of life. Another common component of Pagan worldviews is a belief in the efficacy of magic and **spell casting**.

Pagans think of divinity not only in terms of gods and goddesses, but also as appearing in various other forms. Thus Paganism is well defined as "an affirmation of interactive and polymorphic sacred relationship by individual or community with the tangible, sentient, and nonempirical."[1] The divine is something that Pagans interact with in a variety of ways, through its various forms. In Paganism, there are male and female deities, and some deities for whom gender is not a useful category, being either androgynous and having characteristics both male and female, or not being gendered at all. In discussing Paganism, then, it is not accurate to speak of gods when discussing deities in general. "**Deity**" is a nonspecific word for divine beings, goddesses and gods, and the God and the Goddess. "Divinity" is a more generic word for the sacred, not necessarily quantifiable as a distinct being or class of beings. "Thealogy" and "theology" are terms for the study of deity. "Theology" is the more common term, initially meaning writings about the gods, and, later, god in the monotheistic sense of the one and only God. "Thealogy" is a term used by practitioners, and in religious studies, to describe studies of female divinity.[2] "**Theoilogy**," or "polytheology," are possible generic terms for the study of goddesses and gods in the plural.[3]

Pagan relations with divinity are not focused on belief or worship. Practitioners generally feel that belief in divinity is not a useful way of looking at Pagan religious practice, pointing to the strangeness of the idea that one must "believe" in something to relate to it. To demonstrate the inappropriateness of the question of belief, Starhawk points to the idea of believing in rocks. They simply are what they are, regardless of what humans think about them. This attitude toward belief can be explained, tongue in cheek, by quoting the popular novelist Terry Pratchett: "Most witches don't believe in gods. They know that they exist, of course. They even deal with them occasionally. But they don't believe in them. They know them too well. It would be like believing in the postman."[4] While some Pagans suggest that respectful relations, rather than "worship," are appropriate, others do worship their god/desses. Some **Asatruar** and Druids refer to them as "the high ones" or "the bright ones," feeling that it is appropriate to honor the god/desses, to praise them, in order to win their friendship and support.[5] Many Pagans leave offerings such as fruit, grains, and flowers, which might be interpreted as worship, or simply as leaving gifts.

Theism, meaning belief in God (or god/desses), thus may not be a very useful way of looking at Pagan relations with divinity. Belief in divinity is

Figure 2. Starhawk (press photo)

not necessary for being Pagan, but practitioners usually feel that it is possible for anyone to meet a deity or to encounter the divine. Such encounters need not be mediated by clergy or by dogmatic ideas about what divinity should be like. Pagans trust their own experiences above all else. In
general, Pagans believe that divinity occurs in many forms, which may all
be expressions of a single reality, or which may each be unique beings, not
all of them deities. Pagans do not necessarily conceive of divinities as being supernatural or above humans. Divinities can be "more than human"
in the way that a cat is a more-than-human being. Not all other-than-human beings are gods or goddesses. Pagans understand some of these beings in other terms, such as **landwights**, boggarts, faeries, or "the good
people." Landwights are local nature spirits, and boggarts are house-
dwelling spirits, while faeries might be of either type. These beings are

S tarhawk is a prominent American Witch and author of *The Spiral
Dance*, one of the most popular how-to books in Paganism. For
more information on Starhawk and other prominent Pagans, see
chapter 7.

often understood to be corporeal, but not in the same manner as humans. They might be described as other-than-human persons.

The anthropologist A. Irving Hallowell developed the phrase "other-than-human persons" to describe the understanding of persons by the Ojibwa people he studied. He suggested that, for the Ojibwa he studied, not everything is always a person, but many more things could be a person for them than for most Westerners. He once asked a man if all stones are alive. After some thought, the man replied, "No! But some are." Hallowell thus formed the hypothesis that the people he was studying believed that many more things have the potential to be animate beings than just humans.[6] Contemporary Pagans often see the world as animate in a similar fashion. This sort of perception of the world is sometimes called "animism," indicating a belief that all things are living beings or may possibly be "ensouled." However, Pagans do not conceive of "souls" as animating material bodies in any consistent manner. In fact, the idea that matter needs a soul is repugnant to some Pagans, since this implies a devaluation of the material world, as though it needs to be animated by something transcendent of it.

Some Pagans perceive nature spirits, or local land spirits, called "landwights," or *landvættir* in Norse traditions, as other-than-human people. Nature spirits are beings who share a human territory, helping or hindering depending on the respect given to them by humans, and on whim. In the study of religion, these beings are sometimes referred to by the Latin term *genii loci*, meaning spirits of place. Pagans also refer to such beings as faeries, "little people," or "the good folk." These terms, as well as the names "brownies" and "boggarts" are drawn from English folklore.[7] Brownies and boggarts tend to be associated with houses, while the others are more likely to be found outside or are associated with features of the land, such as hills or **barrows**. Some Pagans use the Native American term *manitous*, meaning "little mysteries," to refer to some nature spirits. In general, nature spirits are associated with particular trees, rocks, or bodies of water. Some practitioners call water spirits "nixies," earth spirits "gnomes," and rock spirits "trolls." Believing in nature spirits makes the world a more meaningful place for Pagans, a world filled with mystery rather than just real estate and suburbs. For some Pagans, especially Asatruar and some Druids, nature spirits may be just as important in ritual, or more so, than the god/desses. Practitioners may find it more necessary, for example, to invite local nature spirits and to obtain the permission of landwights to hold a ritual than it is to address the god/desses.[8]

How Pagans think about nature spirits is often influenced by novels more than by formal theology. Terri Windling's novel *The Wood Wife* and Charles de Lint's short-story collection *The Ivory and the Horn*, for example, describe relations with other-than-human beings that have influenced my own thoughts about and perceptions of such entities. In Windling's novel, the protagonist, Maggie, learns that the extraordinary beings she meets are not created in her interaction with them, but the form they take depends on who is interacting with them. Reading this novel encourages Pagans to think about how nature spirits come into being in part through one's belief in them, while their existence is not wholly dependent on humans. Pagans might believe in them in part simply because they like the idea, but this does not necessarily mean that nature spirits are simply projections of the psyche, even though one's thoughts about them contribute to how one experiences them. Windling conveys a useful analogy in the protagonist's conversation with a character called Fox, between the way poetry describes a landscape and the way one perceives other-than-human persons, emphasizing the way significance takes form through interaction.[9] The perception of nature spirits is somewhat dependent on one's belief in them, but this is in fact part of everyday perception of other humans and the world in general. One cannot interact with another if one does not regard them as real.

In de Lint's stories set in the fictional city of Newford, the characters learn to see people who are sometimes animals, and other "little mysteries." In the story "Bird Bones and Wood Ash," one character asks another if she has to believe in the fairies to see them, and the other character replies, "Land's sakes no. . . . They have to believe in you." She explains, "It's like this . . . You don't think of them as prissy little creatures with wings. That's plain wrong. They're earth spirits—and they don't really have shapes of their own; they just show up looking the way we expect them to look."[10] As in Windling's novel, the existence of these entities is not wholly dependent on human belief—they do not exist only as projections of the mind, but one's beliefs about them do influence how one perceives them, or fails to perceive them.

Other Pagans feel differently about the independent existence of nature spirits and other forms of divinity. There is a certain amount of ambiguity in Pagan thought about whether or not deities have an existence external to what humans think about them. The divinities are understood, even by individual Pagans, as both within humans and as independent forces. Some accept a psychological explanation and regard god/desses and nature spirits as mental projections. Some find it appropriate to act as though the deities are real because they might be, while others are certain that the god/desses have external existences as individual personalities. Pagans may practice a suspension of disbelief during ritual, since participants are not required to express faith or belief in divinities, and they often are skeptical.[11] For some practitioners, it is always appropriate to act as though the divinities are real, and belief is largely irrelevant. This is sometimes regarded as "deep play," in which one pretends or acts as

Figure 3.   The Goddess (Goddess altar, photo by Catherine Kerr)

though the divinities are real.[12] For many Pagans, particularly women focused on the Goddess, the deities are also understood as role models or as
representations of strength within oneself.

The Goddess is the female aspect or embodiment of the divine. She is
often envisioned in the triple form of maiden, mother, and **crone**, corresponding to the three phases of women's lives. This way of imagining the
Goddess is significant for female practitioners, as it symbolically values
women's bodies, including their experiences of menstruation and
menopause, and of birth and lactation if they choose to have children.
Goddess images also value mother-daughter relations and other connections between women. Female images of divinity sanction women's
power. As feminist thealogian Carol Christ has argued, the Goddess sym-
bolizes "the acknowledgment of the legitimacy of female power as a
beneficent and independent power."[13] The Goddess represents the
strength within women, but she can also be an external source of comfort
and support. Starhawk explains, "When I feel weak, She is someone who
can help and protect me. When I feel strong, She is the symbol of my own
power. At other times I feel Her as the natural energy in my body and the
world."[14] She can function this way for men as well, but she can also rep-

resent the female in more sexual terms, and more deeply as mystery: "the eternally desired Other, the Muse, all that he is not."[15]

While there is generally no creator god in Paganism, sometimes the Goddess is understood to function in this capacity. More often, the Goddess is understood as the body of the cosmos or the Earth. Otter G'Zell and Morning Glory, of the organization called the Church of All Worlds, speak of Mother Earth, and **Gaea**, as the "All-Mother," in what they call "the Gaea thesis," an explicitly pantheist understanding of the Earth as a living being akin to James Lovelock and Lynn Margulis' more widely known Gaia hypothesis.[16] Lovelock and Margulis' Gaia hypothesis, a theory that the planet is a self-regulating system and in effect a living being, was first published in 1975, but G'Zell indicates that he had a vision of "the unity of the Earth's planetary biosphere as a single organism on the evening of September 6, 1970."[17]

The Goddess is widely identified with nature in Paganism.[18] The common **liturgy** of the Charge of the Goddess speaks of the Goddess as "the soul of nature that gives life to the universe." Use of the phrase "the earth our mother" is commonplace among Pagans, particularly in environmentally active groups like Britain's Dragon Environmental Group,[19] but it also occurs at mainstream Pagan gatherings like the Avalon East festival. Canadian Maritime Pagans who participated in the festival addressed nature not only as "Mother Earth" but also as "MARI, Mother Sea."[20] In addition, the Goddess is identified not only with the life-giving aspects of nature in regeneration, but also with "the power of death."[21] She "is at once the unploughed field, the full harvest and the dormant, frost-covered Earth."[22] In the Wiccan denomination, nature is conceived as "ensouled, alive, 'divine,'"[23] but not only as mother or even Goddess. Figures such as the Horned God, the Corn God, the Green Man, and the Sun God are also important. In Wicca, nature tends to be perceived in terms of interactions between male and female divinities. The cycle of the seasons is linked to the Goddess's relations with the God through alternately being impregnated by him at the spring equinox, raising him as her child in the summer, and mourning his death at harvest time.

These relations of the God with the Goddess in Wicca are distinguished sometimes by splitting the God into the Holly King and Oak King, as aspects of the Horned God. The Horned God is the lord of the forest, sometimes portrayed as a stag, similar to the horned deity portrayed in the film *Princess Mononoke*.[24] The Horned God is also associated with wildness, virility, and the hunt. Unfortunately, the Horned God has been associated with the Christian Devil. Early Wiccans associated their image of the God with Margaret Murray's accounts of witchcraft in *The Witch Cult* and *The God of the Witches*, originally published in the 1920s and 1930s. These works were immediately criticized by academics, but they had a strong

Figure 4.   The Horned God (Horned God altar, photo by Lloyd Keane)

emotional appeal for their portrayal of the God as a sexual being. Murray argued that there was a Witch cult, a surviving pre-Christian religion in the British Isles. She presented this cult in somewhat negative terms in the first book, but celebrated it in the second. Murray came to believe that witches worshipped a deity, the Horned God, who was demonized into the Devil by Christianity, while really their religion was a joyous, life-affirming faith. The Horned God was initially associated with the Greek god Pan in England but was eclipsed by the Celtic god Cernunnos.[25]

Cernunnos is the Gallic or Celtic god of the forest, associated with deer. Murray took selective evidence of any god with horns across Europe and

Margaret Murray was a British academic, specifically an Egyptologist and folklorist. Her studies of Egyptian culture were well respected, but her work on folklore in Britain was less academically credible. Nonetheless, her writings on folklore were very popular and influenced the early revival of Witchcraft in Britain in the 1940s. For more information on Murray and other literary influences on Paganism, see chapter 6.

the Near East and said they were all aspects of the Horned God, whether they had stag antlers or ram horns. She assimilated the invented witch-craft of the witch hunts with British folk traditions, linking Robin Hood and church carvings with paganism. Murray interpreted female figures in medieval churches as pagan goddesses of fertility, which inspired Lady Raglan, a fellow member of the Folklore Society, to interpret the foliate heads of fourteenth- and fifteenth-century churches as the vegetation god described by James Frazer, calling such images "the Green Man."[26]

Even if the Green Man and other images of the God are largely modern creations, they are meaningful to Pagans. For both male and female prac-titioners, the Horned God provides an alternative to patriarchal symbols of masculinity. The Horned God reenvisions male strength, virility, and power with gentleness and respect for female power. He is neither macho nor effeminate. In Starhawk's words, "He is gentle, tender, and comfort-ing, but He is also the Hunter. He is the Dying God—but his death is al-ways in service of the life force. He is untamed sexuality—but sexuality as a deep, holy, connecting power. He is the power of feeling, and the im-age of what men could be if they were liberated from the constraints of patriarchal culture."[27]

Images of the Green Man, and those of Pan, have influenced contem-porary understandings of the Horned God, but Pagans stress that the Horned God should not be associated with the Christian Devil. Pan is the Greek god of nature, a figure with the legs of a goat, the upper body of a man, and ram's horns. Pan is imaged as wild, exciting, and disturbing. He is associated with "pandemonium" and "panic," words derived from the feelings he incites. He was relatively unimportant in modern times until he was celebrated in the poetry of English Romantics such as Wordsworth, Keats, and Shelley. In their work, he was presented as the personification and guardian of the English countryside as imagined by urbanites on holiday: a pleasant land where it is always summer and where agricultural work is invisible.[28] He appears in this form in Kenneth Grahame's children's book *The Wind in the Willows*. Through the popular-ity of such images in the early 1900s in England, **pantheism** became Pan-theism, the belief in the god Pan as lord of nature.[29] In the 1900s, Pan was imaged as a horned god of nature, sometimes with goat legs and horns, sometimes as part stag. Goats, in Western culture, have long been associ-ated with lust, and Pan thus served as a challenge to Victorian prudery, providing an alternative vision of male divinity to the nonsexual Christ-ian God. Aleister Crowley's "Hymn to Pan," for example, presents Pan in terms of ravenous sexuality.[30]

Pagans associate not only Pan with forests and nature, but also the goddess Diana, following a related evolution of the deity through En-glish Romanticism. Diana was a symbol of chastity and hunting in

Roman culture, as well as in Greek culture, in which she was known as Artemis. In Britain, she came to be associated with the moon, wild animals, and the greenwood (the British sense of natural areas as enchanted leafy glades inhabited by elves or faeries). By about 1810, she had evolved into a mother-earth figure in the works of the English Romantics, most often approached at night through the moon, in the woods.[31] Pagans sometimes understand Diana as a name of the Goddess and associate her with Aradia, the goddess named in Charles G. Leland's *Aradia: or the Gospel of the Witches*. *Aradia*, never taken seriously as folklore in Italy or the United States, is a collection of spells, charms, and liturgy, gathered in 1886, Leland said, through the help of a **hereditary witch**, Maddelena, who had collected lore from the *strega*, or Italian witches. It includes a creation story of Diana fooling Lucifer into fathering Aradia, who becomes the savior of the witches. Eventually, this work provided inspiration for the Charge of the Goddess, which was written in verse form by Doreen Valiente. Starhawk adapted this common prose version of the Charge:

> Listen to the words of the Great Mother, who of old was called Artemis, Astarte, Dione, Melusine, Aphrodite, Ceridwen, Diana, Arionrhod, Brigid, and by many other names:
>
> "Whenever you have need of anything, once in the month, and better it be when the moon is full, you shall assemble in some secret place and adore the spirit of Me who is Queen of all the Wise. You shall be free from slavery, and as a sign that you be free you shall be naked in your rites. Sing, feast, dance, make music and love, all in My presence, for Mine is the ecstasy of the spirit and Mine also is joy on earth. For My law is the cup of wine of life that is the Cauldron of Ceridwen that is the holy grail of immortality. I give the knowledge of the spirit eternal and beyond death I give peace and freedom and reunion with those that have gone before. Nor do I demand aught of sacrifice, for behold, I am the mother of all things and My love is poured upon the earth."
>
> Hear the words of the Star Goddess, the dust of whose feet are the hosts of heaven, whose body encircles the universe:
>
> "I who am the beauty of the green earth and the white moon among the stars and the mysteries of the waters, I call upon your soul to arise and come unto me. For I am the soul of nature that gives life to the universe. From Me all things proceed and unto Me they must return. Let My worship be in the heart that rejoices, for behold—all acts of love and pleasure are My rituals. Let there be beauty and strength, power and compassion, honor and humility, mirth and reverence within you. And you who seek to know Me, know that your seeking and yearning will avail you not, unless you know the Mystery: for if that which you seek, you find not within yourself, you will never find it without. For behold, I have been with you from the beginning, and I am that which is attained at the end of desire."[32]

Whatever its origin, the Charge is an inspiring piece of liturgy for many Pagans and can lead to powerful experiences in ritual. Margot Adler relates that when she first heard this liturgy, "A feeling of power and emotion came over me. . . . The contents of the tape had simply given me *permission* to accept a part of my own psyche that I had denied for years—and then extend it."[33]

For Asatruar, the deities have more distinct personas and are less likely than in other Pagan denominations to be seen as aspects of the God or Goddess. Odin, for example, is envisioned as the All-father, but other gods in the Norse pantheon are not usually thought of as aspects of him. Rather they are friends, lovers, comrades, or enemies. The *gythia*, or Asatru priestess, Diana Paxson describes Odin as one of the three most prominent gods in the northern European pantheon (the others being Thor and Freyr). Odin is the All-father, a multifaced god of poetry and ecstasy, and the giver of the runes.[34] However, Freya Aswynn, an Asatruar dedicated to Odin, suggests that Odin has different aspects. She prefers to call him "Wodan," and she regards the different spellings as referring to different aspects of the god. Aswynn suggests that "Odin" is "Wodan" "in a bad mood," a god of battle. She describes Odin in three forms: Odin, Villi, and Ve, corresponding respectively to his roles as warrior, shaman, and wanderer.[35] However, she does not interpret other Norse deities as aspects of Odin. Odin is best known for hanging on the world tree, Yggdrasil, for nine days; sacrificing one of his eyes; and thus gaining knowledge of the runes (a magical alphabet) and charms (things to say to achieve goals magically).

Yggdrasil, as the world tree, serves as a model of the cosmos in Norse mythology. Some Pagans, having been influenced by writings in comparative religion, principally those of Joseph Campbell and Mircea Eliade, envision the cosmos as organized into three realms linked by a vertical axis, often symbolized by a tree. Eliade describes the worldview of shamanism in this manner as a three-tiered universe having a dark underworld at the bottom, the regular mundane human world in the middle, and a light-filled heavenly world above. Pagans might be more likely to conceive of these as the underworld, middle earth, and the astral plane, with fewer associations of dark and light for the underworld and the astral. Some envision these as the three principle realms of Norse mythology described in relation to the world tree Yggdrasil, rooted in earth, standing in the here and now, and with branches reaching into the sky. In this cosmology, earth is the underworld, where the dead go, at least those who have not died in battle. (Norse mythology actually has a cosmology composed of nine realms, three in each of these basic divisions.) Many Pagans have an integrated sense of the cosmos, without making a sharp separation between the realm of the god/desses and the realm of humans. Even in the Norse cosmology, the god/desses interact with people in all the realms.

Perhaps the greatest unifying feature of Pagan beliefs about the structure of the universe is immanence, the belief that divinity is embodied in the world. Pagans believe that the sacred is inherent in the natural world, meaning that divinity dwells within the physical universe. This is in contrast to a cosmology of transcendence, in which divinity is thought to reside outside or beyond the physical universe, so that God is a supernatural entity. The sacred is not understood as the opposite of the profane in Paganism. To a large degree in Pagan worldviews, nothing is profane, and everything is sacred. "Ordinary" and "extraordinary" are better terms for speaking of the way Pagans understand sacrality and the manifestation of divinity than "profane" and "supernatural." When Pagans create sacred space, they mark it as set apart from the ordinary, but without devaluing the ordinary or hypervaluing the sacred space. For example, Wiccans create sacred space in ritual by casting a circle, envisioned as a sphere formed with a circle traced on the ground or floor as its horizontal circumference. This sphere holds energy raised in ritual until it is ready to be released, and it represents the intention of the participants to let go of their everyday concerns and focus instead on the ritual at hand. When the ritual is finished, the space again becomes ordinary. Some Pagans also describe the sacred as something that has intrinsic value, that is, value apart from or beyond any usefulness ascribed to it by humans. Starhawk, for example, describes the five sacred things, earth, air, fire, water, and spirit, in this manner.[36]

Pagans believe that the immanence of divinity applies to the Earth as well as to human bodies. Many Pagans refer to the Earth as the body of the Goddess, sometimes called Gaia (or Gaea). Pagans see all bodies as divine, whether the body of the Goddess as Earth or the cosmos, or human bodies. The divinity of human bodies is sometimes expressed in the ritual greeting "thou art god" or "thou art goddess." The celebration of the body is intended to revalue embodiment and the natural functioning of bodies, including sex, which Pagans feel have been denigrated by the monotheistic traditions. The belief in immanence similarly revalues the rest of the natural world. If divinity is inherent in the natural world, if the Earth is the body of the Goddess, it is unacceptable to damage ecosystems, to pollute natural systems, or to exploit natural resources.

While Pagans largely agree that the Earth is sacred and commonly say that they revere nature, what they mean by "nature" and their practices in relation with it differ. Practitioners more often understand "nature" as a symbol than as a place or as "the environment." Pagans expect "nature" to be an idea around which they can bond, but they often come into conflict over their diverse understandings of what is natural and how Pagans should relate with the natural world. Pagans came into disagreement, for example, at the Avalon East Pagan gathering of 1995 when some participants roasted a pig, and when Asatruar lit a gasoline-doused raft and set it adrift in the ocean as part of a ritual. Some participants in the festival felt that an attitude of reverence for nature requires vegetarianism, while some felt that it is sufficient that nonhuman others, such as the pig, be shown respect.[37] While Pagans agree in saying that the Earth is sacred and that nature should be revered, they exhibit diverse behavior in their relations with nature.[38]

Some of the differences in Pagan relations with nature arise from differences in their understandings of divinity. While Pagans agree that divinity is immanent in nature, they differ in how they think of divinity and in what they feel are appropriate relations with deities. Some Pagans' understanding of the relation between divinity and the natural world might be described as pantheism, the belief that all is divine (understood in monotheistic religions as all is God, or God is in all things). This is particularly true of those who talk about the Earth as Gaia or Gaea. Some find that since the sacred is immanent in humans as well as in the Earth and is not restricted to deities, then "worship" and "reverence" may not be appropriate ways of relating with other-than-human persons. Many Pagans feel that deities and other-than-human people do not want praise, but respect.[39]

Pagans sometimes speak of an "otherworld" as though it is a distinct place from the natural world, in a way that makes it seem like the natural world is transcended to access something supernatural that is not immanent in nature. This otherworld or "otherland" is understood as a place where people go when they meditate or dream, and sometimes as the land of the dead. Pagan meditations are often guided meditations, structured through imagery to direct participants to a particular sort of experience. Sometimes this is seen as a method of "deep play," or active imagination in the sense intended by Jungian psychology, so that the experience is perceived as imaginal but real. The otherworld that is accessed is not a corporeal place in the same way that New York or London are "real" places, but it nonetheless is a place where things really happen, with real repercussions. Some Pagans think of perception of the otherworld in terms of a state of wonder and being open to possibility. Some explain experiences of the otherworld in terms of altered states of consciousness, saying that one's perception of reality is altered when one goes into a trance state. Eliade describes such experiences as ecstasy, which he presents in terms of the soul standing out of one's body or out of the world. Pagans are just as likely to understand such experiences as standing out of oneself in the sense of out of one's cultural preconceptions, rather than out of the world. In ecstasy, one stands out of the ordinary, but not necessarily out of the natural.

Many Pagans hold what might be termed a monist view of the universe based on scientific understandings of the world. Monism is often understood in contrast to dualism, an understanding of the universe as fundamentally divided between two types of things, such as the natural and the supernatural, or the material and the spiritual. Monism is sometimes described as an understanding of the universe as restricted to the material, but Pagans tend to think of the natural world as not restricted to the quantifiable. If divinity is present in nature, nature does not need to be transcended for divinity to appear. The category of "the supernatural" is then irrelevant, since spirits are beings in and of the natural world. Pagans who subscribe to a monist view of the universe accept the idea that the planet Earth and the physical universe started with the big bang and proceeds according to physical laws, but they tend to think of the physical world as less limited than a strict empiricist view of the world would indicate. Such Pagans note the ambiguities of quantum physics, indicating that we do not fully understand the complexity of the physical workings of the universe. Thus, they conclude that it would not be appropriate to say that the god/desses or magic do not exist simply because their existence has not been proven. Scott Cunningham, for example, says, "Magic is the practice of moving natural (though little-understood) energies to effect needed change."[40]

Pagan cosmologies might be more accurately termed "holistic" than "monist" to describe the Pagan sense that humans are not separate from nature but part of it, in the sense that the personal or the individual is embedded in the cosmic or universal.[41] However, it should be noted that some Pagans do espouse a dualist understanding of the universe. Gardnerian priest Gus diZerega, for example, holds a panentheistic understanding of the universe, which means that he believes that divinity is immanent in the Earth, but also transcendent of it.[42] Some practitioners of Gardnerian Witchcraft believe that all the goddesses are ultimately one Goddess, that all the gods are ultimately one God, and that finally even the Goddess and God emanate from a single absolute reality or source of divinity.

Some Pagans see this emanation as a process that occurs through time, so that the universe proceeds from one point and will conclude toward a final goal or end. This is sometimes called a **teleological** view. Some Hea-

---

Scott Cunningham was an American practitioner of Wicca. He was a prolific writer, best known for his book *Wicca: A Guide for the Solitary Practitioner.*

thens accept the Norse idea of Raganok, a final destruction of the universe, but most Pagans understand time to be cyclical rather than teleological. A cyclical view of time is focused on the cycling of the seasons and has no sense that history is proceeding toward a final end in destruction, final judgment, or redemption. Worldviews with a cyclical conception of time often do not have any sense that there was a beginning of the universe, and hence they do not have creation stories.

Another common feature of Pagan worldviews is a tendency toward **romanticism**. Pagans tend to idealize the past, envisioned as a time when people lived in harmony with one another and with the rest of the natural world and were more in touch with the divine. This time of greater harmony with nature is envisioned alternately as occurring in the rural past, such as in the folk culture of "Merrie Olde England"; the Neolithic, such as the matrifocal (mother-focused) cultures of Old Europe described by the archaeologist Marija Gimbutas; or the Paleolithic, the cultures of prehistory, before the advent of agriculture and living in settled communities. The metaphor of coming "home" is often connected to these images of the past, and practitioners speak of reclaiming their past heritage. In this context, Paganism is understood by some practitioners as a revival of "the Old Religion," whether that is understood as the folk religion of pre-Christian Britain, as the more ancient religions of Greece and Egypt, or as the primal religious practices of shamanism (understood as the original or primal religion of humanity, universally practiced by humans in prehistoric times).

The romanticism of Pagan worldviews is not often a conscious aspect of practitioners' cosmologies; it is more often an implicit belief that is more visible to scholars involved in Pagan studies than it is to practitioners. Similarly, scholars identify Pagan worldviews as "late modern" in terms not commonly expressed consciously by practitioners. Paganism can be categorized as a religion of **late modernity** because it embraces relativism, **globalism**, and skepticism. Pagans espouse relativism in the sense of an acceptance of ambiguity and a lack of certainty about truth. They tend to accept a recognition that everyone perceives reality differently. Pagans engage in globalism in the sense that eclectic practitioners take symbols, deities, and ritual practices from other cultures and use them without the context of their original time and place. Pagan sources of inspiration are global and are not confined to a single culture. This globalism is part of the general cultural milieu of late modernism. While Pagans exhibit a postmodern sense of play, create a pastiche of **cultural borrowings** in their rituals, and tend to question rationality, they are also skeptical in the sense of applying doubt to **Enlightenment** rationalism, and thus they are better described in terms of late modernity rather than postmodernism. However, Pagans also criticize rationalism for its incorporation of patriarchy

and its domination of nature.[43] Most Pagans embrace the modern Western
ideals of democracy, equality, and respect for diversity. In addition, they
support gender equality, sexual diversity, and the feminist value of empowerment more than average Americans do.

In contrast to their implicit beliefs about romanticism and the late modern character of their worldviews, Pagans consciously articulate their beliefs about pain, suffering, and death, and they have written a fair amount
of theology/thealogy about how these feature in their worldviews. In an
early essay discussing ethics, Starhawk provides a **theodicy** (or, more accurately, a *thea*dicy), explaining the role of suffering and pain in her
worldview and how this relates to her understanding of the Goddess. She
explains that suffering and pain are a consequence of actions against laws
of nature. Pain and suffering are not punishments for a violation of God's
law but are natural consequences inherent to the structure of the universe.
She gives the following example: "if I 'break' the law of gravity by jumping out of a third-story window, I may break my neck in consequence, not
because the Goddess is punishing me for my effrontery, but because that
is the way the law of gravity works. So, if we continue to spray our forests
with mutagenic chemicals that leach into local water supplies, we will
continue to see increases in miscarriages and birth defects."[44] The consequences of ecological damage are not necessarily felt by those directly responsible for the harm done to the environment, but Starhawk argues that
this does not indicate a lack of care for individuals on the part of the Goddess. Rather, it teaches us that we are collectively responsible for creating
justice in the world. This belief is in keeping with her cosmology, in which
the Goddess is immanent in the natural world, including humans: "*We*
must create justice and ecological and social balance; this is the prime concern, the bottom line, the nitty gritty of ethics in a worldview that sees deity as immanent in human life and the world we live in."[45] Scott Cunningham presents a similar understanding of suffering and pain as part of
life and part of divinity, suggesting that humans need to work with divinity to try to make the world a better place. He also indicates that for
Wiccans, divinity is not split into a wholly good god and a wholly evil
devil but is mixed in all deities, as in humans. He indicates that the
god/desses have their shadow sides as well.[46]

Death does not require so much explanation as suffering in Pagan
worldviews, since Pagans see death as a natural and necessary part of the
process of life in the natural world. The cycle of life requires death to
make a complete and self-sustaining cycle. Starhawk describes life without death as cancerous, and death without life as war and genocide.[47]
Death is honored in Pagan worldviews, rather than being envisioned as a
negative or destructive force, so old age is celebrated because it is not so
strongly associated with the fear of death. In Pagan myth, death is fea-

tured in stories of a dying god associated with the harvesting of grain. Each being has its own time, and in turn passes on to sustain others. Death is not just an end but also a beginning, a point in a continuing cycle. Pagans commonly believe in reincarnation. The cyclical aspect of reincarnation harmonizes with Pagan worldviews, but it also expresses a seemingly dualist belief in a spirit that is distinct from material bodies, which is hard to reconcile with beliefs about immanence and with Pagans' holistic cosmologies.

The Pagan belief in magic easily fits into Pagan beliefs about the holistic nature of the cosmos, and Pagans explicitly articulate these beliefs. Pagans tend to believe in the interconnectedness of all things, and they often use the metaphor of a web to describe this aspect of their cosmologies. Everything is connected to everything else, regardless of our limited ability to fully understand all the connections, so changing one part of the web has effects that may seem unrelated but that are connected through the web of relations. Pagan belief in magic is rooted in, or is dependent upon, this belief in the interconnectedness of all things in the universe. People who practice magic use the unseen or poorly understood connections of the web of the universe to bring about their desired results. This is not understood as manipulating natural forces, or as bending natural forces against their will, but as shaping a desired result by encouraging the result through petitioning the help of others and by focusing one's desire.

Belief in magic is also based on the idea that the future is constituted by probabilities, not predetermined outcomes: natural laws are not so much laws as probabilities. These probabilities are consistent on the large scale, but less so on smaller scales, such as in quantum physics. Pagans suggest that magic works on similar principles, but where even the probabilities are not well understood. Starhawk, for example, describes the nature of reality by saying that "all things are swirls of energy, vortexes of moving forces." Despite the appearance of separateness and fixity of physical objects, they are "field[s] of energies that congeal, temporarily, into forms." Things appear separate and fixed because of our (regular or ordinary) human perception of things in linear time. She notes the connection with modern physics, arguing that we can perceive the world differently, in "extraordinary consciousness," a way of perceiving the world holistically, as undifferentiated, and seeing patterns and connections instead of distinct objects.[48]

Cunningham remarks that anyone can do magic. Like science, he argues, it is a matter of knowing what to do and how to do it. Pagans believe that some of the connections available to use in magic are based on correspondences between things like certain colors, herbs, images, sounds, phases of the moon, and other astrological phenomenon. Based on such correspondences, some Pagans believe in the efficacy of sympathetic magic, so that action on a part can influence a larger whole. This is sometimes explained in terms of the microcosm being able to affect the macrocosm, symbolically rendered like this: "as above, so below." Cunningham describes a ritual to help pay a hundred-dollar phone bill one cannot afford. He suggests using green candles, patchouli oil and a selection of money-drawing herbs such as cinnamon and sage, parchment paper, and green ink. After lighting the candles and burning the herbs and spices, the practitioner creates an image of the phone bill. Drawing a square around the resulting image, the practitioner establishes control over it. S/he then draws a large X across it to negate its existence, visualizing the bill as being paid.[49]

Starhawk describes how ritual can create a mood that helps one address one's deeper or "Younger" self through symbolic associations of scents, colors, images, and sounds, which are represented by the tangible things used in the ritual. (In her tradition of Witchcraft, the conscious mind is referred to as the "Talking Self," and the unconscious mind accessed in trance and magic is referred to as the "Younger Self.") Some Pagans' beliefs about magic support the use of alternative medicine, so Pagans are more likely than others to practice and utilize the skills of things like herbalism, naturopathy, and Reiki.

FURTHER READING

Cunningham, Scott. *Wicca: A Guide for the Solitary Practitioner*. St. Paul, MN: Llewellyn Publications, 1988.

D'Apremont, Anne-Laure Ferlat, et al. "The Nature of the Divine: Transcendence and Immanence in Contemporary Pagan Theology." *The Pomegranate: The Journal of Pagan Studies* 16 (2001): 4–16.

Harvey, Graham. *Contemporary Paganism: Listening People, Speaking Earth*. New York: New York University Press, 1997.

Starhawk. *The Spiral Dance: A Rebirth of the Ancient Religion of the Great Goddess*. 10th anniversary ed. 1979. New York: HarperSanFrancisco, 1989.

NOTES

1. Michael York, "Defining Paganism," *The Pomegranate: A New Journal of Neopagan Thought* 11 (2000): 9.

2. Naomi Goldenberg introduced the term to religious studies in *Changing of the Gods* (Boston: Beacon Press, 1979), 96. The term also appears in the 1979 edition of Isaac Bonewits' *Real Magic* (Berkeley, CA: Creative Arts Book Company, 1971). He used other forms of the term, such as "thealogian," as early as 1974, in a privately published document, "The Druid Chronicles (Evolved)." The term is an obvious coinage, and it seems to have developed spontaneously in various groups. See Shan Jayran, "Thealogy," *Wikipedia: The Free Encyclopedia*, http://en.wikipedia.org/wiki/Thealogy (accessed November 15, 2004).

3. Graham Harvey suggests the term "theoilogy" in *Contemporary Paganism: Listening People, Speaking Earth* (New York: New York University Press, 1997), 66. Isaac Bonewits used the term "theoilogy" in the 1979 edition of *Real Magic*. Bonewits more frequently uses the term "polytheology" to describe studies of divinity in the context of polytheism. See Jayran, "Thealogy."

4. Quoted in Harvey, *Contemporary Paganism*, 160. For Starhawk's comment about rocks, see Harvey, *Contemporary Paganism*, 176.

5. See, for example, Diana Paxson, "Worshipping the Gods," Hrafnar website, www.hrafnar.org/norse/worship.html (accessed April 22, 2004), originally published in *Idunna* 20 (1993).

6. A. Irving Hallowell, "Ojibwa Ontology Behaviour and World View," in *Primitive Views of the World*, ed. Stanley Diamond (New York: Columbia University Press, 1969), 55.

7. Graham Harvey suggests that belief in nature spirits survives in English folklore as Brownies and boggarts. See Harvey, *Contemporary Paganism*, 56.

8. Jenny Blain, "Contested Meanings: Earth Religion Practitioners and the Everyday," *The Pomegranate: A New Journal of Neopagan Thought* 12 (2000): 19.

9. Terri Windling, *The Wood Wife* (New York: Tor [Tom Doherty Associates], 1996), 99.

10. Charles de Lint, *The Ivory and the Horn* (New York: Tor [Tom Doherty Associates], 1995), 171–72.

11. Helen Berger, *A Community of Witches* (Columbia: University of South Carolina Press, 1999), 33–34.

12. Tanya M. Luhrmann, *Persuasions of the Witch's Craft* (Cambridge, MA: Harvard University Press, 1989), 331–32.

13. Carol Christ, "Why Women Need the Goddess: Phenomenological, Psychological, and Political Reflections," in *The Politics of Women's Spirituality: Essays on the Rise of Spiritual Power within the Feminist Movement*, ed. Charlene Spretnak (Garden City, NY: Anchor Books, 1982), 75.

14. Starhawk, quoted in Christ, "Why Women Need the Goddess," 76.

15. Starhawk, *The Spiral Dance: A Rebirth of the Ancient Religion of the Great Goddess*, 10th anniversary ed. (1979; New York: HarperSanFrancisco, 1989), 99.

16. Otter G'Zell and Morning Glory, "Who on Earth Is the Goddess?" in *Magical Religion and Modern Witchcraft*, ed. James R. Lewis (Albany: State University of New York Press, 1996), 28.

17. Quoted in Joanne Pearson, Richard H. Roberts, and Geoffrey Samuel, *Nature Religion Today: Paganism in the Modern World* (Edinburgh: Edinburgh University Press, 1998), 134. G'Zell's vision is discussed in Gordon J. Melton's *An Iona Anthology* (Isle of Iona, Argyll: New Iona Press, 1990), 183. G'Zell, originally Tim Zell, has more recently changed his name to Oberon Zell-Ravenheart. For the Gaia hypothesis, see J. E. Lovelock's *Gaia: A New Look at Life on Earth* (Oxford: Oxford University Press, 1982).

18. I have discussed divinity in relation to Pagan ideas of nature more fully elsewhere, and I draw on that work here. See Barbara Jane Davy, "Nature," in *The Encyclopedia of Modern Witchcraft and Neo-Paganism*, ed. Shelly Rabinovitch and James Lewis (New York: Citadel, 2002), 165–66.

19. Cited in Andy Letcher, "'Virtual Paganism' or Direct Action? The Implications of Road Protesting for Modern Paganism," *Diskus* 6 (2000), Web edition, http://web.uni-marburg.de/religionswissenschaft/journal/diskus (accessed May 16, 2001).

20. Marion Bowman, "Nature, the Natural, and Pagan Identity," *Diskus* 6 (2000), Web edition, http://web.uni-marburg.de/religionswissenschaft/journal/diskus (accessed May 16, 2001).

21. Starhawk, *Spiral Dance*, 92.

22. Scott Cunningham, *Wicca: A Guide for the Solitary Practitioner* (St. Paul, MN: Llewellyn Publications, 2003), 11.

23. Pearson, Roberts, and Samuel, *Nature Religion Today*, 170.

24. Hayao Miyazaki, *Princess Mononoke* (Miramax Films, 2000).

25. Ronald Hutton, *The Triumph of the Moon: A History of Modern Pagan Witchcraft* (Oxford: Oxford University Press, 1999), 196.

26. Hutton, *Triumph of the Moon*, 198.

27. Starhawk, *Spiral Dance*, 108.

28. Hutton, *Triumph of the Moon*, 44.

29. Hutton, *Triumph of the Moon*, 45.

30. Aleister Crowley, "Hymn to Pan," in *Liber Aba*, 2nd rev. ed., 4:121–22 (York Beach, ME: Samuel Weiser, 1997).

31. Hutton, *Triumph of the Moon*, 33.

32. Starhawk, *Spiral Dance*, 90–91.

33. Margot Adler, *Drawing Down the Moon: Witches, Druids, Goddess-Worshippers, and Other Pagans in America Today*, revised and expanded ed. (Boston: Beacon Press, 1986), 20.

34. Diana Paxson, "The Religion of the North," Hrafnar website, 1996, www.hrafnar.org/norse/tract.html (accessed April 22, 2004).

35. Freya Aswynn, *Northern Mysteries & Magick: Runes & Feminine Powers* (St. Paul, MN: Llewellyn Publications, 1998), 177, 184.

36. Jone Salomonsen, *Enchanted Feminism: The Reclaiming Witches of San Francisco* (London: Routledge, 2002), 2.

37. Bowman, "Nature, the Natural, and Pagan Identity."

38. See Adler, *Drawing Down the Moon*, 399, 400.

39. Harvey, *Contemporary Paganism*, 174.

40. Cunningham, *Wicca: A Guide for the Solitary Practitioner*, 6.

41. "Holistic" is the term Helen Berger uses, *Community of Witches*, 124.

42. Gus diZerega, *Pagans & Christians: The Personal Spiritual Experience* (St. Paul, MN: Llewellyn Publications, 2001).

43. This analysis of Paganism in terms of late modernity is taken from Berger. See especially Berger, *Community of Witches*, 7, 123, 125.

44. Starhawk, "Ethics and Justice in Goddess Religion," in *The Politics of Women's Spirituality: Essays on the Rise of Spiritual Power within the Feminist Movement*, ed. Charlene Spretnak (Garden City, NY: Anchor Press [Doubleday], 1982), 417.

45. Starhawk, "Ethics and Justice," 421.

46. Cunningham, *Wicca: A Guide for the Solitary Practitioner*, 18.

47. Starhawk, *Spiral Dance*, 41.

48. Starhawk, *Spiral Dance*, 32–33.

50. Cunningham, *Wicca: A Guide for the Solitary Practitioner*, 23.

2

Social Organization

Because most Pagans are reluctant to cede religious authority to any centralized structure, institutions develop differently in Paganism than in other world religions. The basic unit of organization in Paganism is small, usually less than a dozen people. Membership in these small groups is fluid, and groups tend to form and disband relatively frequently. Any Pagan can act as his or her own clergyperson or become a priest/ess, so Pagans do not necessarily belong to a religious organization or group of any kind. Consequently, Paganism has more in common with religious activity that has been described as "daily" or "democratized" shamanism than with the institutional forms of monotheistic traditions. The relative lack of formal religious institutions within Paganism has led some ethnographers and sociologists to label it "disorganized" religion, or even "pseudoreligion," and to comment on its seeming tendency to dismantle itself, often dissolving structures and institutions as soon as they start to form.

Paganism is currently undergoing a process of routinization, developing religious institutions and standardized practices as it grows from a new religious movement into a world religion, but there are active countertrends against the normalization of Pagan religious practice. Forms of social organization beyond small groups do develop, but some Pagans feel constrained as soon as they become aware of these structures, and become intensely critical of them—hence Paganism seems to deconstruct itself. However, some Pagans welcome the increasing organization because they feel it will increase the legitimacy of the religion in the eyes of the public and will lead to further legal rights and protections for Pagans.

"Institutions" in religion can be things with physical components, such as buildings like synagogues or mosques, as well as social structures like clergy (religious officials) and **laity** (general participants who are not clergypersons). The institutions of Paganism have several structural differences from the monotheistic religions. Paganism rarely forms sects in the way of the monotheistic traditions, which usually develop as splinter groups on the basis of differences in belief, so the overall structure of Paganism is different as a world religion. Paganism is an umbrella term, which includes multiple denominations and types of Paganisms. Wicca, Asatru, and Druidry, for example, are denominations within Paganism. Eclectics, solitaries, and practitioners of Goddess religion are types of Pagans. The various types and denominations have a family resemblance to one another but do not have a single genesis. There is no originating prophet who revealed the central story or foundation of the religion. (While Gerald Gardner is an important historical figure in Gardnerian Wicca, his Book of Shadows, a book of spells and rituals, does not have unique authority in Paganism. Even within Wicca, each Gardnerian coven creates its own book, and each individual Wiccan adds to her/his own book.) Paganism has multiple points of origin instead of simply diffusing from a single source. Disparate groups appeared here and there throughout North American and Europe, initially inspired largely by books, first by the German and English Romantics, other poets and novelists, and anthropologists such as James Frazer and Margaret Murray, and later by writings specifically on Paganism as a newly revived religion.

Some Pagan groups do form as sects, or splinter groups, founded because of an internal disagreement in a group. However, sects in monotheistic traditions are generally formed due to divisions in beliefs about the fundaments of the faith: a dispute about doctrine or orthodox tradition. Sects often regard each other as heretics. This is not the case between the different types and denominations of Paganism, because there is no orthodox tradition, and adherence to the religion is not conceived in terms of doctrine or beliefs. I use the term "denomination" for different groups within Paganism because it seems less connected to the idea of divisions based on disagreements about doctrine. "Denomination" simply conveys that the groups have different names for themselves. Despite "witch wars," which are emotionally charged local disputes among Pagans, the denominations are not in competition with one another the way that sects often are. Furthermore, unlike the Protestant sects within Christianity,[1] Pagan denominations do not tend to poach members from one another. Participation in one Pagan group does not preclude participation in others, and having multiple memberships in various organizations is common. Pagans do not tend to think that Paganism in general, let alone a specific denomination, is any more true than any other religious tradition.

Practitioners indicate that Paganism provides a symbolic language for relating with divinity, and various languages may be more suitable for different people.[2] Paganism is preferred by practitioners for other reasons, such as for the wealth of female imagery for divinity, for the resources it provides for ritual and for having religious experiences, for its positive valuation of women and nature, and for the celebration of diversity and religious tolerance within it.

Paganism has no sacred text or scripture on which to base claims for authority. For most Pagans, there is no book that serves the same purpose as the Christian Bible: most Pagans do not regard any book as uniquely authoritative, inspirational, or revelatory.[3] Each Pagan can experience the divine directly, so no single book can speak for all. Additionally, personal experiences have more authority than what one reads in a book. However, there is something of a literary canon developing. Many groups have similar recommended reading lists. These lists often begin with the works of Starhawk and Margot Adler. In particular, *The Spiral Dance* and *Drawing Down the Moon*, both originally published in 1979, were frequently the first introduction to the religion for people who became Pagan in the 1980s and early 1990s. This is perhaps less true of more recent converts subsequent to the growth of the Internet in the mid- to late 1990s.

That authority is vested in the individual is a teaching reiterated in virtually all how-to texts produced by Pagans. Pagans are protective of the autonomy and self-determination of the groups in which they participate. They often resist governance by larger federations. Some create official "churches," but others resist the formation of official institutions that might try to dictate what the smaller groups can do. Many Pagans fear that centralized organization of the religion would lead to power imbalances. They feel that all Pagans should be equal, that Paganism is a "priesthood of all believers," with no clergy standing above the laity. In the words of a Wiccan practitioner, "The power is in the hands of every practitioner, not specialized priests or priestesses who perform these feats for the masses. This is what makes Wicca a truly satisfying way of life. We have direct links with the Deities."[4] Some Pagans fear that a centralized organization would lead to the dominance of some Pagans over others, with a consequent loss of freedom of practice and belief.

As a religion characterized by a "priesthood of all believers," Paganism bears some similarity to religious practices described by shamanism, and indeed some Pagans identify their religious practices with shamanism. The term "shamanism" is generally applied to certain practices in indigenous cultures, particularly those cultures wherein people live in small groups and subsist by foraging. It is usually associated with practices of healing and relating with the more-than-human world.[5] It is a scholarly construct, a term applied to cultures by outsiders. Paganism is most similar to shamanism in what some anthropologists refer to as "daily shamanism," the everyday magical activities of people that occur outside of the more spectacular shamanic rituals noted by early anthropologists.[6] People practicing these everyday shamanic activities may be recognized as having specific powers in indigenous cultures, without formal status as shamans. In tribal societies, social roles are not as highly specialized as in modern culture, so it is unsurprising that most adults in these societies engage in activities that might be described as shamanic, for example, divination, magic, and the interpretation of dreams. In the cultures in which shamanism appears, religion is not generally identifiable as something distinct from culture by the people who live within it. The participants do not perceive it as something distinct from the daily activities of hunting, fishing, and entertainment. Among the Nabesna of British Columbia, whose religion exhibits characteristics of daily shamanism, all adults are expected to pay attention to their dreams and communicate with the more-than-human world through them, gaining experience as they get older, until each becomes a "sleep doctor," a *gyenin*, the Nabesna name for a shaman (essentially, one who talks with the spirits).[7]

Perhaps some Pagans would prefer to develop religious structures as in indigenous cultures, such as the traditional religious practices of the Nabesna, where there are religious specialists but not priests. Spiritual power is not vested in a single authority in shamanism, but in people with particularly well-developed religious practices recognized as strong in the ways of the spirits. These people are recognized as elders or shamans rather than as ordained priests. Some Pagan traditions have priests and priestesses, but these are generally initiated rather than ordained. Pagans also recognize elders as sources of religious authority because of their experience. Most Pagans believe that all practitioners have similar potentials to develop spiritually. Pagans do not generally feel that priest/esses and elders have a special relationship with divinity or greater access to the divine, and Pagan priest/esses do not serve as intermediaries between practitioners and the divine.[8] Each Pagan can have direct encounters with divinity, although individuals may develop specific spiritual skills to a greater or lesser degree than other individuals. As in the shamanism of the Nabesna, Pagan practitioners may specialize in certain religious activities, such as divination, ritual leadership, singing, writing liturgies, administration, counseling, and so on, without developing any greater general authority among their coreligionists.

Gardnerian Wiccan initiatory traditions are somewhat different from other Pagan denominations in this respect, since initiatory Wiccans have a greater sense of separation between clergy and laity, emphasized through the secrecy of their priesthood. Not all secrets are revealed until the third degree of initiation. Some other denominations have specific clergy training programs and offer services typical of a clergy serving a laity. One such group is the Fellowship of Isis. In this multifaith organization that includes Pagans, clergy are trained at Lyceums, or schools, that are chartered through the main college of Isis in Ireland, where the Fellowship began. Members of the Fellowship can found a local group, called an Iseum, and offer religious services such as initiation and other celebratory rituals. Each Iseum is dedicated to a deity chosen by the founder, and this deity is thought to shape the development of the Iseum.[9]

Similar to practices of daily shamanism in indigenous cultures, it is not only the high festivals and showy rituals that are religiously significant in Paganism. Pagans keep home altars and shrines and engage in personal spell work outside of the celebration of the seasonal festivals. In addition, the choices made in daily life have religious significance for Pagans. For them, the spiritual is political, just as the personal is political.[10] It is participation in everyday life as a Pagan that makes one a Pagan, as much as doing formal ritual in a group or having experiences mediated through others at public events. The way one prepares one's food, composts, recycles, and shows respect for the more-than-human world on a daily basis is as important as organized ritual.

At least half of all Pagan practitioners do not belong to a group and instead practice as solo practitioners, or solitaries.[11] Solitaries, however, often do participate in the larger Pagan community. The "community" can serve in the place of the church or congregation in Christian traditions for Pagans. "Community," in this context, is understood in a parallel sense to the "gay community," as sharing a sense of alternative lifestyle, life world, and politics. It refers not to a physical community such as a town or a neighborhood, but to a shared life world or worldview, including a perception of reality that accepts the efficacy of magic.[12] The Pagan community can also be described as a "community of memory," wherein a sense of community is fostered by identification with those killed in the witch hunts.[13]

While Pagans in a particular town or city may develop a sense of community, they rarely have public meeting spaces. Pagans usually meet in practitioners' homes or in parks for rituals, or at local coffee shops or pubs for social events. To an extent, the lack of a public building owned by a group functions to make Pagan groups more transient. Owning a building gives a group a focus and requires setting up a certain amount of bureaucratic overhead to allow the group to maintain the building despite fluctuations in membership. Without a dedicated public building, groups more easily disintegrate as individuals lose interest, move away, or leave in anger.[14] A few larger groups, such as Circle Sanctuary, own land. Pagans are generally more interested in purchasing wild or naturalized land than in opening public ritual space within towns and cities. Perhaps over time, wealthy Pagans will build temples to their patron deities, or perhaps

not. Some Pagans express a desire for such public spaces, but many prefer to meet their god/desses at home or in parks and conservation areas.
Some groups try to collect money to hold Pagan festivals, so as to gain
more freedom than is possible in renting campgrounds or camps for these
events.[15] More commonly, though, money is collected at public events for
the specific event attended in order to cover the costs of candles, incense,
snacks, and beverages.

The basic structure of Pagan groups is the circle, which is called a coven
in Wicca and in other traditions of Witchcraft. In Druidry, it is called a
grove, and in Asatru, it is sometimes called a troth, although "troth" may
also refer to a federation of smaller groups and solitary practitioners. Pagan circles tend to be small and intimate, usually consisting of less than a
dozen people. Starhawk's definition of a coven—"a Witches' support
group, consciousness-raising group, psychic study center, clergy-training
program, College of Mysteries, surrogate clan, and religious congregation
all rolled into one"[16]—is descriptive not only of covens but of Pagan circles more generally. She uses the term "circle" for looser-knit ritual groups
that may form into covens,[17] but it also functions as a generic term for Pagan groups. Some circles are affiliated with larger organizations, such as
those described at the end of this chapter. Many circles, however, are local groups not affiliated with any larger federation.

The circle represents the equality of the participants: none stands above
the others, and there is no "front" of the circle. The initiatory traditions of
Gardnerian and Alexandrian Wicca appear to have a more hierarchical
structure than feminist-oriented groups. In Gardnerian and Alexandrian
covens, the group is lead by a high priestess and priest, who ideally act as
a voice for the group's desires rather than dominating the other coveners.
The high priestess in such groups has the highest authority, followed by
the high priest. They are usually both initiates of the third degree. In feminist-oriented groups, the ideal is often to run the group on consensus, but
the emergence of leaders is usually inevitable. This sometimes leads to
anger and accusations of covert control.

In both feminist groups and initiatory traditions, there is often a hierarchy of status, if nothing else.[18] This hierarchy sometimes extends beyond
the coven but operates primarily in terms of lineage rather than control
over what "offspring" covens do. The organization of related groups in a
tradition is generally a branching structure of filiation, not a power structure or an administrative structure. Paganism is decentralized, so that
larger organizations or federations exercise little control over what individual groups do.

Some circles are part of traditions that are structured as **mystery religions**. In initiatory Wicca, for example, there is no laity as such: all participants are either clergy or potential clergypersons as initiates or neo-

phytes training for initiation into the mysteries. A neophyte is a beginner, an apprentice, or a student. The mysteries are protected by secrecy. Gardnerian training, for example, is open at the first level to all interested persons over the age of eighteen, but further training is restricted to those who have been initiated into the first degree. Some researchers have been allowed to attend further training, but not with unlimited access.[19] Second-degree training prepares for initiation into the third degree. Most of the information revealed in this training has been made public, except perhaps some details given to third-degree initiates as oral instruction. The rationale for the secrecy surrounding the training and initiation is to shield the identity of coven members against persecution, but also to protect people from the mysteries. Secret knowledge can be harmful if revealed to those who are not prepared for it or who might misuse it. Secrecy can also help create a sense of trust in covens. Some sociologists note that secrecy fosters group cohesion, creating an in-group and an outgroup.[20] More generally, secrecy functions as a form of institutionalization in Wicca, structuring it into levels of status.

Pagan circles often have a structure of concentric circles, of an inner court and an outer court, so that there are closed or private groups related to public groups. A Pagan women's group, for example, might have public monthly meetings, based on the phases of the moon, at a local bookstore or magical supply shop, which is open to all women. Some of the women who lead rituals in the public group might also hold private celebrations of the festivals in closed covens to which they belong. Many of these women might also celebrate the festivals in public ceremonies open to men and women, perhaps at larger regional gatherings.

Participants in closed Pagan circles often think of the circle in terms of the closeness of family, more intimate than friends.[21] As in families, similar sorts of conflict develop between members. The intensity of the relations in covens, for example, can ultimately lead to the disintegration of the coven. But recombinations are frequent; membership is fluid in closed groups as well as in public groups, but relationships continue with the development of new covens. Some covens continue to exist long after all the original members have left. Despite the sometimes acrimonious partings of the ways between coven members, divided groups can re-form into new covens over time, and relationships developed in covens remain important in the larger community regardless of whether individuals continue to circle together.[22]

The transience of Pagan circles should not be mistaken for superficial bonds. In Wiccan covens, the ideal is to come together in perfect love and perfect trust, creating intense personal relationships. The instability of Pagan groups has led some sociologists to regard Paganism as a quasi-religion, but others suggest that covens should be looked at in the context of extended networks and related associations.[23] Wicca does show trends of growing into an institutionalized religion, which some sociologists suggest is necessary for the survival of the religion. Some scholars theorize that new religious movements tend to disintegrate without formal institutions. However, even if some groups do not continue due to a lack of organizational structure, it appears as though, at the very least, the inclusive groups of Wicca will survive.[24] Wicca is currently undergoing a process of routinization as children are being raised in the traditions developed by their parents, and in some cases, grandparents.[25]

However, there is a strong current in Paganism that resists routinization and the development in the religion of codified traditions. Some would rather see Paganism as a spontaneous way of being religious that does not rely on a received tradition of ritual forms or on the teachings of a bureaucratized clergy. Pagan studies scholar and practitioner Michael York, for example, would seem to prefer that what he calls "paganism" be a spontaneous way of being religious, that it serve as the always new upwelling of religious experience. For York, this is a human universal, visible in folk customs worldwide, including things like tossing coins in a fountain, making wishes, and leaving offerings.[26]

In this sense, "paganism" is largely congruent with Catherine Albanese's understanding of nature religion as a form of religiosity that is largely implicit rather than institutionalized. Albanese, in *Reconsidering Nature Religion*, says that she finds nature religion to dissolve almost as soon as it is identified.[27] Nature religion deconstructs itself because it is implicit, something that people do largely unconsciously or on an ad hoc basis, rather than a formally institutionalized religion with meeting houses and identifiable congregations. Nature religion thus appears in rituals that develop spontaneously at environmental protests, and in some of the folk practices of Pagans. Most of Albanese's discussion of nature religion is about phenomena such as the intense communion with nature described by John Muir, the religious experience of an individual alone in nature, apart from community. She explains that in such phenomena, people feel a sense of kinship of spirit rather than connections based on a common ethnic background or working on common tasks, so that organized religion is less likely to develop as a result.[28] However, in Paganism, more specifically than in the broader religious expressions of nature religion, community is formed around things other than individual revelatory experiences in nature. Shared experiences in the circle are important, but for some Pagans, ethnicity is paramount to their sense of community. This is particularly true in the revival of Pagan traditions in Eastern Europe.[29]

In her discussion of nature religion, Albanese notes the formation of Wicca and other contemporary Pagan groups, but she suggests that these phenomena have the status of a "movement" rather than a religion. She notes that membership changes frequently, that groups are subject to fragmentation, and furthermore that the development of such groups is atypical in Western culture. She argues that "without strongly institutionalized community, without clearly demarcated history, it exists as an inherently *un*stable construct, and it easily *de*constructs into something else." The something else, she says, is politics, or metaphysical sublimation through things like New Age healing. Nature religion does not lead to the development of a "church of nature."[30]

Nature religion, and the Pagan groups expressive of it, may not lead to the development of institutions like the Catholic Church, but this does not mean that other forms of religion will not develop out of nature religion. Paganism follows a different pattern of routinization, developing with a different sense of community and a different sense religious custom through daily practice. Implicit religion is just as common worldwide as institutionalized religion, but it is much less identifiable. In indigenous traditions, for example, there are rarely words that translate into "religion" or "church," yet traditions develop and evolve without these explicitly recognized institutions. Religion does not require central authority as a form of organization. Oral traditions, tribal religions, and shamanism, for example, perpetuate themselves without central authority. Religion can be perpetuated as a nondistinguished aspect of cultural tradition. Some of the institutions of Paganism are identifiable, however, such as the resistance to hierarchy and bureaucratization. This is, paradoxically, an identifiable structure of Pagan religion.

Pagans are often willfully disorganized in their resistance to bureaucracy and hierarchy, which leads some researchers to describe Paganism as "a decentralized religious movement" and a "disorganized religion."[31] Such tendencies are especially evident in feminist Paganism, in overlap with feminist spirituality in groups such as Reclaiming, which is run on consensus, and attempts to reject centralized authority. The religious experiences of Pagans, of direct connection with divinity, counter the processes of routinization as the religion is constantly renewed through new encounters with divinity. The belief that anyone can have such experiences makes it impossible for any single person or organization to claim to speak with authority about what experiences are legitimate or about what are proper Pagan experiences. This belief that all Pagans can encounter the divine directly is part of how Pagan religion legitimizes itself: authority resides in the individual, not in approval of external clergy or elders.

Some Pagans reject the label of "religion," preferring "spirituality," in common with more general trends in religiosity.[32] Pagans often reject "religion" or "organized religion," by which they usually mean Christianity and Judaism. First-generation Pagans tend to be converts out of

Christianity or Judaism and are critical of those traditions. Their practice of Paganism is "religion" in the sense that they are now participating in Paganism instead of in the organized religion to which they used to belong. Canadian legislation conflates religion with "a formal boundary-maintaining structure through which that religion is administered."[33] Pagan religion is not like this, so identification of Pagans is largely dependent on their identifying themselves as Pagan. This creates a problem of how to restrict who is Pagan among practitioners, as well as how to identify practitioners for scholars studying Pagans. There is no creed to identify Pagans, and individuals bear only a family resemblance to one another.

The desire for Paganism to continue as "disorganized religion," or to develop formal religious institutions, divides Pagans. Within Paganism, there is "tension between a desire to appropriate the religious language and the legitimacy it confers, while repudiating the cultural and institutional baggage that [practitioners] perceive as attached to 'religion' more generally."[34] Some Pagans fear that for Paganism to gain recognition as a legitimate religion, it will have to change to resemble the organized religions that people left in coming to Paganism. They want to retain the countercultural tendencies of Paganism and for it to challenge social norms and act as the social conscience of the surrounding culture in terms of the environment and acceptance of ethnic and lifestyle diversity, for example. Others want Paganism to become unremarkable, just another of the world religions, with the same legal rights and freedoms as other religions.[35]

Contemporary Paganism has always been somewhat critical of its surrounding culture. Wicca has "always posed an implicit powerful challenge to social and religious norms."[36] Wicca was inspired in part by the Romantic movement against the Victorian repression of sexuality. However, rather than being countercultural in the sense of the American movement of the 1960s, this Paganism rejected modernity. "Pagan witchcraft travelled from Britain to the United States as a branch of radical conservatism; it returned as a branch of radical socialism" after being influenced by Starhawk and other feminist witches.[37] The tension between conservatives who regard Paganism as a private matter and those who want it to change the world continues.

Pagan parents are somewhat more likely than other practitioners to want Paganism to be accepted by the surrounding culture as legitimate.[38] It is primarily in the context of raising children that researchers talk about the process of routinization in Wicca, and Paganism more generally. Some suggest that the birth of the second generation of Pagans is causing the religious movement to mature.[39] Based on the supposition that there are approximately 200,000 adult Pagans in the United States, probably more than 82,600 children are currently being raised as Pagans.[40] Raising children in the religion requires teaching them and creating new traditions, and, "because children enjoy repetition, the rituals are likely to become systematized."[41] This routinization process causes some tension with the mystery religion aspect of Wicca. As a mystery religion, Wicca is somewhat oriented toward gaining new members through the training and initiation of neophytes, rather than maintaining the faith through the development of family traditions.[42]

Another motivation for institutionalization in Paganism is the desire of some practitioners for greater legal rights and protections, as well as services.[43] Some Pagans express concerns about freedom of religion, fearing persecution through things like having burning crosses erected on their lawns and discrimination in child custody cases. Pagans have also had problems with being allowed to take religious holidays for Pagan festivals. Students have been refused permission to write exams before Samhain when the tests are scheduled for November 1.[44] In Wicca, November 1 is much like New Year's Day in the secular calendar, a day to recover after the festivities of the night before.

Some Pagans want the same services that are available to members of other religious groups, such as formal seminary training of clergy and legal recognition of chaplains for military and correctional institutions (jails and penitentiaries). Some also want to be able to perform legal marriages (sometimes called handfastings in Paganism). Other Pagans fear that legal regulations of services might follow recognition of legal status.[45] The legal recognition of groups presents a problem for administration on the government side, as well as for practitioners, most of whom do not belong to large federated organizations. There is also a problem in deciding who should be awarded legal rights to perform marriages. Many Pagans would rather that no groups have legal status, if it would mean that others would be denied it, since this would create a certain hegemonic authority in legally recognized groups, which is contrary to the spirit of individual authority in Paganism.[46]

Perhaps more than any other Pagan organization in Canada, the Wiccan Church of Canada has developed structures common to other religious organizations. The Wiccan Church of Canada of southern Ontario is run with a central authority rather than through a regular coven structure. The training of clergy is structured through a formal curriculum, and candidates are judged by a committee of priesthood.[47] This structure allows the development of a laity—people who want to participate in the religious tradition but without becoming initiated into it. Yet even with these concessions to mainstream religion, the Wiccan Church of Canada continues to be denied tax-exempt status.[48] A number of Pagan groups in the United States have achieved tax-exempt status.

In other branches of Wicca, and in Paganism more generally, the process of routinization does not follow the familiar models of the monotheistic traditions. Berger compares the routinization of Wicca as a religious movement with Max Weber's writings on the routinization of charisma. In Weber's understanding of routinization, the teachings of a charismatic prophet or religious leader are standardized and codified by her/his disciples. In Paganism, however, it is competent administrators who contribute most to the standardization of religious practice, through things like producing newsletters and organizing festivals.[49] Paganism does have celebrities, such as Starhawk and Fiona Horne, but while they are charismatic leaders, Pagans do not follow them the way Weber describes charismatics. The modern media, by exposing all the foibles of public personages, mitigates the influence of charismatic leaders, and the context of late modernity contributes to a general attitude of skepticism in regard to leaders, and to the rejection of hierarchy.[50]

Pagan practices converge in at least three ways in processes of routinization and standardization: coercive, mimetic, and normative isomorphism.[51] Isomorphism refers to a convergence of diverse types into a more homogenous type. Coercive isomorphism, a response to outside pressures to conform to certain standards, is the least active process of homogenization in Paganism. There are some legal requirements for obtaining tax-exempt status and the right to conduct marriages, but these pressures do not form a significant impetus to conformity of religious practice in Wicca.[52]

Mimetic isomorphism, much more common in Paganism, is the result of diverse groups learning from one another and copying or mimicking the practices of other groups and individuals. Homogenization in Paganism develops with the spread of chants and liturgies through individual contact at festivals.[53] Festivals contribute to mimetic isomorphism by bringing together large groups of Pagans, who participate in workshops, teach each other songs and chants, and perform rituals. Almost half of festival participants in one study attended large festivals.[54] Another sort of mimetic isomorphism occurs through print media. The influence of Starhawk's books is enormous, but periodicals are also popular. There are more than a hundred Pagan journals in the United States.[55] However, the explosive growth of Paganism in the 1990s coincided with advances in desktop publishing and the popular growth of the Internet, and this has become a significant medium for many Pagans to share their ideas and communicate with one another.

Normative isomorphism occurs through the growth of professionalism, including the creation of experts and standards for experts. The growth of seminaries and training programs for clergy, such as Cherry Hill Seminary in Vermont, is part of this process of normative isomorphism in Paganism. The rapid growth of Paganism contributes to routinization, because with increased numbers of new practitioners, the demand for formalized training and access to services increases. In the process, individuals have less control over the development of the religion. This contributes to divisions between those who want Paganism to be countercultural and those who seek legitimacy for it, as well as between those who have been involved in Paganism for decades and those who are new to the religion.

A number of large organizations have developed in Paganism in the form of federations. These federations are generally networking organizations, sometimes created to conduct **antidefamation** work, to provide accurate information on Paganism to media people and governmental and policing authorities, and to protect the religious rights of Pagans. Membership usually requires payment of small annual fees, which often cover the cost of producing a newsletter or publishing a magazine or journal.

The Pagan Federation in the United Kingdom, founded in 1971, is one of the oldest still-existing federations. It produces a journal called *The Pagan Dawn*, formerly called *The Wiccan*, and holds an annual conference, as well as more frequent regional gatherings. Membership is open to all adults over the age of eighteen who accept the principles of love and kinship with nature; who follow the ethical principle of "if it harms none, do what you will"; and who acknowledge both female and male aspects of the divine. They began as an antidefamation organization and developed into a networking organization. They now also provide some chaplaincy support. The Pagan Federation is run by an elected board of directors called "the Council."[56] The Pagan Federation International serves as an international liaison between the Pagan Federation in the United Kingdom and related groups around the world, such as the Pagan Federation/ Fédération Païenne Canada (PFPC) in Canada.[57] In Australia, a group called the Pagan Alliance functions in much the same way as the Pagan Federation, and membership is based on acceptance of the principles outlined by the Pagan Federation. The Pagan Alliance, founded in 1991, has become a nationally incorporated networking organization in order to produce the magazine *Pagan Times*.[58]

Circle Sanctuary, founded in 1974 by Selena Fox and Jim Alan, is the largest Pagan organization in the United States. Circle is based in Wisconsin and owns land there. It has legal status as a church, and it sponsors paid clergy. Circle produces *Circle Network News*, a magazine with a circulation of 15,000, and hosts the annual Pagan Spirit Gathering festival.[59] The Covenant of the Goddess (CoG) is another American organization. It was founded in 1975 and is based in California. It aims to protect the legal rights of various Pagans in a nondenominational manner. As a federation, CoG does not train clergy or conduct initiations. However, it can give individuals legal status to conduct marriages in some states. CoG has individual members and coven members that conduct training and initiation.[60]

For some Pagans, the Covenant of Unitarian Universalist Pagans (CU-UPs) serves as a larger organization. CUUPs formed within the Unitarian Church in 1987. As part of the Unitarian Universalists, they can provide the security of a well-established church infrastructure, including seminary training, church buildings, two publishing houses, and a money base. However, not all congregations within the Unitarian Universalist Church are happy with the development of CUUPs within it.[61]

There are also a number of explicitly Craft organizations that serve as federations. One of the best known of these is Reclaiming. Reclaiming formed in the late 1970s in San Francisco as a collective that grew out of classes taught by Starhawk and Diane Baker. It is an explicitly feminist Witchcraft organization and is open to men as well as women. Reclaiming has continued to offer courses, organize public rituals, and produce a quarterly newsletter, as well as run weeklong Witch camps, which are training retreats. The Reclaiming Collective, as it first existed, was run on consensus and pursued projects through largely autonomous cells. Membership in these cells was based on participation and on getting to know people in the group. This created tension as the group grew and it became harder to get to know people in what became an inner circle. In 1997, the Collective reformed itself, creating an explicit leadership and administration center for the San Francisco area, and maintaining tax-exempt status. Reclaiming groups in other areas operate completely independently but subscribe to the principles of unity developed collectively in 1997.[62]

The Wiccan Church of Canada (WCC) is based in Toronto, and its membership is largely restricted to southern Ontario. Like the Aquarian Tabernacle Church (ATC) in the United States, the WCC is not an umbrella organization, unlike most larger organizations in Paganism. The ATC was founded in Washington in 1979 and has spread into British Columbia, with an affiliate organization founded there in 1994.[63]

EarthSpirit Community, another Wiccan organization, was founded in the Boston area by Andras Corban Arthen in the early 1980s as a network of covens originating in the Athanor Fellowship, which has now dissolved, although related groups continue. EarthSpirit had a structure of an inner circle made up of the coven members of Athanor Fellowship, who ran a magazine they used to produce and did most of the organization work for public rituals; a middle circle of volunteers; and an outer circle of people with a limited sense of commitment to the organization. EarthSpirit attempted to gather financial support for paying administrative staff and for buying land to host the Rites of Spring festival, but the plan failed, primarily due to fears that people who paid money would not have control over how it was spent, as well as because of the fear that a class of paid clergy would develop. Dissatisfaction with a similar process in Circle Sanctuary may have contributed to the failure of EarthSpirit to attain a similar sort of structural organization.[64]

There are also Druid and Heathen organizations. Ár nDraíocht Féin (pronounced "arn ree-ocht fane") is Gaelic for "Our Own Druidism," but it is often referred to as "A Druid Fellowship," or by the acronym **ADF**. ADF is an international organization of Druids founded by Isaac Bonewits.[65] Members of ADF practice Druidry or Druidism as a revived religion based on up-to-date scholarly research on the Celts and other Indo-European groups. ADF runs a comprehensive training program for clergy through distance education. They also run guilds for teaching various performing arts, such as storytelling and music, fine arts and crafts, and magical arts. Until recently, ADF published the journal *Oak Leaves*. They have rules for grove membership in the larger federation, including the payment of fees, maintenance of a membership list, and the requirement to hold open rituals, due to legal requirements for maintaining tax-exempt status in the United States.[66]

The Troth is an international Asatru organization based in Texas, where they are incorporated as "The Ring of Troth" and have tax-exempt status. Their bylaws refer to them as a "church" for legal reasons: they clarify that "church" means "nonprofit religious organization." The Troth is run by an elected board of directors called "the High Rede." "Troth" means loyalty to the gods, specifically the deities of the Norse pantheon. Due to racist activities in other Norse-inspired groups, the Troth is explicitly antiracist. The Troth runs a training program, certifies elders, and hosts an annual gathering called Trothmoot. They publish the journal *Idunna* and the newsletter *Mimir's Well*, as well as a comprehensive website.[67]

The Church of All Worlds (CAW) is another large organization, whose members are mostly Pagan. It began in 1962, inspired by Robert Heinlein's novel *Stranger in a Strange Land*. In the novel, a human who was raised in an alien culture comes back to Earth and studies human culture as an alien anthropologist. He creates the Church of All Worlds to teach humans about how he was raised with the values of ecological integrity, recognizing divinity in one another, and ensuring that the necessities of life are available to all. After reading this novel, Tim Zell (later known as Otter G'Zell and, more recently, Oberon Zell-Ravenheart) and Richard Lance Christie decided to create the church in reality. CAW became a federally recognized church in the United States in 1970 and for many years produced the popular Pagan magazine *Green Egg*. Some members are not Pagan, but their magazine and their ritual practices related to stewardship of the Earth have been quite influential in American Paganism.

FURTHER READING

Berger, Helen. *A Community of Witches*. Columbia: University of South Carolina Press, 1999.
Reid, Siân Lee MacDonald. *Disorganized Religion: An Exploration of the Neopagan Craft in Canada*. Doctoral thesis, Carleton University, Ottawa, 2001.
Salomonsen, Jone. *Enchanted Feminism: The Reclaiming Witches of San Francisco*. London: Routledge, 2002.

NOTES

1. See Reginald Bibby, *Unknown Gods: The Ongoing Story of Religion in Canada* (Toronto: Stoddart, 1993), 44.
2. Siân Lee MacDonald Reid, "Disorganized Religion: An Exploration of the Neopagan Craft in Canada" (Doctoral thesis, Carleton University, Ottawa, 2001), 178.
3. Some Pagans in Eastern Europe regard written sources such as the *Book of Veles* and the *Maha Vira* as scripture. See Adrian Ivakhiv, "In Search of Deeper Identities: Neopaganism and 'Native Faith' in Contemporary Ukraine," *Nova Religio* 8, no. 3 (March 2005): 7–38.
4. Scott Cunnigham, *Wicca: A Guide for the Solitary Practitioner* (St. Paul, MN: Llewellyn Publications, 1988), 13.
5. The "more-than-human world" is a phrase introduced by David Abram in *The Spell of the Sensuous: Perception and Language in a More-Than-Human World* (New York: Vintage [Random House], 1996); it refers to the world beyond superficial human perception of it as "nature" or "the environment," to an animate world filled with other intelligences.
6. See, for example, Marie-Françoise Guédon, *Le Rêve et la Forêt: Histoires de Chamanes chez les Nabesnas et Leurs Voisins* (Québéc: Presses de l'Université Laval, 2004).
7. Guédon, *Le Rêve et la Forêt*.
8. Reid, "Disorganized Religion," 200.
9. Wendy Griffin, "Goddess Spirituality and Wicca," in *Her Voice, Her Faith: Women Speak on World Religions*, ed. Arvind Sharma and Katherine K. Young, 243–81 (Boulder, CO: Westview Press, 2004).
10. Helen Berger, *A Community of Witches* (Columbia: University of South Carolina Press, 1999), 8.
11. Berger, *Community of Witches*, 50.
12. Berger, *Community of Witches*, 66, 69.
13. Berger, *Community of Witches*, 70–71.
14. Berger, *Community of Witches*, 55.
15. Berger discusses the failed plans of EarthSpirit Community to purchase land, in *Community of Witches*, 104–10.
16. Starhawk, *The Spiral Dance: A Rebirth of the Ancient Religion of the Great Goddess*, 10th anniversary ed. (New York: HarperSanFrancisco, 1989), 49.
17. Starhawk, *Spiral Dance*, 220.
18. See Jone Salomonsen, *Enchanted Feminism: The Reclaiming Witches of San Francisco* (London: Routledge, 2002), 42. Initiation is an aspect of some feminist groups, such as Reclaiming, but it is not required for participation and is not structured the same way as in Gardnerian and Alexandrian groups.
19. See Berger, *Community of Witches*, 56.
20. Berger, *Community of Witches*, 62.
21. Berger, *Community of Witches*, 50.

22. Berger, *Community of Witches*, 62–64.

23. See, for example, Berger *Community of Witches*.

24. See Berger, *Community of Witches*, 13–14. She suggests that women's only groups are less likely to survive.

25. Berger, *Community of Witches*, 14.

26. Michael York, *Pagan Theology: Paganism as a World Religion* (New York: New York University Press, 2003).

27. Catherine L. Albanese, *Reconsidering Nature Religion* (Harrisburg, PA: Trinity Press International, 2002), x.

28. Albanese, *Reconsidering Nature Religion*, 32.

29. See Michael Strmiska, "The Music of the Past in Modern Baltic Paganism," *Nova Religio: The Journal of Alternative and Emergent Religions* 8 (2005).

30. Albanese, *Reconsidering Nature Religion*, 31–33.

31. Reid, "Disorganized Religion."

32. See Reid, "Disorganized Religion," 161; William Closson James, *Locations of the Sacred: Essays on Religion, Literature, and Canadian Culture* (Waterloo: Wilfrid Laurier Press, 1998), 4.

33. Reid, "Disorganized Religion," 169.

34. Reid, "Disorganized Religion," 177.

35. Reid, "Disorganized Religion," 193.

36. Ronald Hutton, *The Triumph of the Moon: A History of Modern Pagan Witchcraft* (Oxford: Oxford University Press, 1999), 360.

37. Hutton, *Triumph of the Moon*, 361.

38. Berger, *Community of Witches*, 99.

39. Berger, *Community of Witches*, 86.

40. Berger, *Community of Witches*, 133, 83.

41. Berger, *Community of Witches*, 86.

42. Berger, *Community of Witches*, 15.

43. See chapter 10 for further discussion of these issues.

44. See, for example, Reid, "Disorganized Religion," 174.

45. Reid, "Disorganized Religion," 193.

46. Reid, "Disorganized Religion," 194–95.

47. Reid, "Disorganized Religion," 197.

48. Reid, "Disorganized Religion," 172.

49. Berger, *Community of Witches*, xiv.

50. Berger, *Community of Witches*, 101.

51. This analysis is drawn directly from Berger, *Community of Witches*, 102–3.

52. Berger, *Community of Witches*, 103.

53. Berger, *Community of Witches*, 103.

54. See Berger, *Community of Witches*, 72–75.

55. Berger, *Community of Witches*, 76.

56. See Pagan Federation, *The Pagan Federation*, 2003–2004, www.paganfed.org (accessed May 14, 2004).

57. See PFPC, *Pagan Federation/Fédération Païenne Canada*, 2004, www.pfpc.ca (accessed May 14, 2004).

58. See Pagan Alliance, *Pagan Alliance, Inc.*, 2001, http://paganalliance.lasielle .net/index.html (accessed May 14, 2004).

59. Berger, *Community of Witches*, 110.

60. Reid, "Disorganized Religion," 216.

61. Berger, *Community of Witches*, 114–19.

62. Vibra Willow, "A Brief History of Reclaiming," Reclaiming website, 2000, www.reclaiming.org (accessed May 14, 2004). Earlier version published in *Reclaiming Quarterly* 76

(Fall 1999). See also Jone Salomonsen, *Enchanted Feminism: The Reclaiming Witches of San Francisco* (London: Routledge, 2002).

63. Reid, "Disorganized Religion," 217.

64. Berger, *Community Witches*, 104–10.

65. Bonewits' influence on the development of contemporary Paganism is further discussed in chapter 7.

66. ADF, *Ár nDraíocht Féin/A Druid Fellowship*, 2004, www.adf.org/core (accessed May 14, 2004).

67. Troth, *The Ring of Troth Official Home Page*, 1995–2004, www.thetroth.org (accessed May 14, 2004).

3

Individual and Family Practices

Although Pagans are in many ways indistinguishable from the general population, there are certain practices and ritual activities that they engage in that set them apart and make them identifiable as Pagans. This chapter explores some of the more common religious practices that Pagans engage in individually, in their homes, and with their families, and describes related tools and accoutrements. For some solitary practitioners, these practices may be the sum of their religious activities, but others may also practice individual forms of the group activities discussed in the chapter 4. Solitaries, for example, may initiate themselves rather than be initiated into a group. The most obvious practice of Pagans that sets them apart from the general population is their use of magic and spell casting. However, Pagan lifeways also include celebrating the changing of the seasons through the seasonal festival cycle, keeping home altars and shrines, giving offerings, **scrying** and other divination, as well as other meditation and trance work.

Pagans understand magic differently from how it has been defined in the history of religion. Western scholars, for the most part Christian or post-Christian secularists, have interpreted magic as a "primitive" form of religion. Early sociology and anthropology texts define magic in terms of "manipulating" deities and the spiritual world to achieve desired goals. Religion, in contrast, is presented as worship, involving requests rather than demands, in the work of influential scholars such as Emile Durkeim and Bronislaw Malinowski. However, for Pagans, magic is integral to the practice of their religion.[1] For Pagans, magic is a means of personal growth and self-expression, not a degeneration of religion into "superstition."[2]

The practices of magic in Paganism are expressive of the worldview of Paganism, an understanding that everything is connected and that there is more to the world than humans understand. Magic is not something separate from the regular activities of Pagans.[3] Pagans see everyday life as magical, "significant, imbued with value, sacred or paradoxically suffused with transcendence."[4] The occurrence of this sort of magic is partly a matter of interpretation. A Pagan might think, for example, that if a friend calls just when s/he is thinking of the friend, this is a result of magic.[5] Pagans prefer to live in a meaningful world and to believe that there are no meaningless coincidences.

Pagans' practices of magic are most often directed at healing, whether oneself, friends and family, or the environment.[6] Pagan rituals do not always involve doing magic, but they often do. Their rituals are generally directed toward creating a specific sort of experience in the participants, as opposed to what they perceive as "empty" rituals of repeated formulas and going through the motions in other religious traditions. Magic can be done as a formal event in ritual, but also as spontaneous, unscripted, and unrehearsed acts. Pagan ritual is often conducted as a performance in public venues by groups, but in the home it is less performative than a spontaneous expression and practice of a Pagan worldview integrated into daily life. Magic can be as simple as stirring a pot widdershins (counterclockwise), symbolically the direction of decrease, to rid it of lumps, or planting seeds during the waxing of the moon, symbolically a time of increase.

Pagan practices of magic are not like the fairy godmothers of animated Disney films or the special-effects magic of the witches in the television shows *Charmed* and *Buffy the Vampire Slayer*, or the film *The Craft*. Pagans do not just wave a wand to make things appear or transform. Their practice of magic is based on the belief that all things in the universe are connected, that changing one thing can potentially change others, even at a distance. A thought, for example, can have a physical outcome, not in the sense of creating something out of nothing but of transforming a situation by working with possibilities. Pagans believe that magic works through hidden connections, correspondences, and sympathy. In their rituals, they use correspondences, symbolic connections between sometimes seemingly disparate things, to work with the hidden connections, as in the spell to pay a phone bill described in chapter 1.

Pagans also use ritual to create metaphors for accomplishing goals with something tangible to remind them of their commitment to a particular objective and to encourage them to take pragmatic action in pursuit of it. At the spring equinox, for example, a group of feminist Witches planted seeds in conjunction with a guided meditation in which each of the women focused on what she wanted to grow in her life, such as a new job or a quality in herself, like assertiveness or patience. After the initial ritual, each woman took her potted seed home to tend it. As the women ritually watered their plants, they were reminded and encouraged to take practical steps toward accomplishing the goals they had identified at the spring equinox, which symbolically and literally is a time of renewal and growth. As their plants grew, they visualized and worked toward their goals becoming manifest. If the plant did not flourish, or if the planned goal did not come to fruition, the woman considered why, thinking about how the timing of the desired outcome might be inappropriate, or how her commitment, or lack of it, had contributed.[7]

Magic is so integrated into the regular activities of Pagans that many of them describe their religion as a "way of life."[8] As in indigenous religions, Pagan religious practices are as much lifeways as they are overtly religious. Pagans do not see daily life as mundane or profane as opposed some more spiritual concern. For Pagans, spirit and matter are one in Earth. As one practitioner remarks, "Nearly everything we do at home can be done with Wicca in mind. From rearranging a room to brushing hair."[9] Spirituality is integrated into their daily life in work and leisure. For many Pagans, an important aspect of this is their relationship with the natural world. Pauline Campanelli's *The Wheel of the Year: Living the Magical Life* describes the practices she and her husband have developed as solitaries, following the seasons. She gives instructions for craft projects, recipes, and spells, as well as for growing, harvesting, and eating food with spiritual awareness.

For some Pagans, growing and harvesting some of their own food is an important part of their religious observances. For many, this primarily involves gardening, but some Pagans also raise livestock, and some find gathering wild foods, as well as hunting, important. All aspects of gardening can be imbued with religious significance in Pagan practice, from planning the garden to preparing the beds, planting, tending, and harvesting. Campanelli gives a charm to make an herb garden grow. After the soil has been prepared, she suggests walking sunwise (clockwise in the Northern Hemisphere) around the garden while asperging (sprinkling) the edge with a fir branch dipped in fresh water. She suggests visualizing lush growth and **chanting,**

> Herbs that charm
> Herbs that heal
> Grow now
> Spring till Fall.[10]

In general, Pagans tend to talk to their plants, encouraging them to grow.

For harvesting potatoes, Campanelli describes carving a potato into the shape of the Earth Mother, envisaged as in ancient fertility statues, and burying it in a mound, saying,

> O Great Earth Mother
> From whom we receive all nourishment
> And the flesh of our bodies,
> We your loving children
> Make this offering in your honor
> In love and in gratefulness
> Blessed be![11]

She also gives a charm to say when gathering seeds for the next year's planting: "From this Life / Life to come."[12]

Food preparation has particularly strong religious significance for some Pagans, linking them to their ancestors and to their patron deities. Diana Paxson, a prominent Heathen practitioner, describes how cooking and one's kitchen can connect Heathen women to the *dísir*, female ancestral spirits. She relates that she met an ancestor spirit who was willing to work with her on the condition that she clean up her kitchen:

> I encountered a sturdy blonde woman who called herself Helga, said she was a Frisian, and agreed to be one of my disir and help me learn about Germanic women's mysteries—but only if I did something about my kitchen! In true Germanic tradition, she refused to cross my threshold so long as the heart of the house was a grubby room with pocked walls and woodwork and linoleum so ancient that when I tried to clean the floor, it would dissolve.[13]

Other Pagans might develop relationships with the *matronae*, a similar group of deities in Roman religion, or connections to Heartha, the Roman goddess of the hearth. Some Pagans talk to their food as they are preparing it, for example urging the yeast to grow in making bread. Campanelli gives a recipe for making ritual bread with freshly sprouted wheat to represent the regeneration of the dying god associated with the grain ground for the bread. She includes instructions for blessing the loaf by incising a pentagram on it with a ritual knife, saying, "I invoke thee beloved Spirit of the Grain / Be present in this Sacred Loaf."[14]

Pagans also use food in ritual as a means of grounding oneself, returning to ordinary consciousness after ritual activity. Some Pagans say a blessing on food at regular meals, but more commonly on food eaten in ritual. They also use food for offerings to deities and nature spirits. Offerings to landwights and household deities, whether in the city or in rural areas, serve as a reminder of human dependence on the Earth for food, air, and water. Usually before or after eating during ritual, a portion is given

Technically, a libation is a liquid poured as an offering, although Pagans often put solid food in libation bowls as well.

Figure 5.   **Leaving offerings (photo by Barbara Jane Davy)**

as an offering. For indoor rituals, the offering might be left on the altar in a libation bowl (and later disposed of). Pagans often pour the first bit of wine, mead (wine made from honey), milk, water, or whatever beverage is used in a ritual, on the ground for the divinities, or collect it in a libation bowl to be poured on the ground later. Pagans often leave offerings outside, with the understanding that squirrels, birds, or raccoons will eat the offerings. Sometimes Pagans bury food offerings. Food is probably the most common offering, but sometimes cut flowers or branches serve as an offering. Pagans associate specific offerings with certain deities, such as barley for Demeter, red wine for Dionysus, or roses for Aphrodite. Some Pagans also give votive offerings, offerings given to consecrate a vow or oath, or in fulfillment of an oath.

Pagans are somewhat more likely than others in the modern secular population to embrace alternative lifestyles. Pagans tend to pay greater attention to spiritual aspects of life. They have a greater willingness to believe in paranormal events, to see significance in dreams, and to pursue alternative healing. Some Pagan parents make dream pillows for their children's use on nights of the full moon as a way of teaching them to pay attention to dreams. Many Pagans use herbal teas in preference to over-the-counter drugs and are more likely to use other aspects of naturopathic medicine, including, for example, therapeutic massage. Pagan mothers tend to prefer natural childbirth and the services of midwives, where available.

For some Pagans, being Pagan means being politically active. Many Pagans live their politics on a daily basis in keeping with what some scholars call "life politics," which are political orientations and actions that are played out in daily life because of one's awareness of the connections between oneself and larger or global political issues. Life politics are the politics of choice and the decisions of daily life.[15] This sort of life politics has become integrated into Wicca and is present to some degree throughout Paganism, since integrity is a central Pagan value. Many Pagans feel that if ethics and politics are not lived, then hypocrisy results.

Pagan life politics are particularly evident in terms of feminism and environmentalism. Many Witches, as well as other Pagans, feel that reverence for the Goddess and nature requires living "a life that is consistent with the needs of the environment and to be aware of women's issues."[16] Some practitioners suggest that Pagans should live such that anyone coming into their homes will know immediately that they practice an earth religion, that their homes should reflect the environmental sensitivity of their religion.[17] Such practitioners feel that a Pagan worldview requires active participation in ethics and politics. Living in harmony with nature means more than celebrating the changing of the seasons, but also trying to implement environmental ideals on a daily basis. For some practitioners, this harmony can be expressed through growing grain for Lammas, or herbs in pots, and "killing and dressing our own meat—at least occasionally."[18] However, for some Pagans, living environmental ideals on a day-to-day basis requires vegetarianism.[19] As discussed further in chapter 9, while Pagans generally support a degree of feminism and environmentalism, how they put their politics into practice varies.

One of the more obvious markers of who is Pagan is their observation of a seasonal festival cycle. Many Pagans celebrate eight seasonal festivals, sometimes called **sabbats**, which are linked to the changing seasons, one every six weeks over the year, but not all Pagans celebrate the same festival cycle. Heathen practices in particular do not follow the same pattern as other Pagan groups, but the Wiccan wheel of the year is dominant in Paganism. The wheel of the year is called a wheel because the festivals are represented through the image of an eight-spoked wheel, metaphorically emphasizing a circular sense of time. Four of the festivals are held at the solstices and equinoxes and are referred to as the solar holidays. The ex-

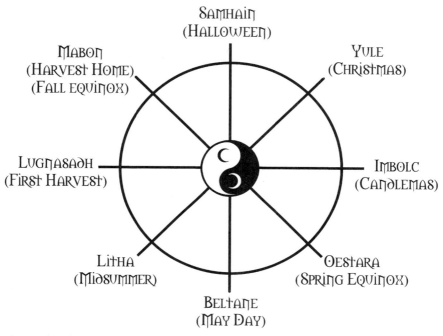

Figure 6.   Wheel of the Year (Northern Hemisphere) (image created by Catherine Kerr)

act dates of the festivals vary from year to year because of discrepancies between the calendar and the varying relationship between the sun and the Earth. The other holidays, sometimes referred to as the "cross-quarter" holidays, are more fixed, although regional and tradition-based differences exist. This festival cycle is of Celtic origin. The celebration of the solstices has a long history in Celtic cultures, but recognition of the equinoxes is a modern addition.[20] In the Southern Hemisphere, where summer arrives in December, Pagans usually invert the Celtic seasonal festival cycle to coincide with the local seasons.

Some Pagans celebrate these festivals privately with their families, and some celebrate them individually apart from their families. Some solitaries are truly solitary, in the sense that their religious practice is intensely private, not shared with family, friends, or coreligionists. Other Pagans who belong to circles may also celebrate the sabbats with their groups, or celebrate them only through group practice. Within families and groups, often a few festivals will take precedence, involving more elaborate festivities, and others will be recognized more simply.[21] In Canada, for example, the fall equinox often receives little attention, probably because of the importance of Thanksgiving as a harvest festival in mainstream culture. (In Canada, unlike in the United States, Thanksgiving is not associated with Pilgrims and the founding of the nation but is essentially a celebration of the fall harvest.)

The wheel of the year begins with Samhain, an Irish Gaelic word pronounced "sow-ain" or "sow-een." In the Northern Hemisphere, Samhain is held on the evening of October 31, coinciding with Hallowe'en. Traditionally, Samhain is the Wiccan New Year's celebration. It is the beginning of winter in Celtic traditions, wherein the year is divided into two seasons, winter and summer. Pagans see it as a time when "the veil between the worlds is thin," a time when communication with the dead, the faeries, and/or spirits is easier. Some Pagans set up a special altar to honor the recently dead and/or their ancestors. Samhain marks the end of the harvest and a time to begin to turn inward, spending more time in one's house and contemplating one's mental inner space.

Yule is held in December, between the twentieth and the twenty-third, at the time of the winter solstice, the longest night of the year in the Northern Hemisphere. Some Pagans celebrate Yule with their families through the common Western activities associated with Christmas, noting that practices such as bringing greenery into the home and decorating trees were originally pre-Christian pagan practices. For contemporary Pagans, Yule marks the dreaming time of the year. The Earth sleeps, and no new vegetative life appears outside. It is a time of meditation and introspection. The days immediately begin to get longer even as the Earth settles into winter. By association, Pagans suggest that the body sleeps, but the mind is active.

Imbolc (also spelled "Oimelg") is Irish Gaelic for "lactation," in reference to the birth of lambs. This festival is also sometimes called Candlemas, or the Feast of Brigid, and is held about February 1 in the Northern Hemisphere. For Pagans who observe the festival as Candlemas, it is a festival of lights, and they place candles in the windows of their homes. These represent the returning strength of the sun and the wakening of the Earth. In Britain, Imbolc marks the beginning of spring. In Canada and the northern United States, spring is not yet visible, but there are stirrings. For Pagans, it is a time of purification, often marked by early spring-cleaning. It is the end of the contemplative time of the year and the beginning of the time of action.

Oestre or Oestara marks the vernal (spring) equinox, which occurs around March 20 to 23 in the Northern Hemisphere. As a time of equal day and equal night, it represents balance. It is the beginning of the change of season, but balanced now between winter and summer. For Pagans, it is a time of planning, when people are eager for action but it is not quite time to plant the garden or start other new projects. Oestre is related to the Christian celebration of Easter, and Pagans celebrate the pre-Christian practices and associations of Easter, such as decorating eggs and making or eating chocolate rabbits. Both eggs and rabbits are symbolic of fecundity, which Pagans celebrate at this festival.

Beltain (also spelled "Beltane" and "Beltaine") is Gaelic for "bright fire." It is held on April 30 or May 1 in the Northern Hemisphere. In nature, it is a time of bursting potential, as the buds swell with the running sap and all the birds and other wildlife seem to be having sex. For Pagans, it is a time to celebrate human sexuality.

The summer solstice, sometimes referred to as Midsummer, is the longest day of the year, occurring around June 20 to 23 in the Northern Hemisphere. Some Pagans celebrate it as Litha. In Celtic traditions, it is the beginning of summer. The Sun is at its zenith but is about to lessen in strength. For agriculturalists and gardeners, the rush of activity of planting will be followed by a time of tending. It is a time of much physical work, but this day is taken to celebrate. Pagans sometimes associate this time of the year with the Goddess as pregnant, a time of fullness not yet come to fruition.

Lammas or Lughnasadh is often held on July 31 in the Northern Hemisphere, although historically the date has varied depending on the time of the first harvesting of grain. The name "Lammas" comes from the Old English *half-maesse*, meaning "loaf mass," in reference to a special bread made from the first fruits of the harvest. Pagans see this time of year as a time of coming to fruition, and hence the ending of potentiality. Lammas celebrates the first fruits of the harvest, and the festival often includes a symbolic representation of the sacrifice of the vegetative life that supports human life. Some Pagans use the British folk character of John Barleycorn for this purpose. Other Pagans focus on the god Lugh at this time and call the festival "Lughnasadh," in reference to "the mourning of the many-talented God Lugh."[22]

The autumnal equinox, sometimes called Mabon, falls around September 20 to 23 in the Northern Hemisphere. As the vernal equinox, it is a time balance, of equal day and night. The seasonal change from summer to winter begins. It is a time of harvest and thankfulness for the plants and animals sacrificed to sustain human life. Many North American Pagans celebrate a harvest festival with their families at Thanksgiving, in October in Canada, and in November in the United States, instead of at the equinox.

Another recognizable feature of Paganism is that most Pagans keep altars in their homes.[23] An altar is a place to keep ritual tools, and a surface to use in casting spells and conducting rituals. It often includes religious symbols, such as an object representing each of the four elements or directions. A rock or bit of earth in a pot might represent north and the element of earth, for example. Incense often represents air and the east, and

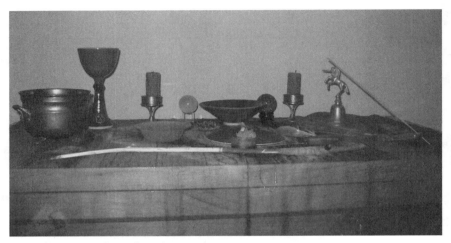

Figure 7.   Home altar (photo by Mandy Furney)

a candle often represents the south and fire. Seashells sometimes represent water and the west on Pagan altars. While practitioners often use the terms "shrine" and "altar" interchangeably and the two often are not distinguished in contemporary Pagan practice, technically a shrine is dedicated to a particular deity and often includes images of the deity or deities.

Practitioners usually start with one altar, but they may proliferate to one in each room of the house or apartment. A Pagan altar might consist of a single shelf or dresser top that holds ritual and symbolic items. Tokens, or significant found objects such as feathers, stones, and pinecones, are kept on altars. Pagans often have a personal altar in the bedroom for individual use, and a house altar in the kitchen for family use. Some individuals and families have a ritual room, temple, or meditation room set aside for magical rites.

The form of magic practiced most by Pagans at home is probably simple spell casting. These are magical acts designed to improve one's life, or the lives of friends or family members. Pagans may, for example, cast spells for money, for a new job, or to find a new lover. However, as previously mentioned, spells are most often directed toward healing. Pagans often also use rituals to aid them in making life transitions, and not just the rites of passage discussed in chapter 4, but also the smaller transitions of life, such as moving into a new house or apartment. A new residence can be purified before moving in by ritually sweeping it in conjunction with cleaning it. One how-to guide suggests creating a broom specifically for this purpose, taking a branch from a tree before dawn and leaving an offering of a coin or a semiprecious stone. To the branch, the practitioner ties a bunch of flowers to fashion a broom. The practitioner then sweeps each room of the new residence, visualizing the flowers absorbing negative influences out of the house or apartment, and then disposes of the ritual broom at a crossroads before the sun comes up.[24]

One method of spell casting used by Pagans involves making talismans. A talisman is an object made to protect an individual from a particular sort of harm, or to draw a particular sort of energy to a person. It can include crystals or other stones, feathers, bodily fluids, and herbs, and may involve inscribing an object with runes, a bind rune, or a sigil. Sigils and bind runes combine letters or characters to form a pattern that represents a desired outcome. Dragon Environmental Group, for example, uses a bind rune for its logo, incorporating the runes Laguz, Fehu, Tiwaz, Kaunaz, Algiz, and Isa, representing health, healing, love, protection, growth, and harmonious relationships between humanity and the rest of nature. Talismans take effect through meditating on the talisman during its creation, and, for personal talismans, wearing it or keeping it close to where one sleeps. For talismans aimed at others, they may be left where they will be seen by others, or burned.[25]

Pagans often seek inspiration for spells and rituals in how-to books, but they tend to be creative in designing them. A basic ritual involves creating sacred space, invoking divinities, raising and directing energy, grounding, thanking and dismissing divinities, and returning the space and participants to ordinary life. First, the practitioner prepares for the ritual, sometimes with a ritual bath and by putting on ritual clothing. Often the practitioner proceeds with grounding and centering (a short meditation to focus on the ritual, leaving the other concerns of one's life aside for the time being). Some Druids leave an offering outside the ritual area for those beings they do not want to attend the rite. Wiccan practitioners create sacred space by casting a circle, tracing a circle around the space used for the ritual with a ritual knife, wand, or finger, or by simply walking around the space. The circle is visualized in three dimensions, to make a sphere around the ritual space. The circle holds in the energy raised until it is ready to be released, and it keeps out distractions.

Next, the practitioner invokes the directions, usually the four cardinal directions, each associated with an element: often, but not always, north with earth, east with air, south with fire, and west with water. The invocation of the directions in Wiccan circles tends to be verbal, repeating a liturgy or speaking some extemporized words. In some ecologically focused groups such as Dragon Environmental Group, the directions are invoked through more performative actions, such as actions to mimic the sound of fire, and waving motions to mimic the dance of flames.[26] Some groups vary this to suit local geography, and some follow other associations of directions and elements and may include invocations of the additional directions above, below, and center, or within.

The practitioner invokes whatever deities are desired in the rite, if any, and sometimes the ancestors, particularly in Druid circles, Heathen rituals, and the Reclaiming tradition. Next, the practitioner proceeds with the work of the ritual, whether it is a healing spell, a spell to gain or rid oneself of something, a spell to create a talisman, or a spell to celebrate an event or season. Energy is generally raised in the work of the ritual. This can be accomplished through things like dancing, drumming, singing, or meditation. Energy is directed into the work, and then the practitioner grounds her/himself again, often by eating and drinking. This part of the ritual is sometimes referred to as "cakes and wine" but can include any food and drink. A small offering is usually given to the divinity invoked. Grounding, that is, returning any remaining excess energy to the Earth, helps return the participant to ordinary consciousness. Dismissing those divinities invoked ends the rite.

Pagans use a variety of tools in casting spells and in conducting more formal rituals. Some Pagans express the curious idea that "when buying magical tools, [one should] never haggle over the price."[27] It is often suggested that it is better to make one's own tools whenever possible, or that "found" tools are better than bought tools. Unfortunately, this has led some people to steal ritual tools, particularly **Tarot cards**, due to the belief that if you buy them they will not work as well. While it is an often-repeated folk tradition that bought tools do not work as well as others, the solution is not to steal them, but to make them or to receive them as gifts. Some covens give ritual tools as gifts to initiates.[28] An exception to the practice of giving tools is sometimes made for knives, due to the folk belief that giving a knife cuts the friendship. Thus, the recipient of a ritual knife symbolically gives the giver a coin to pay for it.[29] This practice is inverted in other areas and traditions so that the giver includes a coin with the blade so as not to cut off the relationship.

Ritual tools are often consecrated, blessed, and dedicated to ritual activity. To consecrate ritual tools, some Pagans first bury them in the Earth for a time, or they place them in a box of salt, to regenerate the tool, to remove influences of any previous owner, or to purify manufactured tools. Consecration consists in then blessing the tool using the elements earth, air, fire, and water, and sometimes a pentacle, particularly in Wiccan practice, and perhaps invoking the blessing of a deity or deities. Some Pagans keep ritual tools separate from regular household tools. Others use the same tools for multiple purposes, feeling that it consecrates daily life to use the same tools in the kitchen and at the altar. Pagans suggest that while none of the tools are necessary for doing magic, they can help create an appropriate mood in ritual.

A few of the common tools Pagans use in their religious practice are often kept near, but not on their altars. These include the drum, the broom, and the cauldron. For some Pagans, drums are important tools for trance work, as discussed below. The broom is used for ritual cleaning to sweep out "bad" energy, sometimes with the help of salt. For Wiccans, the broom represents the union and balance of male and female energies through the sexual symbolism of shaft in thatch. Many Pagans favor a type of broom called a "besom," an old English word for broom. These brooms are generally round, with the bristles gathered all the way around the shaft instead of extending in a line parallel to it. In addition to ritual cleaning or the symbolic clearing of space for ritual, Wiccans use brooms in handfasting ceremonies. To jump the broom with one's partner is to become handfasted, making a commitment for a year, or as long as the love shall last.

A cauldron is a heavy round pot. Pagan ritual cauldrons are often black, are made of cast iron, and are supported on three legs. The typical round shape with a narrowed neck is symbolic of the womb of the Goddess. Celtic-influenced practitioners associate the cauldron with the goddess Ceridwen's cauldron of wisdom, and with the cauldron of regeneration from stories in Welsh and Irish mythology. Pagans often use cauldrons to contain fires used in ritual rather than for brewing potions with fire beneath. The cauldron is often too heavy to store on an altar, but a similar symbolic significance is attached to the chalice, a ritual cup, which is usually kept on the altar. It is generally goblet shaped, like a wineglass. The chalice is often filled with water during ritual, to represent that element. In Wiccan ritual, salt is added to the water in the chalice to represent the sea and the waters of life. Salt is also used for purification, and sometimes in casting the circle. Salt kept in a bowl on the altar represents the element of earth.

Pagans often place incense and candles on the altar to represent the elements of air and fire. Incense purifies and scents the air, and it can facilitate trance work. Pagans use candles of various colors for symbolic associations in spell casting—for example, red for passion, pink for love, white for cleansing and healing, and green for fertility and money. However, some prefer to use only natural beeswax candles. Pagans sometimes inscribe candles with runes or other symbolic figures, anoint them with oils, and bless them for spell work.

Some Wiccan Pagans keep an athame, a double-edged ritual knife, on their altars. It is often black handled, and the blade is usually magnetized to bring it into harmony with the Earth. Wiccans use the athame to cast the circle and to draw pentagrams in the air in invocation of each of the four directions and in closing the ritual. Some Pagans use a sword to cast their circles. The blades of such athames and swords are generally dull, and they are used only for ritual purposes, not for cutting. However, Pagans who do not keep ritual tools distinct from regular working tools might use the same knife for casting the circle as for cutting materials in their spell work, and for chopping vegetables in the kitchen. Some Pagans, particularly Wiccans, have a separate knife for cutting in ritual activities, called a bolline. This knife is often white handled and is used for inscribing and sometimes for cutting herbs. Some Pagans prefer to use a copper sickle, which has a curved blade in the shape of a crescent moon, or a regular jackknife to cut herbs. A wand sometimes replaces the athame, to be used in ritual as a pointing tool and to focus intent, but wands are often not used by Pagans who find them too stereotypical or too reminiscent of magical use in popular culture.

Despite this distaste for stereotype, Pagans often wear robes for rituals. Ritual robes frequently have long flowing sleeves, are sometimes hooded, and are often medieval in inspiration. Some Pagan robes are simple garments sewn from bedsheets, but others are well tailored and elaborately decorated. Many Wiccans have adopted the pentacle, a five-pointed star enclosed in a circle, as a symbol of their religious affiliation, and they wear silver pendants in this shape as Christians wear crosses and as Jews wear the Star of David. As well as being a symbol of Wicca, the pentacle represents earth and protection. Medieval magical practitioners thought it was protective because it can be drawn with one continuous line, preventing any evil influences from entering a place protected with it. Wiccans find it significant that an apple cut crosswise reveals a natural pentacle. Both the apple and the pentacle are symbols of the Goddess.

Pagans may also keep tools for divination on or near their altars. Pagans use a number of different oracular devices and systems to prophesy, that is, to predict the future, interpret the present, and understand the past. One of the more common divination systems in Paganism is the Tarot. The Tarot is a set of seventy-eight cards, similar to playing cards in having four suits that are numbered ace, two to ten, king, and queen, but with pages added, and with knights in place of jacks. The suits are cups (hearts), wands (clubs), swords (spades), and pentacles (diamonds). These cards, called the minor arcana, make up the majority of the deck. The other twenty-two cards, called the major arcana, are said to be derived from the work of Hermes Trismegistus, and they correspond to the letters of the Hebrew alphabet. The major arcana are numbered zero to twenty-one, and each has a name, which, to an extent, describes the spiritual growth of an adept in the mystical arts. The images on the cards are Neo-Platonic in inspiration, following the traditions of Western alchemists who were influenced by Egyptian mythology and Jewish mysticism. The images contain highly overdetermined symbols. There are many elements to consider in each picture, and many possible meanings, so the cards provide a structure through which to apply one's intuition for understanding the past, interpreting the present, and predicting and directing the future.

Another type of oracular system that Pagans use is the runes, either Germanic (Norse) or Celtic. Germanic runes are based on the Norse alphabet, and Celtic on Ogham, sometimes called the tree alphabet. The Norse runes originally consisted of twenty-four letters, generally incised or carved on pieces of wood or clay, but sometimes on stone or metal. Using the runes requires a greater knowledge of symbolic associations than the Tarot does, because the simple letters are not as evocative as the pictures on the cards. Runes may not historically have been used for divination so much as for other magical purposes, such as for enchanting objects by putting spells on them to increase their usefulness, for example, on a weapon to make it strike true, or on a cup to increase the drinker's health. Druids often use Ogham runes for divination during their rituals.

Many Pagans practice some form of scrying for divination purposes. Scrying involves looking into a crystal ball, or more often into a pool of water, a cauldron, or flames, to focus one's intuition. Practitioners scry to see events at a distance, to interpret the situation at hand, to see the future, and to reveal what is hidden. This form of divination possibly requires more facility with trance than do other divination techniques, since there is less to inspire the imagination in scrying than in reading Tarot cards or runes.

Pagans use a variety of means to alter their consciousness to go into trance. Two of these are meditation and drumming. Pagans use guided meditation, called "pathworking" in Britain, more often than they use Buddhist-style meditation. For Pagans, the aim is often to guide the mind to a particular sort of experience or state rather than to empty the mind. Stilling the mind is still a goal, though, in order to gain the discipline necessary to follow guided meditations or to direct oneself to particular goals rather than just sitting and daydreaming. One might pursue a guided meditation in which one journeys down a path and into a cave in order to become aware of things one's conscious mind is hiding from one's awareness. Meditation facilitates problem solving in a different manner from conscious thought, through accessing what Pagans sometimes call the "Deep Self." In learning meditation techniques, Pagans usually begin with visualization. A commonly used exercise is to try to visualize an apple with one's eyes shut, starting with the shape, the texture, and the color, and then adding the scent, the sound of cutting it, and the revelation of the pentacle within. The practitioner next tries to visualize the apple with his or her eyes open.

In a guided meditation in a feminist Witchcraft group, the women were asked to imagine themselves "in a beautiful garden, to discover a path and to follow it, to enter a warm enveloping mist, and then to emerge on the other side of the mist where [they] met the Goddess," who gave them each a gift. The women described gifts such as meeting the Goddess and recognizing that she was "me." Another said, "In my trance the Goddess gave me a book. It was the story of my life and it was only half written. It

A dedicant is one who has expressed an interest in learning about a tradition and has made an oath dedicating her/himself to growing in that particular tradition.

was for me to write the rest." Such experiences in guided meditation give participants a strong sense of the sacred, as well as emotional experiences that feed their work in ritual.[30]

Ár nDraíocht Féin, a Druid organization, suggests using a guided meditation for practitioners to identify their patron deities, and they include a text to use in their Dedicant Program handbook, the manual given to those who are learning to become Druids. A coreligionist can guide a new practitioner, or the practitioner can also make an audio recording of the text of the guided meditation. To conduct the ritual using the meditation, the practitioner first makes an offering, asking to be shown the way to the patrons. Next, the practitioner assumes her or his meditation posture, a position in which the practitioner is comfortable and relaxed. The meditation begins with a metaphor of descending through mist, and proceeds, narrated in the second person: "At last you drift down toward a great rolling meadow."[31] The narration guides the **dedicant** into a forest, and then into a temple, which contains all the world's deities. The dedicant chooses her or his patrons from those in the temple and places their images in a place of honor at the front of the temple.

Guided meditations such as this use metaphor to transform the practitioner's consciousness into trance and then back into regular consciousness. Pagans often enhance this process through drumming. Starhawk suggests that the drum is frequently the most important ritual tool in groups, since it provides an effective way to alter consciousness through rhythm and easily keeps the group together.[32] Some practitioners, following the work of Michael Harner, refer to the drum as the vehicle that transports shamanic practitioners into the "Shamanic State of Consciousness."[33] This can also be accomplished through singing. Like drumming, singing facilitates group cohesion and formation of the "group mind," and it keeps everyone together on the same "wavelength." Dance is also used for this purpose, particularly at summer festivals, as discussed in chapter 4.

FURTHER READING

Buckland, Raymond. *Buckland's Complete Book of Witchcraft.* St. Paul, MN: Llewellyn Publications, 1986.

Cunningham, Scott. *Wicca: A Guide for the Solitary Practitioner*. St. Paul, MN: Llewellyn Publications, 2003.

Starhawk. *The Spiral Dance: A Rebirth of the Ancient Religion of the Great Goddess*. 10th anniversary ed. San Francisco: HarperSanFrancisco, 1989.

NOTES

1. Helen Berger, Evan A. Leach, and Leigh S. Shaffer, *Voices from the Pagan Census: A National Survey of Witches and Neo-Pagans in the United States* (Columbia: University of South Carolina Press, 2003), 39.

2. Graham Harvey, *Contemporary Paganism: Listening People, Speaking Earth* (New York: New York University Press, 1997), 89.

3. Harvey, *Contemporary Paganism*, 101.

4. Harvey, *Contemporary Paganism*, 87.

5. See Berger, Leach, and Shaffer, *Voices from the Pagan Census*, 38.

6. Berger, Leach, and Shaffer, *Voices from the Pagan Census*, 37.

7. Kathryn Rountree, *Embracing the Witch and the Goddess: Feminist Ritual-Makers in New Zealand* (London: Routledge, 2004), 175.

8. Margot Adler, *Drawing Down the Moon: Witches, Druids, Goddess-Worshippers, and Other Pagans in America Today*, revised and expanded ed. (Boston: Beacon Press, 1986), 372.

9. Quoted in Helen Berger, *A Community of Witches* (Columbia: University of South Carolina Press, 1999), 96–97.

10. Pauline Campanelli, *Wheel of the Year: Living the Magical Life* (St. Paul, MN: Llewellyn Publications, 1989), 62.

11. Campanelli, *Wheel of the Year*, 108.

12. Campanelli, *Wheel of the Year*, 127.

13. Diana Paxson, "The Matronæ," Hrafnar website, www.hrafnar.org/goddesses/matronae.html (accessed April 22, 2004), originally published in *Sage Woman*, Fall 1999.

14. Campanelli, *Wheel of the Year*, 114–15.

15. Helen Berger applies Anthony Giddens' concept of "life politics" to Wicca in *Community of Witches*, 78–79.

16. Berger, *Community of Witches*, 79.

17. See, for example, Chas S. Clifton, "Witches and the Earth," in *Witchcraft Today, Book One: The Modern Craft Movement*, ed. Chas S. Clifton (St. Paul, MN: Llewellyn Publications, 1992), 126.

18. Clifton, "Witches and the Earth," 129–30.

19. See Marion Bowman, "Nature, the Natural, and Pagan Identity," *Diskus* 6, Web edition, 2000, http://web.uni-marburg.de/religionswissenschaft/journal/diskus (accessed May 16, 2001).

20. See Ronald Hutton, *Stations of the Sun: A History of the Ritual Year in Britain* (Oxford: Oxford University Press, 1996).

21. Starhawk, Diane Baker, and Anne Hill, *Circle Round: Raising Children in Goddess Traditions* (New York: Bantam, 1998), 19.

22. Harvey, *Contemporary Paganism*, 12.

23. Berger, *Community of Witches*, 32.

24. Scott Cunningham and David Harrington, *The Magical Household: Spells & Rituals for the Home* (St. Paul, MN: Llewellyn Publications, 2003), 125, 127.

25. Harvey, *Contemporary Paganism*, 101.

26. Harvey, *Contemporary Paganism*, 103.

27. Starhawk, *The Spiral Dance: A Rebirth of the Ancient Religion of the Great Goddess*, 10th anniversary ed. (New York: HarperSanFrancisco, 1989), 76; Zsuzsanna Budapest, *The Holy Book of Women's Mysteries* (Oakland, CA: Wingbow Press, 1989), 12.

28. Starhawk, *Spiral Dance*, 76.

29. Starhawk, *Spiral Dance*, 227.

30. Rountree, *Embracing the Witch and the Goddess*, 153.

31. Ian Corrigan et al., ADF Dedicant Program, document produced by Ár nDraíocht Féin: A Druid Fellowship, 1997, 40.

32. Starhawk, *Spiral Dance*, 227.

33. Michael Harner, *The Way of the Shaman* (New York: HarperSanFrancisco, 1990), 51.

4

Group Practices

The individual and family practices discussed in chapter 3 carry over into the group practices of Pagans, but they may be more structured to facilitate group activities. For example, group celebrations of the sabbats, the seasonal festivals, are more likely to have a script to keep everyone together. Pagan groups may conduct rituals in closed or public formats for each of the eight seasonal festivals, and at the full or dark phases of the moon, depending on the group. Some Pagans also attend large regional festivals in the summer months. In addition, Pagans recognize rites of passage in their groups, including birth, puberty, other coming-of-age rites, initiations, handfastings, cronings, and death.

Some Pagans celebrate the sabbats with their circles, or in open public rituals, as well as in their homes. Others celebrate the sabbats only at home or privately, or, conversely, only through attending public rituals, sometimes participating only as loosely affiliated laity. Some solitaries attend large public rituals to gain a sense of belonging to the community, but not all Pagans celebrate all the sabbats. Heathens in particular are more likely to celebrate festivals more closely related to their traditions than those based on the British festival cycle.

Group rituals tend to follow a similar pattern to the basic ritual designs discussed in chapter 3, but group sabbat celebrations tend to be more performative and theatrical than private sabbat observances and may involve props, costumes, and masks. The ritual may be planned communally in small groups, or by a committee for larger events. Sometimes ritual scripts are written by one member of the group, who is then responsible for organizing and leading the ritual. A single organizer might plan the ritual, circulate a script, and ask people to choose parts. Alternatively, a group might prefer to work from an outline around which they improvise. Inspiration for the ritual structure and ideas for the event might come from a group's Book of Shadows or from any of the multitude of how-to books on Paganism. As in individual and family practices, creating a ritual can be an intensely creative process. Scripts in how-to books usually suggest using the script as a jumping-off point, an idea of where to start, rather than as something to be applied by rote.

In Ottawa, Samhain is publicly celebrated in a large open ritual called the "Witches' Gathering," usually held on the Saturday closest to Samhain. It is open to the community, including the public, as well as to those who identify as part of the Pagan community. This festival is held at Barrymore's Music Hall, an atmospheric old theatre that has been converted into a bar. The bar has a Gothic ambience of gilt mirrors, ornate plaster moldings, and chandeliers. Hundreds of people come out for the celebration dressed in extravagantly elaborate costumes. The organizers, eclectic Pagans, describe it as the largest Pagan event in Canada. Like many other public Pagan events, the number of participants is determined by the venue. The organizers indicate that the capacity of Barrymore's is 500, but the booking agent for the bar says 375.[1] The ritual itself is largely performative and is conducted onstage with little audience participation. In this respect, Samhain is atypical of other festivals, largely due to the openness of Samhain events to the general public. Consequently, organizers cannot expect all the attendees to know how to participate. This is similarly true of the large Spiral Dance rituals held each Samhain in San Francisco organized by the Reclaiming community. For Ottawa's Witches' Gathering, there is a cover charge for attendance, with the proceeds donated to charities such as the Ottawa Food Bank, Brighter Futures for Children of Young Single Parents, or the Wild Bird Care Center, as have been chosen in recent years. Because of the secular association of witches with Hallowe'en, Pagans often use Samhain as an opportunity for public education. Media representatives seek out Witches to interview, and some Pagans oblige them with the intention of dispelling stereotypes and misconceptions about Paganism.

Some groups mark Yule by observing all-night vigils, staying up through the longest night. Some groups, such as a closed women's circle in Ottawa, celebrate the winter solstice by discarding items they do not want to keep, sometimes as an exchange in which others who want any of the items may take them, with leftovers donated to charity. Everyone in the group brings an object that she is finished with or would like to discard to the circle, and each can choose to take whatever others leave. In other groups, winter-solstice exchanges may be more metaphorical. In New Zealand, a group of feminist Witches went to a cave for their winter-solstice ritual to sacrifice unwanted, "outmoded, negative or unconstructive thoughts, attitudes, or behaviour patterns." Some of the women later wrote poems about their experiences:

> Senses totally stimulated—the power of the sea calling me inside myself. The safety of the cave and the sense of love and belonging drawing me close to the other women. Feeling my baby stirring within my womb, and knowing I have come home.

> The journey beginning with oneself
> Among the dunes of Bethell's
> Being in one's inner darkness
> Letting go unwanted thoughts, feelings
> Being there . . . .
> At home in the bosom of the Great Mother.[2]

Imbolc is the time at which some groups make or anoint all their candles for the year as part of celebrating the festival. Anglicans in Britain celebrate the Christian festival of Candlemas at this time, and some Gardnerians celebrate the festival similarly as a festival of lights. In Gardnerian ritual, a woman representing the Goddess as mother wears a headdress with candles in the ritual celebration of Imbolc. The ritual involves sweeping away "all that is old and outworn." At the conclusion of the ritual, the priest symbolically burns two evergreen twigs and says a ritual **chant** to banish winter.[3]

Some groups reenact the myth of Demeter and Kore (or Persephone) in celebrating Oestre. In this story, Kore disappears to the underworld, and her mother Demeter is so upset that she causes the Earth to become cold and barren, creating winter. Eventually an agreement is made that Kore will return to visit her mother for half the year each year, and as Kore returns each year, Demeter releases the Earth from winter, bringing spring. Some groups celebrate a Pagan version of the Jewish holiday of Passover, or they celebrate Passover with their extended families each spring. It is often still too cold to celebrate Oestre outdoors in Canada and the northern states, but sometimes groups do hold their sabbats outside, particularly when trying to connect with the local features of the land. For example, Red Maple Grove, a Druid group affiliated with Ár nDraíocht Féin, held an outdoor spring equinox ritual in Ottawa in 2003 to connect with the watershed and its history. The ritual began with offerings to the Rideau River and included a pledge to petition the local and regional governments against the use of pesticides and chemical fertilizers, and to help clean up garbage in the park where the ritual was held. The group requested that the river let the melting snow and ice gently pass through the city to avoid flooding, which had been a problem in the area in the past.

Figure 8.   The Goddess as mother at Imbolc, wearing a Brigid headdress of candles (from Farrar and Farrar, *A Witches' Bible*)

Beltain celebrations sometimes include a Maypole festival, which involves erecting a pole planted in the Earth and weaving ribbons around it. Often the group of celebrants is divided so that men go in one direction and women the other, weaving the ribbons into a complex pattern around the pole. Some participants joke about going "a-maying" after the ritual, spending the night out in the woods with one's partner or a partner of the night. However, although most are aware of Marion Zimmer Bradley's description of such a Beltain celebration in her popular novel *The Mists of Avalon*, not many celebrate it in that fashion. Sometimes celebrations of Beltain on May Day are connected to the political demonstrations held on the same date called "*M'aidez*," a play on the French imperative phrase meaning "help me."

Figure 9.   Maypole (photo by M. Macha Nightmare)

In Britain, Stonehenge is the place to be for the summer solstice, although Pagans' use of the site has been much contested with heritage authorities. Stonehenge is protected as a heritage site, but people demand access, not just Druids and other Pagans, but hundreds of other "travelers," the name given to people who live in caravans or trailers and move from place to place. Some travelers are Pagan and see the annual journey as a sort of pilgrimage. The celebration of the solstice at Stonehenge consists of an all-night party concluding with watching the sun come up. The People's Free Festival was held there beginning in the early 1970s but was banned in the mid-1980s.[4] Access has since been allowed again.

Group observances of Lammas, or Lughnasadh, often involve some form of a sacrificial death of a god figure. For Gardnerians, Lughnasadh is the time of the rebirth of the Holly King and his mating with the Goddess, symbolically enacted in ritual by the high priest and priestess. Gardnerians see the Holly King as the dark half of the Horned God, the god of the waning year.[5] Lughnasadh is the only time in Gardnerian groups that the high priestess invokes the Goddess in herself instead of the high priest invoking the Goddess in her.[6]

Many Pagans celebrate a fall festival around the time of the autumnal equinox through family gatherings of thankfulness for the harvest, particularly in North America, but some also conduct group celebrations. Pagan women in New Zealand braid wool girdles, incorporating symbols of personal harvest or what they want to carry forward into the next season.[7] The fall equinox is a time to celebrate the Goddess in her Crone aspect and to recognize the value of older women. It is also a time to "do what is necessary to achieve balance in one's life."[8]

In addition to local circle-based or city-based celebrations of the eight seasonal festivals, some Pagan groups host large outdoor festivals in the summer months, which often do not fall on the sabbats. Wic-Can Fest, usually held the week before the summer solstice, is Canada's oldest and longest-running Pagan festival. It is a family-oriented festival held in southern Ontario, near Toronto, at a private campground. Attendance at the festival is restricted by the capacity of the campground to about three hundred people. Scheduled activities at Wic-Can Fest include workshops, lectures, demonstrations, and concerts and rituals, as well as a market area and an impressive musical lineup.

The Rites of Spring is similarly a large festival, hosted by the EarthSpirit Community each May at a camp near Boston, Massachusetts. Some participants stay in the cabins of the camp, and additional participants stay in tents. Activities at the festival include rituals, workshops, and socializing.[9] The festival develops a strong village atmosphere, partly through communal food preparation and a common dining area.[10]

ELFest, a festival sponsored by the Elf Lore Family (ELF) at a place they call Lothlorien, has been described in detail by researcher Sarah Pike:

> Clusters of colorful tents were set up under the canopy of trees. Small campers and vans lined the circular gravel driveway. Festival goers were roaming informally around campsites, gathering at tables covered with books on witchcraft and long, hooded robes for sale or talking with and greeting friends. A woman who smelled of incense and rose and whose naked body was more than half covered with tattoos of flowers and dragons, smiled broadly at me. Two men wearing black leather boots and dark cloaks walked by, deep in conversation. Farther along the road, a young man with bronzed skin juggled balls as he talked to another man wrapped at the waist in a tie-dye cloth and carrying a rainbow-colored parasol. The festival was alive with music, quiet conversation, naked skin, and bodies adorned with costumes and elaborate jewelry.[11]

Most Pagan festivals in the United States follow a common pattern of activities, including an opening ceremony, workshops during the days, rituals and performances in the evenings, and drumming and dancing at night, as well as a community feast and closing ritual.[12]

Regional festivals are usually open to all who pay the registration fees. At some festivals, registrants are expected to contribute some volunteer time with the festival, either with directing parking, looking after children, or cooking. Festivals last anywhere from a weekend to a week, and vary in size, with the bigger festivals drawing a few hundred attendees.[13] Alternative dress is common at festivals, and nudity is frequent, although officially restricted to certain areas of the festival grounds, such as the beach and fire pit. Many people, including men, wear sarongs. Cloaks are more common if the weather is cooler. Robes are often worn in ritual, regardless of the temperature.

Almost half of all Pagans attend large regional festivals, whether they usually engage in solitary practice or are affiliated with circles.[14] Solitaries are somewhat less likely to attend festivals: 43.1 percent of attendees at festivals belong to groups, and 35.8 percent are solitaries. The largest segment of attendees are in their thirties (33.9 percent), followed by those in their forties (26.7 percent) and those in their twenties (24.1 percent). There are more women than men at festivals, but the proportion of men attending festivals is higher than in the general Pagan population.[15]

Although festival participants tend to be more politically active than other Pagans, festivals are not popular forums for political activity. People might mention pride parades and environmental concerns, but such issues are not central at festivals. Spiritual and magical concerns are more important, although political views are often implicit in rituals.[16] Festivals provide participants with a forum for re-creating themselves as Pagans, to forge new identities.[17] Some Pagans who are deeply in the "broom closet," that is, hiding their Pagan identity in their day-to-day lives, are openly Pagan only while attending festivals. At festivals, Pagans are not marginal but are at the center of the community. The consensus reality of a festival community supports Pagan understandings of the world. At festivals, "where the rules of everyday interaction are suspended, they imagine finding an ideal community and an ideal self."[18]

Some Pagans regard festivals as liminal spaces, in anthropologist Victor Turner's sense of being outside of time. Summer festivals are a "vacation" from participants' usual lives, and some expect that the judgment of others will be suspended around things like nudity, sexual activity, gender boundaries, and sometimes drugs.[19] However, festivals do not escape cultural conditioning to the degree that some participants hope and expect: "festival goers expect festivals to reflect their vision of a more egalitarian, less sexist society. Construction of men's and women's identities within this ritual space is coded in varieties of bodily expression. The languages of movement and body decoration reveal that while ritual work within Neo-Pagan festivals involves gender play and gender reversal, its transformative effects are more limited than participants anticipate."[20] In addition, the perceived freedom and license of the festival atmosphere has been marred by occurrences of sexual harassment at some festivals, including incidents of rude flirting and grabbing. Women have appealed to festival organizers to prevent such activities. Some participants also have concerns about excessive drinking around fire pits, preferring to preserve them as ritual spaces. However, while some participants express desires that festivals be a "safe space," others prefer an "anything goes" atmosphere.[21]

In addition to regional and seasonal festivals, some Pagans meet in groups at particular phases of the moon. These meetings are sometimes called esbats, particularly by Wiccans. Esbats are the "work" meetings of Pagan circles, as opposed to the more celebratory sabbats. Esbats are the regular ritual meetings of a coven in Wicca. If a member wants to conduct a healing ritual, for instance, it would more likely be at one of these meetings than during a sabbat celebration (or they might do a ritual specifically for a healing). Such meetings are closed to the public; that is, they are restricted to group members. In the Reclaiming community, esbats tend to be gender-segregated closed events, while the sabbats are public.[22]

Wiccans usually meet once a month, when the moon is full, as specified in the liturgy of the Charge of the Goddess. Some Pagan groups regularly perform the ritual of drawing down the moon at the full moon, and it is often conducted at regional festivals. In this ritual, a woman invites the Goddess to speak through her. In Wicca, a man either invokes the Goddess in the priestess, or the woman evokes the Goddess from within.[23]

Some Pagans understand this in terms of possession, and others in terms of the woman becoming an incarnation of the Goddess. Some practitioners prefer to say that they do not "invoke" or "become" the Goddess, but that they manifest the part of the Goddess that is already in them.[24] During the ritual, the priestess goes into trance and may prophesy after the Goddess is invoked, or she may speak the words of the liturgy of the Charge of the Goddess. Some say that the words spoken vary somewhat in practice, as appropriate to the occasion. In some traditions, such as Reclaiming, the Goddess may be drawn down into men as well as women.[25] The ritual of drawing down the moon, and the liturgy of the Charge, spread from Gardnerian Wicca and was derived from *Aradia*. Doreen Valiente wrote the original verse version used in Gardnerian Wicca, and Starhawk wrote the prose version that is in common circulation. Wiccans suggest that some form of the ritual of drawing down the moon was practiced in ancient Greece.

Many Pagans associate the phases of the moon with women's menstrual cycles, which are of approximately the same length, and with the three aspects of the Goddess. The waxing or new moon is associated with the maiden, the full moon with the mother, and the waning moon with the crone. There is a fourth phase of the moon, the dark moon, which is not visible. This is sometimes also associated with the crone. Some women's-only groups prefer to meet at the dark of the moon, or the new moon. Sometimes women who are menstruating during such meetings wear bracelets of red wool to indicate their special state so that it can be recognized and honored by the others present. Menstruation is thought to occasion a "psychic opening" and to increase women's intuitive powers.[26]

Pagans also conduct group ceremonies acknowledging rites of passage for individuals in their communities. Rites of passage recognize changes in social roles, status, or identity. In general, such rituals require community recognition through a group event of some sort. As Paganism has matured from a movement into a world religion, Pagans have developed rituals for rites of passage in all stages of life, from birth to death. Most of these involve some community component, but some rites of passage are

---

Doreen Valiente, author of a number of popular books on Witchcraft, was a member of Gerald Gardner's coven beginning in the 1940s. She extensively rewrote Gardner's Book of Shadows, parts of which have diffused into contemporary Paganism without recognition of her authorship. More information on Valiente can be found in chapter 7.

more family oriented, such as recognition of the change from baby to child.[27] Some puberty rites are also more oriented toward family than group recognition.

Many Pagans conduct formal rituals to welcome babies into their communities, but they also speak of more spontaneous rituals to introduce infants to the world. Charlene Spretnak recounts a story of taking her daughter outside for the first time, into a garden outside the hospital, and introducing her to the pine trees, the flowers, the moon, and the stars, and them to her. She felt a need to welcome her child to the cosmos in a ritual fashion.[28] Pagans tell similar stories of the spontaneous impulse to introduce their children or god/dess children to the natural world.

Welcoming rituals for introducing new babies into Pagan groups are variously called "Wiccaning," "saining," or "Paganing." These rituals introduce the child to the community and the deities, to ask for their blessings on the child and to introduce the child to ritual. No promises are made to commit the child to the religion, although god/dess parents may be appointed.[29] For example, at a Wiccaning, a Wiccan welcoming ritual, a group met in a suburban state park, where they often held rituals, to Wiccan a month-old child. Dressed in the family's baptism gown, the child was introduced to the four directions and the elements. The afterbirth and birth blood, frozen to preserve it and thawed for the ritual, were used. The afterbirth was buried, and the blood was used to anoint the child, as well as a white cord. The cord symbolically linked the child to the Earth, just as his umbilical cord had linked him to his mother in the womb. As part of the ceremony, each of the group members made a wish for the child, represented by a colored ribbon tied to a branch. After the ritual, the group shared a picnic lunch, and gifts were given for the baby.[30]

Pagans have developed coming-of-age rituals for two stages of transition into adulthood: puberty and leaving home. Puberty rituals tend to be limited to members of the youth's sex for at least one stage of the ritual, but may subsequently involve welcoming by both men and women into the community. Some male puberty rites involve an ordeal as a symbolic confrontation with mortality.[31] The influence of readings in anthropology is evident in the development of such Pagan puberty rituals for males. Rituals recognizing menarche, the onset of menstruation, often include a component designed to counter popular images expressive of the beauty myth. *Circle Round*, a family guide prepared by members of the Reclaiming community, includes a number of exercises to use in preparation for puberty rituals. It includes, for example, meditations on what to leave behind and what to carry forward, meditations on accepting that one will not be good at certain activities, and meditations on refusing to accept prejudgments of others about one's capacities. The authors suggest, for example, perhaps deciding to quit taking piano lessons if one is not willing to take the time to practice, or deciding to take up singing again, despite the inappropriate ridicule of a teacher who criticized one's voice.[32] *Circle Round* also includes blessing liturgies for male and female puberty rites. These liturgies are symmetrical in structure and include wishes that the adolescent always find her/his body "a temple of love and pleasure," use her/his reproductive powers responsibly, and recognize her/his unique value.[33]

Rituals for leaving home tend to be family oriented and can be as much about the parents letting go as about the youth coming of age. These rituals recognize the separation of a youth from her/his parents, and the youth's passage into full responsibility for her/his own life. In *Circle Round*, Calla Unsworth describes a coming-of-age ritual for her son Tor. The family shared stories and wishes for Tor's future and ritually tied a cord between him and each of his parents to symbolize their bonds, allowing him to cut the ropes when he was ready.[34] A similar practice can be used as part of a ritual to recognize menarche, the onset of menstruation and of a girl becoming a woman. In the Reclaiming community, a young woman named Sonia who was celebrating menarche was anointed with waters gathered from around the world, marking her forehead, breasts, belly, and genitals, as Starhawk said, "Remember, nobody can give you power. You already have the power within." A cord was tied around Sonia's and her mother's wrists. Sonia's grandmother likened this cord to Sonia's umbilical cord, saying that, like it, the cord needed to be cut so that the daughter could live on her own, but that their "bond of the heart" would endure. Sonia and her mother were asked to run for as long as they could while tied together. Her mother eventually could not keep up with Sonia's youthful speed. Her grandmother cut the cord with a ritual knife, which was then presented to Sonia as a gift.[35]

Pagans also sometimes conduct rites of passage to confer new or magical names. These are rituals of self-transformation. Adopting a magical name, or changing it, can help one grow emotionally or spiritually, providing a focus for working to change oneself.[36] Recognizing the name change in community can help reinforce one's commitment to change. If one does it alone, there is no one to notice if one does not sustain the change. Some Pagans adopt magical or Craft names in place of their legal names. Starhawk, born Miriam Simos, is a prominent example. Pagans make fun of their tendency to adopt fanciful magical names,[37] but magical names can signify personal growth. To change one's name is to change oneself, to recognize a change, to preserve it, or to encourage it. For example, through an initiation ceremony, a man changed his magical name from "White Water" to "Three Blade Jaguar," to recognize his change from being full of undirected energy, like white water, early in his religious practice, to perceiving himself as growing in the role of protector of his wife and child.[38] Such uses of magical names can foster a positive image of the gendered self, in this case a romantic but positive image of masculinity.[39]

Some Pagans participate in initiatory denominations of Paganism, which are traditions that require initiation into the group or tradition for full participation of its members. Even those who do not belong to an initiatory denomination sometimes speak of being initiated by the Goddess or by their patron deities. Initiation ceremonies often involve a symbolic death and rebirth, and they usually require the initiate to make a commitment to the Goddess, to his/her patrons, or to the tradition. Gardnerian and Alexandrian Wicca require initiation into "the mysteries." Only adults can be initiated into Wicca, and generally one must be over eighteen to receive instruction leading up to initiation. Pagans speak of training for "a year and a day," but this is a traditional phrase that indicates that initiation requires a sustained period of training. Interest in training does not automatically lead to initiation.

Gardnerian and Alexandrian Wiccans have three degrees of initiation. The first-degree ceremony involves being nude, including the removal of all jewelry, as well as being blindfolded and bound. The ritual is partly inspired by the Sumerian myth of Inanna's descent into the underworld, where she sheds all her clothing and jewelry as symbols of her social status, in recognition of the equalizing power of death. In Gardnerian tradition, men can only be initiated by women, and vice versa.

More generally in Craft traditions, initiation ritualizes acceptance into a coven, and ideally, if timed properly, personal growth.[40] The Faery tradition has two levels of initiation, and the Reclaiming tradition adapts this to one level, which is optional for practitioners in the tradition. In the Reclaiming tradition, one must ask for initiation; it is not spontaneously offered.[41] Gender polarity is not necessary in Reclaiming initiations, so women can initiate women, and men can initiate men. The essence of the Reclaiming initiation is the surrender of one's will to the Goddess, represented in the authority of one's initiators. In undertaking initiation, the apprentice invites the initiator to challenge her/him, that is, to help her/him confront her/his "shadow," in the Jungian sense of the parts of oneself that one would like to hide, ignore, or repress and deny.[42] The aim of the process is to help the apprentice grow so that the initiation will be a personal transformation, recognizing a maturation of the self in the tradition.

The teaching or apprenticeship phase of initiation into the Reclaiming tradition can last more than two years, and the ritual itself can be very long—nine hours in the case of a woman called Catherine. Catherine asked five women to be her initiators. The challenges they specified for her included participation in other Wiccan rituals: to be sky clad (nude) as much as possible, to forgo wearing contact lenses or a watch for a year and a day, to develop ritual materials for children, and to explore her shadow through rituals based on each of the four elements. Preparation for the ritual involved writing her magical will and obtaining magical tools for her initiators to give to her upon initiation. (She had not previously used ritual tools.) The ritual itself began with her going alone to a park in the evening and meditating there by herself for a few hours. Her initiators then came and blindfolded her and took her to the ocean. There they administered tests of each of the four elements. Next, they took her back to one of the initiator's houses, where a bathroom was prepared as a temple. There she took a ritual bath, still blindfolded. Her initiators left her alone for a while to find a new name, and then they led her to the circle to be welcomed as a full initiate and allowed to know all the secrets. She made promises and experienced an emotional dedication to the Goddess. The ritual concluded with an exchange of gifts between the initiate and the initiators. After the initiation, Catherine felt that her relationship with her lover was transformed, and that her relations with others who were initiated had changed, but that her relations with others who had not been initiated were unaffected. She relates, "The only secret is that it is so intimate; that's what cannot be shared. It is just that it is so personal"[43]

Pagans recognize the rite of passage into committed loving relationships through marriages or handfastings. Handfastings are ritual recognitions of love relationships that involve a dedication of the partners to a commitment for a year and day, or for as long as the love lasts. However, most handfastings are understood as marriage in terms of making a permanent commitment. In some places where Pagans have the right to become licensed clerics, handfastings can be legal marriages. Rituals for handfasting generally include a ritual binding of the hands of the partners, representing the symbolic unity or lasting bonds of the couple. The ritual may involve questions to the couple from other attendants. In a Druid handfasting, for example, questions were posed from each of the four directions or elements. The partners were questioned regarding facing "the difficulties of 'the clear light of day,' 'the harsh fires of change,' 'the ebb and flow of feeling' and 'the times of stillness and restriction.'" Following the commitment of the couple, each element blessed the union.[44] Some handfastings, particularly in Wiccan traditions, include a ritual of "jumping the broom" as a symbol of sexual union. The cleric may ask the groom to look at the bride and recognize the goddess in her, and ask the bride to look at the groom and recognize the god in him.[45] In Britain, Beltain is a popular time for handfastings.[46] However, some other Pagans say that it is unlucky to get married in May, because the Goddess marries the God at Beltain in a marriage of Earth and Sun. To get married at the same time as the Goddess, they say, would be presumptuous and would bring bad luck.

Figure 10.   Handfasting (photo from Mandy Furney)

Handfasting can involve blessing a variety of types of love relationships, including not only heterosexual pairings but also homosexual and
polyamorous committed relationships (group marriages). Although few
Pagans practice group marriage, most support its legalization.[47] In some
countries, such as Canada, homosexuals can be legally married. Statistics
on homosexual handfastings are not available, but 4.8 percent of Pagans
surveyed are married ritually, 33.3 percent are legally married, 13.8 percent cohabitate, and 0.4 percent are part of a group marriage.[48]

Largely due to its overlap with feminist-influenced women's spirituality, Paganism has developed a rite of passage to recognize the elderhood
of women, often at menopause, the ending of menstruation. These rituals,
called "croning," recognize the strength, wisdom, and power of older
women, challenging the patriarchal image of the old woman as a with-
ered useless hag. Some Pagans associate croning with a particular age because some women continue to menstruate into their sixties, and some
stop menstruating for a variety of reasons in their thirties or sooner. Z. Budapest gives a ritual for the end of menstruation, but also a separate croning ritual.[49] Budapest suggests that a croning ritual should be done at age
56, astrologically reasoning that the ritual should be done when "Saturn
has returned twice to [the woman's] natal point," which "happens to
everybody at age 56."

> suzsanna Budapest, commonly known as "Z." Budapest, is a Hungarian immigrant to the United States who has greatly influenced the development of contemporary Paganism and feminist spirituality. For more information on Z. Budapest, see chapter 7.

Croning rituals for groups of women are sometimes held at summer festivals. At one of these, although both men and women attended the festival, only women participated in the croning ritual. The ritual focused on the strength of women and their connections with other women, discussing the problems inherent in living in a culture that does not value women or their independence. Some croning rituals are attended by both men and women.[50] A Goddess-oriented group in California conducted a ritual for a group of women to "claim" their Cronehood after a six-month series of workshops on the Goddess as Crone. The ritual was held in late October, inside a rented church. About a hundred people, mostly dressed in black, attended the event, including men, women, and children. The crones were welcomed in, dressed entirely in black, with their faces partially covered by black veils. The procession began with two crones carrying a large cauldron, as a symbol of wisdom, death, and regeneration. As part of the ritual, each introduced herself, saying where she was from and what she contributed to the community. One woman said, "I am Marilyn, daughter of Dorothy, granddaughter of Judith, great granddaughter of Laura, who was a daughter of Hecate. If you would seek wisdom with a Crone, seek me." Some participants mentioned sexuality, which was a revelation for some of the younger women attending the ritual. Breaking the stereotype of old women as useless and weak, the crones presented aging as something to look forward to. They served as an example to the younger women that each could look forward to "an old age where she could be respected and valued by her community, an old age where she could be serious, playful, sexual, wise, powerful, political, and humorous, should she so choose."[51]

Croning is a new rite of passage in Paganism, developing as the religion ages. There are few ethnographic accounts published, but new rituals are developing, with new liturgies being written. There is, for example, a new Charge of the Crone circulating on the Internet, which begins,

> Hear the words of the Grandmother of Time:
> She who has been known as
> Hecate, Erishkagel, Cerridwen, Kali-Ma,
> Anna, Perenna, Spider Woman,

and many other names
—some feared, and some loved,
but none ever ignored.
She it is who brings wisdom and
the awareness of eternity.[52]

Pagans are also developing rituals to recognize the transition of men into elders.[53]

The final rite of passage is death. As Starhawk notes in her preface to *The Pagan Book of Living and Dying*, when a family member dies, one does not have the energy to create new rituals. It is easier to fall back on tradition, which did not exist when her mother died. Thus, she began to collect materials for a book. The result, *The Pagan Book of Living and Dying* (1997), coauthored with M. Macha Nightmare and the Reclaiming Collective, includes not only a script for a funeral or memorial service, but also resource material for comforting the dying and the bereaved. The basic message of the book is that death is part of life, a biological necessity. Life is a cycle, and death is honored in Pagan traditions, sometimes even welcomed as an end to suffering. Pagans feel that death is a transformation, not just an ending. The Reclaiming tradition, following the teaching of the Faery tradition, teaches that part of one's self survives death. The Reclaiming tradition holds that there are three aspects to the self, what Starhawk calls the "Talking Self" (one's rational consciousness), the "Younger Self" (the emotional and instinctive self), and the "Deep Self" (one's core). It is the Deep Self, they believe, that is reincarnated.[54] This aspect of one's self is not spirit as opposed to matter. It is part of extraordinary reality, not cut off or separate from ordinary reality, but not always perceptible. Pagans speak of this extraordinary reality, sometimes called the otherland, in the Celtic-influenced sense of a place imaged as the realm of Faerie, the Summerland, Avalon, or the Isle of Apples.[55] *The Pagan Book of Living and Dying* suggests that the realm of the dead is nonlinear; one's ancestors remain available even when they have been reborn, because the Deep Self is timeless.[56]

Following the Faery tradition, some Reclaiming Witches teach that one should align the three selves (Talking, Younger, and Deep) to increase one's health, but also so that after death no parts of one's self get

---

Like Buddhists, many Pagans believe in reincarnation, but without the goal of release from rebirth. A popular Pagan T-shirt proudly declares that the wearer is a "born again Pagan."

left behind as ghosts.[57] Because there is no standard dogma in Paganism, or even necessarily within the Pagan denominations, practitioners' accounts of death, and their ideas of what Pagan communities should do following a death, vary. Some suggest that the rituals are more about comforting the living than about guiding the Deep Self into the afterlife, saying that the Deep Self needs no guide, because it is at home in extraordinary reality.

Diane Baker, in *Circle Round*, speaks of the miscarriage of a baby in terms of a lost spirit, asking the ancestors to help it on its journey, but the focus of the ritual remains on the woman's loss. Baker suggests addressing the goddess Hecate, saying, "Lady, the reaper, I am empty. You've taken life from my womb, life I wanted, life I invited. Come now and comfort me."[58] Elsewhere, the book suggests that "offerings of food, lighted candles, or libations poured out on the earth are tangible gifts of energy to help bring the dead to a place of renewal," and that the expression of grief gives the dead the energy to reach the otherland.[59]

Victor Anderson, of the Faery tradition, taught that the soul lingers for three days, so the body should not be left alone, and the rooms of the deceased should not be cleaned out during that time. This period gives the bereaved an opportunity to say last things to the one crossing over.[60] Anderson also instructed that souls can stray in cases of sudden or violent death, or they may not know that they are dead, and he suggested that prayer and ritual can help a soul move on. This straying can be a lingering near the body or home, or a failing to find the desired aspect of the otherland. Anderson felt that all images of the afterlife exist, and he indicated that you go where you expect to go: if you imagine you will go to hell, then you will go there, but you can proceed to a more pleasant place, such as the land of the ancestors.[61]

The Pagan Book of Living and Dying provides a comprehensive guide for Pagans dealing with death. It includes prayers for palliative caregivers to say, as well as prayers for the dying to say. It also provides a healing ritual for following an abortion, prayers for use in assisted suicide, and a ritual for removing life support. Rituals for washing the body, a blessing to say, and instructions for smudging or censing the body are also supplied. In addition, *The Pagan Book of Living and Dying* furnishes a complete ritual script, including music, for a funeral or memorial, which can be adapted as necessary or appropriate. It provides instructions for dealing with non-Pagan participants in funeral services. The funeral service begins with offerings to the land, asking it to receive the body. Offerings are made to the ancestors, asking them to guide the dead, and the ritual leader tells the deceased that s/he is dead. Then the attendees share stories of the life of the deceased. Finally, the attendees ritually release the deceased and ask for her/his rebirth.[62]

FURTHER READING

Pike, Sarah. *Earthly Bodies, Magical Selves: Contemporary Pagans and the Search for Community.* Berkeley and Los Angeles: University of California Press, 2001.

Starhawk, M. Macha Nightmare, and the Reclaiming Collective. *The Pagan Book of Living and Dying: Practical Rituals, Prayers, Blessings, and Meditations on Crossing Over.* San Francisco: HarperSanFrancisco, 1997.

Starhawk, Diane Baker, and Anne Hill. *Circle Round: Raising Children in Goddess Traditions.* New York: Bantam, 1998.

NOTES

1. See the Witches' Gathering, www.witches-gathering.com (accessed June 8, 2004); Murielle Varhelyi, personal correspondence, June 8, 2004.

2. Kathryn Rountree, *Embracing the Witch and the Goddess: Feminist Ritual-Makers in New Zealand* (London: Routledge, 2004), 139, 162.

3. Stewart Farrar and Janet Farrar, *A Witches' Bible: The Complete Witches' Handbook* (Custer, WA: Phoenix Publishing, 1996), 66–71.

4. Adrian Ivakhiv, *Claiming Sacred Ground: Pilgrims and Politics at Glastonbury and Sedona* (Bloomington: Indiana University Press, 2001), 13.

5. Farrar and Farrar, *A Witches' Bible*, 24, 111.

6. Farrar and Farrar, *A Witches' Bible*, 27.

7. See Rountree, *Embracing the Witch and the Goddess*, 155.

8. Rountree, *Embracing the Witch and the Goddess*, 142.

9. Helen Berger, *A Community of Witches* (Columbia: University of South Carolina Press, 1999), 59.

10. Berger, *Community of Witches*, 73.

11. Sarah Pike, *Earthly Bodies, Magical Selves: Contemporary Pagans and the Search for Community* (Berkeley: University of California Press, 2001), 1–2.

12. Pike, *Earthly Bodies, Magical Selves*, 3.

13. Helen Berger, Evan A. Leach, and Leigh S. Shaffer. *Voices from the Pagan Census: A National Survey of Witches and Neo-Pagans in the United States* (Columbia: University of South Carolina Press, 2003), 203, 206.

14. Berger, *Community of Witches*, 75.

15. These statistics are from Berger, Leach, and Shaffer, *Voices from the Pagan Census*, 208, 205, 210.

16. Berger, Leach, and Shaffer, *Voices from the Pagan Census*, 215.

17. Sarah Pike, "Forging Magical Selves: Gendered Bodies and Ritual Fires at Neo-Pagan Festivals," in *Magical Religion and Modern Witchcraft*, ed. James R. Lewis (Albany: State University of New York Press, 1996), 121.

18. Pike, "Forging Magical Selves," 126.

19. Pike, "Forging Magical Selves," 123.

20. Pike, "Forging Magical Selves," 122.

21. Pike, "Forging Magical Selves," 134–36.

22. Jone Salomonsen, *Enchanted Feminism: The Reclaiming Witches of San Francisco* (London: Routledge, 2002), 47.

23. Margot Adler, *Drawing Down the Moon: Witches, Druids, Goddess-Worshippers, and Other Pagans in America Today*, revised and expanded ed. (Boston: Beacon Press, 1986), 19.

24. Wendy Griffin, "The Embodied Goddess: Feminist Witchcraft and Female Divinity," *Sociology of Religion* 56 (1995): 35–49, www.csulb.edu/~wgriffin/embodied.html (accessed June 15, 2004).

25. Graham Harvey, *Contemporary Paganism: Listening People, Speaking Earth* (New York: New York University Press, 1997), 41.

26. Rountree, *Embracing the Witch and the Goddess*, 143.

27. See Starhawk, Diane Baker, and Anne Hill, *Circle Round: Raising Children in Goddess Traditions* (New York: Bantam, 1998), 306–10.

28. Charlene Spretnak, "Ecofeminism: Our Roots and Flowering," in *Reweaving the World: The Emergence of Ecofeminism*, ed. Irene Diamond and Gloria Feman Orenstein (San Francisco: Sierra Club Books, 1990), 13.

29. Berger, *Community of Witches*, 90.

30. Berger, *Community of Witches*, 1–3.

31. See Berger, *Community of Witches*, 91.

32. Starhawk, Baker, and Hill, *Circle Round*, 316–17.

33. Starhawk, Baker, and Hill, *Circle Round*, 325–27.

34. Starhawk, Baker, and Hill, *Circle Round*, 331–33.

35. Salomonsen, *Enchanted Feminism*, 33.

36. Berger, *Community of Witches*, 35.

37. See, for example, Lady Pixie Moondrip's Pagan name generator, "Lady Pixie Moondrip's Guide to Craft Names," *Widdershins*, www.widdershins.org/vol3iss4/m9710.htm (accessed June 24, 2004).

38. Berger, *Community of Witches*, 27.

39. Berger, *Community of Witches*, 36.

40. Starhawk, *The Spiral Dance: A Rebirth of the Ancient Religion of the Great Goddess*, 10th anniversary ed. (New York: HarperSanFrancisco, 1989), 173.

41. Salomonsen, *Enchanted Feminism*, 248–49.

42. Salomonsen, *Enchanted Feminism*, 250–51.

43. Salomonsen, *Enchanted Feminism*, 256–72.

44. Harvey, *Contemporary Paganism*, 202.

45. Berger, *Community of Witches*, 33.

46. Harvey, *Contemporary Paganism*, 11.

47. Berger, Leach, and Shaffer, *Voices from the Pagan Census*, 142.

48. Berger, Leach, and Shaffer, *Voices from the Pagan Census*, 28–29.

49. Zsuzsanna Budapest, *The Holy Book of Women's Mysteries* (Oakland, CA: Wingbow Press, 1989), 77–78, 85–86.

50. Berger, *Community of Witches*, 38–40.

51. Griffin, "The Embodied Goddess."

52. This piece is usually attributed to Gypsy, "The Charge of the Crone," Tryskelion, ed. Lady Shayra, www.Tryskelion.com (accessed June 24, 2004), but other sites say that it was co-written by Hank Shadow in about 1996. See, for example, Amethyst, "The Charge of the Crone," Amethyst's Wicca, www.angelfire.com/realm2/amethystbt/chargeofthecrone.html (accessed June 24, 2004).

53. See, for example, Drowynn Forrest Torgerson, "Elder Ritual for Men," *PanGaia* 39 (2004): 57–59.

54. Starhawk, M. Macha Nightmare, and the Reclaiming Collective, *The Pagan Book of Living and Dying: Practical Rituals, Prayers, Blessings, and Meditations on Crossing Over* (San Francisco: HarperSanFrancisco, 1997), 73.

55. Starhawk, Nightmare, and the Reclaiming Collective, *The Pagan Book of Living and Dying*, 80.

56. Starhawk, Nightmare, and the Reclaiming Collective, *The Pagan Book of Living and Dying*, 104.

57. Starhawk, Nightmare, and the Reclaiming Collective, *The Pagan Book of Living and Dying*, 76.

58. Starhawk, Nightmare, and the Reclaiming Collective, *The Pagan Book of Living and Dying*, 300.

59. Starhawk, Nightmare, and the Reclaiming Collective, *The Pagan Book of Living and Dying*, 81, 148.

60. Starhawk, Nightmare, and the Reclaiming Collective, *The Pagan Book of Living and Dying*, 154.

61. Starhawk, Nightmare, and the Reclaiming Collective, *The Pagan Book of Living and Dying*, 154.

62. Starhawk, Nightmare, and the Reclaiming Collective, *The Pagan Book of Living and Dying*, 161–72.

5

Myths and Historical Origins

Sabbat celebrations, as well as other Pagan rituals and gatherings, often include allusions to, or retellings of, certain stories, myths, and understandings of their history. The relationship of myth with history is often blurred in the various world religions' origin myths, and this is also true of Paganism. However, myth should not be understood simply as bad history. The common meaning of "myth" is that it is something false or fictional, while history is generally felt to be a more objective account of what really happened. However, in religious studies, "myth" is understood in the sense of being a sacred or significant story. Myths are inspirational stories for practitioners, some say with **archetypal** content. Practitioners might argue that myths are true and describe a more real account of why things are the way they are in the same manner that some people say that a novel can tell more truth about human life than any purported nonfiction account.

In Paganism, as in other religions, myths function as tools of inspiration and legitimation and may serve other political ends. These uses of myth are not necessarily manipulative, but they indicate why the stories are retold: because they mean something to the tellers and the listeners. Some practitioners feel threatened by questions of historical accuracy, while others prefer to regard the myths primarily as stories that teach and inspire. Questions of historical accuracy apply to understandings of Pagan religion as "the Old Religion," beliefs in the theory of pagan "survivals," interpretations of the medieval witch hunts as the "Burning Times," and feminist revisionings of history, including what is sometimes called the myth of the matriarchies. Other prominent mythological stories in Paganism that have less controversial relationships with history are the stories of the Wild Hunt, Ceridwen's cauldron, Odin's hanging on Yggdrasil, and Inanna's descent into the underworld.

Contemporary Pagans have often repeated a story of historical origins that presents their religion as "the Old Religion." According to this story, Wicca, or Paganism more generally, represents the survival of pre-Christian pagan traditions into modern times. In this story, "the Old Religion" often refers to the religion of the British Isles before Christian colonization, imagined to be unchanged from the Stone Age. A typical 1970s expression of the myth can be found in a Church of All Worlds pamphlet written by Tim Zell, titled "Neo-Paganism: An Old Religion for a New Age." Zell there expresses the belief that "Pagan" properly describes a natural folk religion, an indigenous religion of the original inhabitants of the British Isles, the "faeries" or "heathens" who were persecuted by the church following the Saxon invasions. The pamphlet also makes reference to the church killing nine million people in these persecutions, known as the "Burning Times."[1] Many Pagans have discarded any claim to continuity with pre-Christian traditions due to academic criticism, saying that their religion is not a survival of pre-Christian traditions but part of a revival and reconstruction of ancient religious practices. Some retain the phrase "the Old Religion" but change its meaning to refer to the religion of the culture of Old Europe from the Neolithic period of prehistory.

The idea of "the Old Religion" began at least as early as the German Romantics, in the late 1800s and early 1900s, long before the development of contemporary Paganism as a religion. The German Romantics saw "the Old Religion" as the original, natural religion of humanity before the Fall (of humanity from the grace of God in the garden of Eden). They present it as a religion not of reason but of poetry and mythology, and as a religion that idolizes the ideal feminine. Friedrich Schlegel, for example, used the phrase "the old religion" for this understanding of nature religion in his 1799 novel *Lucinde*, in which a man, Julius, encourages a woman, Lucinde, to discard her social sensibilities and embrace her passionate nature. The novel refers to them as priest and priestess of a religion of free love. Lucinde is associated with the light of the moon, as is the Goddess in later developments of Paganism. Her name alludes to the Latin word for light (*lux*) and to Lucina, the Roman goddess of birth. Schlegel writes in a poetic style that is inspirational to contemporary Pagans: "The religion I have returned to is the oldest, the most childlike and simple. I worship fire as being the best symbol of the Godhead. And where is there a lovelier fire than the one nature has locked deeply into the soft breast of woman?"[2]

For Schlegel, as for contemporary Pagans, this religion is at once "the Old Religion" and new. It is the original nature religion, but newly imagined after the embracing of reason; it is a new religion following urbanization and the repression of the Victorian era. Schlegel's presentation of "the Old Religion" had a popular appeal that spoke to the English Romantics who, in common with the German Romantics, expressed an idealized vision of life in the country. Schlegel wrote that "in the country—if everything were as it ought to be—lovely houses and charming cottages could adorn the green earth like fresh plants and flowers, and make it a garden worthy of God."[3] Popular nostalgia for rural England began at the end of the eighteenth century with the rise of urbanization, it reached a height in the 1850s, and it has continued ever since.[4] Contemporary Paganism embraces this popular nostalgia, especially in Britain.

The popular appeal of romantic images of the countryside in Britain combined with the appeal of the idea of "Merrie Olde England." This was a popular myth of the 1800s that "characterized pre-industrial England as a land of social stability and harmony, operating above all through communal festivity."[5] It idealized the culture of medieval and Tudor England as pagan, despite the fact that it was Christian. It presented "Merrie England" as eternal and changeless, ignoring the upheavals of Christianization and the Reformation (the splitting of the church into Catholic and Protestant sects).[6] It was not contemporary Pagans who created this myth, but they have embraced it, supported by the theory of pagan survivals. In the late Victorian and Edwardian eras in England, the idea of folk-religion survivals, the idea that folk traditions were living fossils of the past, was popular. This idea was based on the theory that social strata could be interpreted as geological strata, so that the lower classes were thought to represent cultural fossils, survivals of preliterate culture. This theory was rejected in archaeology and anthropology in favor of the comparative method, but it continued in studies of folklore much longer.[7]

The French historian Jules Michelet, in his anti-Catholic book of 1862, *La Sorcière*, presented witchcraft as a pagan survival. In it, he argued that women were the natural representatives of a religion of nature, and he presented the witch as a symbol of spiritual freedom and of the rights of women and the working class. Michelet asserted that those killed in the witch hunts practiced a pre-Christian fertility religion.[8] The American journalist and folklorist Charles Godfrey Leland claimed to have found existing practices in Italy of the pre-Christian religion described by Michelet, which he says his informants called "the old religion." This was not an organized religion, he said, but a set of magical practices, which he described as "something more than a sorcery, and something less than a faith."[9]

Pagans are somewhat unlikely to be directly familiar with the writings of Michelet and Leland, but they are usually aware of the theory of Pagan survivals through the work of Margaret Murray. Murray was an anthropologist who specialized in Egypt, but she also wrote on the folklore of Britain and the witch hunts. Murray argued that the ancient pre-Christian

religion of Western Europe was Witchcraft. In *The Witch-Cult in Western
Europe*, she contends that "it was a definite religion with beliefs, ritual,
and organization as highly developed as that of any other cult in the
world."[10] She posits that the religion was organized into a hierarchy, with
slight local differences, as in other cultures, and she presented it as a fertility religion.[11] Wiccans adopted her suppositions that the religion was
that of the "fairy" or "primitive" race, that these people survived up to
less than three hundred years in the past, and that practitioners were
known as witches.[12] Wiccans expanded her argument into a sacred myth,
beginning with Gerald Gardner. Gardner espoused the idea that the
fairies were the earlier settlers of the British Isles in his book *Witchcraft Today*, first published in 1954, a book for which Murray wrote a preface. This
story is still current in Paganism, repeated, for example, in Ly de Angeles'
When I See the Wild God: Encountering Urban Celtic Witchcraft.[13]

Although Wicca bears little resemblance to the witchcraft described by
Murray on the basis of the witch trials, practitioners use terms found
in Murray's work, such as "esbat," "sabbat" (or "sabbath"), and "coven."
Murray's theories were quite influential in stimulating the early development of Wicca and may have been directly responsible for the creation of
some British covens.[14] Murray changed her presentation of the witch cult
between writing *The Witch-Cult in Western Europe*, first published in 1921,
and *The God of the Witches*, first published in 1933, from a description of a
demonic devil-worshipping religion to the celebration of a fertility religion that worshipped Pan. She adopted the phrase "the Old Religion" in
The God of the Witches, possibly from Leland's work.[15] *The God of the
Witches* became a best seller in the 1940s, right before the modern Craft
movement emerged.[16]

Although Murray's work was criticized by witch-trial specialists at
the time of its first publication, her argument that the witch hunts were
a persecution against a pre-Christian religion was accepted by many academics into the 1970s.[17] Additionally, Murray wrote the *Encyclopedia
Britannica* article on "Witchcraft" for the 1929 edition, which gave her a
lasting influence outside of academia.[18] Gerald Gardner, the first popularizer of modern Paganism as Wicca, accepted and promulgated Murray's arguments about the survival of pagan religion in the British Isles
into modern times. Gardner indicates that "witchcraft is simply the remains of the old pagan religion of Western Europe, dating back to the
Stone Age, and that the reason for the Church's persecution of it was
that it was a dangerous rival."[19] Gardner claimed to have found remnants of this ancient religion and to have been initiated into an existing
coven in 1939. However, academic historians have never taken this
claim seriously, because his description of the religion was so dissimilar
from the witchcraft of English folklore.[20]

The myth promulgated by Gerald Gardner was accepted as factual by Wiccans for some time but was publicly challenged beginning in the 1980s by Aiden Kelly. Kelly circulated a manuscript describing the history of Gardnerian Witchcraft, which has since been through many revisions and is now titled "Inventing Witchcraft." He presents some of his findings in *Crafting the Art of Magic: A History of Modern Witchcraft, 1939–1964.* Kelly applied the same methods of textual criticism that have been applied to the Bible to Gardner's Book of Shadows and concluded that Wicca is a modern creation, not a survival of an old religion.[21]

Some Wiccans continue to accept Gardner's account of his initiation and the authenticity of his historical claims as factual, in a parallel fashion to the belief of some Christians in the literal truth of the biblical stories of Jesus. The belief that Paganism is the survival of an ancient religion into modern times, rather than something created in the 1940s and 1950s, provides a sense of legitimacy for some practitioners. It allows them to make similar claims to those of other world religions to a long history and lasting traditions. Some practitioners fear that if the religion is new, then it is just made up, a fantasy without substance, which will not last. However, others celebrate the idea of creating a new religion that is not tied to patriarchal institutions, that freely allows experimentation and the development of rituals enabling religious experience.

Practitioners of contemporary Paganism have long described their religion as both old and new. As previously mentioned, Tim Zell wrote about Paganism in these terms in the 1970s. Starhawk has reframed her use of these terms somewhat, from her early presentation of Witchcraft as the pre-Christian religion persecuted in the witch hunts, to the older religion of "Old Europe." She began by making the debatable claim of an ancient heritage for the Craft, framing it as the Old Religion as Margaret Murray understood it.[22] However, she has also maintained from the beginning that "Goddess religion is unimaginably old, but contemporary Witchcraft could just as accurately be called the New Religion. The Craft, today, is undergoing more than a revival, it is experiencing a renaissance, a recreation."[23] Starhawk now prefers to cite the anthropologist Marija Gimbutas, and the referent of "the Old Religion" is blurred and assimilated into the culture of what Gimbutas calls "Old Europe." Investigating the origins of her religion has never been as important to Starhawk as the politics of her spirituality. She exhibits little interest in the recent history of the development of Wicca and Witchcraft.[24]

Some practitioners distinguish between spiritual roots and historical roots in discussing the history of Wicca. While the literal truth of the continuity of forms of religious practices from pre-Christian times is questionable, the past certainly inspires the content of beliefs in Wicca,[25] and old practices inspire the creation of new forms. Arguably, Prudence Jones and Nigel Pennick's *A History of Pagan Europe* (1995) renders the debate about connections between ancient and contemporary Paganisms moot by elaborating how Pagan ideas have persisted in Europe and North America.[26] Some Pagans feel that pagan folk practices persisted with a Christian veneer, and that this thin covering has been shed by a number of people who have come to identify with contemporary Paganism. It is likely that there are no hereditary Witches in the sense of being raised in a survival of Murray's witch cult, and that if there are practices with pre-Murray origins, the people involved did not call themselves witches or have the accoutrements of modern Witches.[27] However, it is possible that those who describe themselves as hereditary Witches do have family traditions that have been passed on for generations, and that these people sometimes become Witches by shedding a Christian symbol system that includes folkloric magical practices. Some of the practices described by Raven Grimassi, Z. Budapest, and others who have claimed that they learned their traditions from family members—such as techniques for removing or averting the evil eye, divination, healing, and tonics—may well be part of folk traditions that were not identified with any particular religious tradition but were passed down within families and have recently been interpreted as pagan survivals. Some practitioners happily refer to learning their craft from an aunt or grandmother who read tea leaves or Tarot cards, saying that the fact that such relatives did not know they were Witches does not invalidate the teaching.

Part of the stories that Pagans tell about pagan survivals is the story of the "Burning Times," which links contemporary Pagans to those who were killed in the medieval witch hunts. In 1979, when *The Spiral Dance* was first published, Starhawk described the terrors of the "Burning Times," citing the estimate of "nine million Witches executed."[28] In the notes that she added for the tenth-anniversary edition, Starhawk indicates that low estimates run at about 100,000, and that the 9 million figure is "probably high."[29] She also mentions the development of secrecy around the practices of Witchcraft during the "Burning Times," without further clarification.[30]

The exaggerations of what happened in the witch hunts are not generally the creations of Pagans but are the result of long-standing misinformation. The volume of data from trial records is enormous, and only since the 1970s have academics started to examine it in detail. Early research on the trial records examined only "3% of the available evidence. And that 3% was vastly different from the other 97%."[31] Because no one had methodically counted the deaths resulting from the witch hunts, some speculations were greatly inflated. The nineteenth-century American women's rights activist Matilda Joslyn Gage accepted Michelet's account of the witch hunts, adding the speculation that nine million women were killed.

Her 1893 book, *Woman, Church, and State,* is the origin of that inflated number. Gage connected these women to the then-current theory that cultures of prehistory were matriarchal,[32] providing food for later developments of myth in feminist spirituality.

Academic understandings of the European witch hunts changed with the revelation of the forgeries of a few famous medieval witch trials of southern France. Etienne Leon de Lamothe-Langon reported falsely that the Inquisition killed four hundred women in a single day. He was not a historian but a sensationalist writer of horror tales. However, later nonacademic readers of his work did not necessarily know this. His account became frequently mentioned, and while no one cites him directly, the story continues to be retold without reference to him, for example in popular books such as Z. Budapest's *The Holy Book of Women's Mysteries* and Raven Grimassi's *The Wiccan Mysteries.*[33] Scholars Norman Cohn and Richard Kieckhefer exposed the fabrication beginning in 1972.[34]

Based on scholarly analysis of the trial records, probably not more than 100,000 people were actually killed in the witch hunts.[35] This is still a lot of people, but it does not constitute a women's holocaust, as some have claimed. Some Pagan accounts present the witch hunts as a politically motivated campaign against women's power as midwives, healers, and wisewomen, or witches. The majority of those killed (between 75 and 80 percent) were women but not healers. Between 2 and 20 percent, depending on the region, were healers. Magical practitioners were actually more likely to accuse their rivals than were doctors or church officials. In central Europe, many more women than men were accused, but in Scandinavia the numbers were more balanced, and in some areas, such as Iceland, men were targeted more than women, constituting 90 percent of the accused.[36]

The witch hunts were not part of an organized campaign of persecution but were a sporadic series of episodes. It was not the Inquisition or other establishments of the Catholic Church that were responsible for the majority of the killings. Areas under the control of the popes were relatively free of persecution. It was in the areas more distant from the papacy, with less-certain religious identities, that the witch hunts were most vicious. Religious officials "based in the Italian states relentlessly harried people reported to it for resorting to magical practices or for holding unorthodox beliefs, with penances, fines, and imprisonment," but not death.[37] Christian peasants (Protestant or Catholic) were more likely to accuse their neighbors than were church officials. Local secular courts did most of the killings, and "the worst horrors occurred where central authority had broken down."[38] The Inquisition rejected the procedures recommended in the *Malleus Maleficarum,* the "Hammer against the Witches," a work sometimes cited by Pagans as evidence of church persecution. Secular courts used this work, not religious ones.[39]

In popular perception, the witch hunts occurred in the Middle Ages (the fifth to fourteenth centuries), but the most intense period of the witch hunts was not then, when church power was spreading into new areas, nor at its height of power (in the eleventh to fourteenth centuries), but from 1550 to 1650, the time described as the Age of Reason. It was at this time that church power was waning in favor of secular rationality and the church was destabilized by the Reformation, the splitting of the Christian Church into Catholic and Protestant sects.[40] The worst persecutions "took place in areas like Switzerland and Germany, where rival Christian sects fought to impose their religious views on each other."[41]

Stories of the "Burning Times" appeal to some contemporary Pagans in part because it legitimates them through a sense of moral superiority. It allows them to present themselves as victims, justifying a righteous hatred of oppressive Christianity. Some Pagans reject the idea that those killed in the witch hunts practiced a pre-Christian religion, but they continue to feel a sense of solidarity with the victims, who were wrongly accused of malevolent magical acts and other heresies.

Another aspect of the appeal of stories of the "Burning Times," and other ideas related to the theory of pagan survivals, is the desire of many Pagans to be in continuity with the Celtic past of Britain. All things "Celtic," including clothes, jewelry, magical names, and the pantheon of Celtic deities, are immensely popular in Paganism. Many Pagans feel nostalgia for a supposed golden age identified with the Celts. This is imagined as a simpler time of greater connection to the land, with a stronger sense of fellowship and community. Such images of Celtic culture and the Celts are part of the romantic appeal of the "noble savage."[42] The noble savage is a stereotype of "primitive man" as morally superior to modern humanity. It is generally a symbol of the innate goodness of humans when free of the corrupting influence of civilization. The idealization of the noble savage is particularly associated with the Romantics of the eighteenth and nineteenth centuries, especially Jean-Jacques Rousseau. People continue to identify with such images, wanting to become noble savages, understood as a primitive ideal in critique of modern civilization. Just as the stereotype of "the Indian" presents North American Native Peoples as living in accordance with nature, the Celt is presented as an exemplary human in the natural state: strong, heroic, stoic, and healthy.

Some Pagans collapse all indigenous cultures into one category and freely mix Celtic with Native American spirituality.[43] Some practitioners seem to feel that the Celt as noble savage is an image that white people can adopt without issues of appropriation. This possibility of indigenous roots without appropriation has a strong appeal to many North Americans of European descent, all of whom are immigrants. However, Irish and Scottish people are not so sure it is not appropriation when Americans, or even the English, call themselves Celts. The romanticism of the Celts homogenizes various peoples into a pan-Celtic culture, supposedly led by wise Druids, in harmony with nature and the faeries. Some Pagans feel that there is a continuity of belief, practice, and worldview across Celtic cultures, so that a myth or tradition from one place and time can be combined with that of others within pan-Celtic culture. Some Pagans embrace the idea of pan-European Celtic culture, but some practice regionally specific reconstructionist traditions.[44] Many practitioners within Ár nDraíocht Féin (ADF), for example, prefer to focus on the traditions of specific regions and to reconstruct a more culturally specific tradition. While ADF supports the idea of broad similarities between all Indo-European cultures spanning Europe and Asia, practitioners usually adopt (or are adopted by) a specific patron deity or pantheon and work within that specific cultural milieu in their rituals.

The romanticism of the Celts is not restricted to the past. Some New Age and Pagan practitioners avow that contemporary Celts are more intuitive than others. This leads to a general perception that Celtic heritage bestows greater magical abilities, such as clairvoyance, and lends authenticity to religious practice.[45] A number of practitioners suggest that they feel a sense of returning to their spiritual home in visiting Scotland or Ireland, and express a belief that they lived there in a past life or lives.

The romantic view of the Celts is part of larger social trends in Britain and North America, not restricted to Paganism. In the British Isles, the label "Celt" used to apply only to Gaelic speakers (Scots Highlanders and Islanders, and the Irish, Welsh, Manx, and Northumbrians). More recently, all Scots and Irish, and even all the English, are perceived by some as Celts. The perception of who are and were the Celts is changing. Increasingly, "Celticity is coming to be seen as a quality or a matter of choice rather than an issue of history, geography, language or ethnicity; it is 'a thing of spirit not of heritage.'"[46] People who self-identify as Celts in this sense may be called "Cardiac Celts," people who "feel in their hearts that they are Celts," regardless of their genetic heritage and where they live.[47] They identify with Celticity and the British Isles as their spiritual home. People often express this sense of Celtic identity through consumerism. Celticity is intensely commodified: there are not only Celtic Tarot, books on Celtic totem animals, tree alphabets and deities, jewelry, and ritual tools, but also magazines, coasters, watches, socks, clocks, mugs, T-shirts, and ties.[48] Modern geographic mobility has also caused a renewed interest in pilgrimage to "Celtic" sites, which are often remote areas of great natural beauty.[49]

Identifying as Celts allows practitioners to distance themselves from the mainstream culture of late-modern urban life and to express their disaffection (social, political, or spiritual) from the dominant culture.[50] It provides them with a sense of legitimacy as practitioners of indigenous religion. Some practitioners seem to feel that Paganism is a more proper or fitting religion than Christianity for those of the British Isles or those of British ancestry, suggesting that Paganism represents the religion of the land and its people before Christian (or Roman) colonization. Celticity is sometimes held up as a better alternative than Eastern mysticism, as the proper mysticism of the West.[51] Embracing Celticity has an appeal in common with other Pagan revivals in Europe, where ethnicity, history, and nationalism are often more important than the environmental and feminist values supported by Paganism in North America, Australia, and New Zealand (colonized areas where ethnicity tends to be more mixed). Embracing Celtic culture is often more socially acceptable than Norse or Germanic culture because of the co-optation of German folk culture by Nazi Germany.

Despite the questions of historical accuracy posed against practitioners' interpretations of their religion as "the Old Religion," and their romantic interpretations of Celtic culture and nostalgia for "Merrie England," these myths appeal to many Pagans because they allow people to imagine being part of a culture other than the consumerist modern industrial culture of the contemporary Western world. Even if the continuity of contemporary practices with medieval folklore and older traditions is questioned by scholars and practitioners, ideas of the past continue to inspire contemporary Pagans. Such myths root Pagan traditions spiritually, if not historically, creating a community of memory, a sense of a shared history, and a common pool of cultural symbols.

Even for those who do not specifically adopt an identity as Celtic, stories of Celtic origin are popular in Paganism. Many of the myths with enduring appeal in Paganism, such as the Wild Hunt and Ceridwen's cauldron, are of Celtic origin. The Wild Hunt is a widespread Celtic myth, common in folklore throughout Western Europe. Generically, it is a terrifying pack of hounds or men, or spirits of them, led by the Wild Huntsman. The Huntsman has historically been identified as Herne the Hunter in southern England, Odin in Scandinavia and Germany, and Gwyn ap Nudd, ruler of Annwn, the underworld, in Wales. Contemporary Pagans identify the leader of the Wild Hunt as Herne the Hunter as a later form of Cernunnos, the Horned God, or as a Celtic Pan, god of nature and animals.[52] Alternatively, some Pagans say that the goddess Diana, whom some Wiccans equate with Aradia, leads the Wild Hunt. Some Pagans indicate that the Wild Hunt can be summoned, albeit at risk, to avenge "extreme wrongs against the earth."[53]

Ceridwen's cauldron is part of the Welsh story of Taliesin. Ceridwen, a witch in the story, although often understood as a goddess in Paganism, brews a potion to give wisdom to her ugly son to help him attract a mate.

The potion needs to brew in her cauldron for a year and a day, and she asks a child, Gwion Bach, to tend it. Three drops of the brew boil out of the pot and land on his finger. Being burned, he puts his finger in his mouth to soothe the pain and immediately knows that Ceridwen will kill him for stealing the magical understanding meant for her son. He flees, changing form to try to escape. First, he becomes a hare, and Ceridwen pursues him as a hound. He changes into a fish, and Ceridwen pursues him as an otter. He changes into a bird and she into a hawk. He flies into a granary and changes himself into a grain of wheat, and Ceridwen changes herself into a hen and eats him. Nine months later, she gives birth to a child so beautiful that she cannot bear to kill him as she had planned, knowing it was Gwion Bach reborn. She sews him into a leather sack and sets him adrift in the sea. A boy finds the child and pulls him out, and he becomes the chief bard of his adoptive tribe, who name him Taliesin, meaning "radiant brow."[54]

It is perhaps because Ceridwen's cauldron is associated with the rebirth of Taliesin that some say it is also Ceridwen's cauldron that appears in *Branwen*, the second branch of the *Mabinogion*, a collection of Welsh stories and Celtic legends. It is in this cauldron, which was drawn out of a lake in Ireland, that fallen warriors could be regenerated overnight, albeit no longer able to speak.[55] Ceridwen is said to keep her cauldron of wisdom, named Amen, at the bottom of Bala Lake (or Llyn Tegid) in North Wales.[56] Starhawk refers to Ceridwen's cauldron of "rebirth and inspiration" that restored fallen warriors to life.[57]

Other popular myths in Paganism are the story of Odin's hanging on Yggdrasil, the story of Demeter and Persephone, and the descent of Inanna. Each of these involves a journey to the underworld to gain occult knowledge, and thus the stories are often understood to describe initiation. As such, they appeal in particular to practitioners of mystery traditions in Paganism. Odin's hanging on Yggdrasil is a Norse story in which the god Odin sacrifices himself in the manner in which sacrifice was offered to him. In Norse myth, Yggdrasil is an ash tree and is the axis of the world, a symbol of the cosmos. It is rooted in the underworld, the trunk is in middle earth, and the upper reaches are in the sky. The word "Yggdrasil" refers to "Odin's horse," or, more literally, the horse (*drasil*) of the terrible one (*Ygg*). Odin hung on Yggdrasil for nine nights, pierced by a spear, to gain wisdom. Being pierced with a spear dedicated his death to Odin, sacrificing himself to himself. He is also said to have sacrificed an eye to drink from the well of the underworld, to which he journeyed while hanging on the tree. There he learned nine charms or songs from his uncle, his mother's brother, the giant Bolthor. He also learned eighteen runes, which are not specified apart from their uses: to heal, to calm storms, to seduce women, and so on.[58]

The descent of Inanna, originally a Sumerian myth, and the story of Demeter and Persephone, a Greek myth, both involve a seasonal trip to the underworld. Starhawk recounts the story of Inanna's descent into the underworld and the story of Demeter and Persephone in *Circle Round*.[59] Both stories provide an explanation for the division of the year into winter and summer, and both are associated with grain, which lies dormant in the ground for the winter, sprouts and grows in the summer, and is then cut down again at each harvest. They are myths of dying and rising again in the cycle of the seasons, and Pagans associate these stories with regeneration and rebirth, but also with initiation into the mysteries. The myth of Demeter and Persephone was enacted as part of the Eleusinian mysteries in ancient Greece. These stories also have feminist appeal through the importance of female deities in them: Inanna as Queen of Heaven, and Demeter as mother of the fertile earth. Similarly, Ceridwen is a powerful female figure as the owner of the cauldron of "rebirth and inspiration." Contemporary Pagan women find such images of female power inspirational, and some gain a sense of legitimacy through appealing to stories of prepatriarchal goddesses such as Inanna.

For some Pagans, particularly those whose religious affiliation overlaps with Goddess religion and feminist spirituality, the ideas of prepatriarchal goddesses and prepatriarchal culture are crucial to their sense of identity. Some believe in a golden age of matriarchy, when goddesses were revered and women were respected, until the destruction of their way of life by patriarchal invasion. This is sometimes referred to as the myth of the matriarchies, and it serves as a myth of origin for some Pagans. However, most practitioners of Goddess religion, feminist spirituality, and Paganism do not believe in the historical existence of matriarchal culture.

The myth of the matriarchies serves as the feminist spirituality movement's sacred history. It provides an origin myth that encapsulates the thealogy, ethics, and politics of women's spirituality, telling the story of the sacred matriarchal past and the invasion of patriarchy.[60] The feminist use of this myth gives a revaluation to the idea of matriarchal prehistory first espoused by early anthropologists and cultural historians in the nineteenth century, such as J. J. Bachofen, Robert Briffault, and Erich Neumann. These non-Pagan writers suggested that human history shows a near-universal tendency toward ancestor worship, and that the lack of knowledge of the male role in procreation would naturally have led to divinization of a mother goddess. This theory was supported by Near East archaeological findings after World War II.[61]

Nineteenth-century proponents of theories of a matriarchal prehistory presented it as an inferior prelude to later civilizations. The myth of the matriarchies revisions the history of human culture as "herstory," and celebrates the idea of prepatriarchal goddess worship. According to the myth, women in prehistory were respected and honored. Most Pagans and practitioners of women's spirituality do not use the term "matriarchy" to describe the cultures of prehistory, but some do believe in a matriarchal culture controlled by women. Some versions of this narrative include the idea that women invented agriculture, and they present prepatriarchal societies as uniformly peaceful.[62] This mythic past is presented as a paradise for women *and* men, not as the inverse of patriarchy with women dominating men, but as egalitarian.

Practitioners who value this myth point to archaeologist Marija Gimbutas' theories about the culture of "Old Europe" as evidence. Gimbutas' work presents an image of a Neolithic culture in Europe that was peaceful and egalitarian. Gimbutas describes the symbolism of this culture, which she calls Old Europe, as matrifocal rather than matriarchal, by which she means that it was mother or women focused. Her research suggests that Old Europe was matrilineal and matrilocal, meaning that descent was traced through the female line, with men moving to live with their wives' people. She indicates that the culture of Old Europe was characterized by a Goddess of regeneration and was overrun by Indo-European patriarchal society, which revered a sky-god, through a series of invasions over a long period of time. Through these invasions, the denigration of women and nature was introduced throughout Europe. Some practitioners take this history of ancient matrifocal culture as a narrative that explains women's oppression and the destruction of the environment. Some point to the Indo-European revolution as the origin of the estrangement from nature and the desacralization of nature coincident with the beginning of androcentrism (male-centered culture) in Europe around 4500 BCE.[63]

The idea that all Neolithic culture was without war is demonstrably false, and the supposition of an idyllic culture in which people lived in harmony with one another and with the natural world is speculative. Even the nature of the culture of Old Europe, and the manner of its ending, are debatable. Some interpretations of the data indicate that the culture of Old Europe was Indo-European and that change came from within rather than through foreign invasion. However, the usefulness of the myth is not in its historical truth but in its poetic appeal and its psychological and political value. The validity of the story depends not on archaeological evidence but on its usefulness to contemporary women. Like the Christian myth of the Fall of humanity from the grace of God in the story of the Garden of Eden, the story of prepatriarchal culture is only partly historical in nature. It is also metaphor and myth. Its power is in envisaging an alternative to patriarchal culture.[64]

Practitioners continue to repeat stories of a matriarchal or matrifocal past because these narratives have political implications. Not all practitioners use or understand the stories in the same way. Some practitioners are more critical and skeptical than others. Some are well informed about changing theories based on current archaeological evidence, and they focus on what is known about specific goddesses and cultures of the Middle East. For some, it is good enough that such cultures can be imagined for them inspire political action. Practitioners suggest that what once was can be again, and that what we can imagine we can create. Supporters of the myth draw inspiration from the possibility of a culture that honors women. In her novel *The Fifth Sacred Thing*, Starhawk suggests that, if such a culture existed once, "it is possible."[65] Others similarly comment that "we have lived sanely before, we can do it again."[66]

FURTHER READING

Eller, Cynthia. *The Myth of Matriarchal Prehistory: Why an Invented Past Won't Give Women a Future*. Boston: Beacon Press, 2000.
Gibbons, Jenny. "Recent Developments in the Study of the Great European Witch Hunt." *The Pomegranate: A New Journal of Neopagan Thought* 5 (1998): 2–16.
Rees, Kenneth. "The Tangled Skein: The Role of Myth in Paganism." In *Paganism Today*, ed. Charlotte Hardman and Graham Harvey, 16–31. London: Thorsons (HarperCollins), 1996.

NOTES

1. Cited in Chas S. Clifton, *Her Hidden Children* (Lanham, MD: AltaMira Press, 2006), 78.
2. Friedrich Schlegel, *Lucinde and the Fragments*, trans. Peter Firchow (Minneapolis: University of Minnesota Press, 1971), 61.
3. Schlegel, *Lucinde and the Fragments*, 108.
4. Ronald Hutton, *The Triumph of the Moon: A History of Modern Pagan Witchcraft* (Oxford: Oxford University Press, 1999), 117.
5. Hutton, *Triumph of the Moon*, 118.
6. Hutton, *Triumph of the Moon*, 120.
7. Hutton, *Triumph of the Moon*, 112–13.
8. Hutton, *Triumph of the Moon*, 138–39.
9. Hutton, *Triumph of the Moon*, 144.
10. Margaret Murray, *The Witch-Cult in Western Europe: A Study in Anthropology* (Oxford: Clarendon [Oxford University Press], 1921), 12.
11. Murray, *The Witch-Cult in Western Europe*, 13–14.
12. Murray, *The Witch-Cult in Western Europe*, 238.
13. Ly de Angeles, *When I See the Wild God: Encountering Urban Celtic Witchcraft* (St. Paul, MN: Llewellyn Publications, 2004).
14. Margot Adler, *Drawing Down the Moon: Witches, Druids, Goddess-Worshippers, and Other Pagans in America Today*, revised and expanded ed. (Boston: Beacon Press, 1986), 56.
15. Hutton, *Triumph of the Moon*, 196.
16. Hutton, *Triumph of the Moon*, 200.

17. Hutton, *Triumph of the Moon*, 198; Jone Salomonsen, *Enchanted Feminism: The Reclaiming Witches of San Francisco* (London: Routledge, 2002), 89.

18. Clifton, *Her Hidden Children*, 74.

19. Gerald Gardner, *The Meaning of Witchcraft* (New York: Magical Childe Publishing, 1959), 9.

20. Hutton, *Triumph of the Moon*, 206.

21. Clifton, *Her Hidden Children*, 85–86.

22. Starhawk, *The Spiral Dance: A Rebirth of the Ancient Religion of the Great Goddess*, 10th anniversary ed. (New York: HarperSanFrancisco, 1989), 16.

23. Starhawk, *Spiral Dance*, 22.

24. Salomonsen, *Enchanged Feminism*, 90.

25. Salomonsen, *Enchanted Feminism*, 90.

26. Hutton, *Triumph of the Moon*, 381.

27. Shelly Rabinovitch, "'An' Ye Harm None, Do What Ye Will': Neo-Pagans and Witches in Canada" (Master's thesis, Carleton University, Ottawa, 1992), 66–68.

28. Starhawk, *Spiral Dance*, 20.

29. Starhawk, *Spiral Dance*, 214.

30. Starhawk, *Spiral Dance*, 50, 72.

31. Jenny Gibbons, "Recent Developments in the Study of the Great European Witch Hunt," *The Pomegranate: A New Journal of Neopagan Thought* 5 (1998): 4.

32. Hutton, *Triumph of the Moon*, 141.

33. Gibbons, "Recent Developments," 6.

34. Gibbons, "Recent Developments," 5.

35. Gibbons, "Recent Developments," 15.

36. Gibbons, "Recent Developments," 13.

37. Hutton, *Triumph of the Moon*, 146.

38. Gibbons, "Recent Developments," 8–9.

39. Gibbons, "Recent Developments," 10–11.

40. Gibbons, "Recent Developments," 6.

41. Gibbons, "Recent Developments," 8.

42. This argument is developed in Marion Bowman, "Cardiac Celts: Images of the Celts in Paganism," in *Paganism Today*, ed. Charlotte Hardman and Graham Harvey, 242–51 (London: Thorsons [HarperCollins], 1996).

43. Bowman, "Cardiac Celts," 247.

44. Bowman, "Cardiac Celts," 247.

45. Bowman, "Cardiac Celts," 244.

46. Bowman, "Cardiac Celts," 245.

47. Bowman, "Cardiac Celts," 246.

48. Bowman, "Cardiac Celts," 249.

49. Bowman, "Cardiac Celts," 246.

50. Bowman, "Cardiac Celts," 247.

51. Bowman, "Cardiac Celts," 248.

52. Stewart Farrar and Janet Farrar, *A Witches' Bible: The Complete Witches' Handbook* (Custer, WA: Phoenix Publishing, 1996), 81.

53. Ly de Angeles, *When I See the Wild God*, 75.

54. See James MacKillop, ed., "Taliesin," in *Dictionary of Celtic Mythology* (Oxford: Oxford University Press, 1998), 353–54. For a Pagan retelling, see Starhawk, Diane Baker, and Anne Hill, *Circle Round: Raising Children in Goddess Traditions* (New York: Bantam, 1998), 134–37.

55. Alwyn Rees and Brinley Rees, *Celtic Heritage: Ancient Tradition in Ireland and Wales* (New York: Thames & Hudson, 1961), 47.

56. James MacKillop, "Ceridwen, " in *Dictionary of Celtic Mythology* (Oxford: Oxford University Press, 1998), 76.

57. Starhawk, Baker, and Hill, *Circle Round*, 97–98.

58. See Kevin Crossley-Holland, *The Penguin Book of Norse Myths: Gods of the Vikings* (London: Penguin Books, 1980), 15–17, 186–88.

59. Starhawk, Baker, and Hill, *Circle Round*, 237–40, 151–56.

60. Cynthia Eller, *Living in the Lap of the Goddess: The Feminist Spirituality Movement in America* (Boston: Beacon Press, 1995), 151.

61. Eller, *Living in the Lap of the Goddess*, 152.

62. Eller, *Living in the Lap of the Goddess*, 159.

63. See Charlene Spretnak, "Ecofeminism: Our Roots and Flowering," in *Reweaving the World: The Emergence of Ecofeminism*, ed. Irene Diamond and Gloria Feman Orenstein (San Francisco: Sierra Club Books, 1990), 11. It is somewhat ironic that some practitioners blame Indo-European culture for the destruction of the cultures of matriarchal prehistory, while others embrace it as the ancient root of Celtic culture.

64. Kathryn Rountree, *Embracing the Witch and the Goddess: Feminist Ritual Makers in New Zealand* (London: Routledge, 2004), 56, 70, 63.

65. Starhawk, *The Fifth Sacred Thing* (New York: Bantam, 1993), 111.

66. Charlene Spretnak, "Toward an Ecofeminist Spirituality," *Healing the Wounds: The Promise of Ecofeminism*, ed. Judith Plant (Toronto: Between the Lines, 1989), 131.

6

Literary Origins
and Influences

Although most Pagans do not regard any particular text as scripture, written sources are enormously important in Paganism. Pagans are voracious readers, not only of popular texts on Paganism, but also of academic texts from the disciplines of folklore, anthropology, and religion. (This is perhaps less true of recent converts to Paganism who have learned more from Internet sources.) Some groups created themselves entirely out of literary and academic sources, such as the Witchcraft group in California called the New Reformed Orthodox Order of the Golden Dawn (NROOGD). In Britain in the 1940s and 1950s, Wicca developed largely out of early writings in anthropology and folklore, the inspiration of poetry and poetic myth, and what is sometimes called the Western esoteric tradition.

"Esoteric" means obscure, something understood only by those with special knowledge or training. In this context, it also usually means "occult," which means hidden. Esoteric knowledge is kept hidden from the mainstream. The Western esoteric tradition is made up of a group of texts on magic and occult groups that developed magical practices based on their interpretations of previous works, particularly Neo-Platonism and texts attributed to Hermes Trismegistus. Some of these texts can be seen as early prefigurations of Paganism. Other texts, particularly in folklore, are believed to have inspired the creation of Wicca as a reinvention of what were presented as survivals of pre-Christian pagan traditions. Poetry and novels continue to inspire and inform contemporary Pagans' understandings of divinity and their ritual practices.

Hermes Trismegistus is a title meaning "Hermes thrice greatest." Authorship of numerous texts on astrology, magic, and alchemy are attributed to Hermes Trismegistus. Hermes is the messenger of the gods in Greek mythology. According to the Western esoteric tradition, the ancient Greeks called the Egyptian god Thoth "scribe to the gods," and attributed authorship of sacred writings derived from Egypt to him. Post-Christian writings, some of which may originate in translations of this earlier material, were attributed to Hermes Trismegistus in a similar fashion. These writings form a body of writings known as Hermetic literature.[1]

The histories of Paganism and of folklore studies are entwined through their common purpose of critiquing the Enlightenment.[2] Paganism began in the context of the early twentieth century, after urbanization and changes in British culture resulting from modern life and the Enlightenment. "The Enlightenment" is a term used to describe the period in European history when rationalism was coming to replace unquestioned faith in the authority of church and state. There was a great deal of faith put into reason to make people's lives better, but at the same time the changes toward democracy from feudalism (rule by aristocracy) destabilized European society. As people were forced to come to cities to find work, some became nostalgic for a simpler life. Some people became critical of the Enlightenment and instead celebrated aspects of cultures that were perceived as "other," including non-European cultures and peasant- or working-class cultures within Europe. During the Enlightenment, European writers developed relationships with other peoples based on the idea of racial and class differences.[3] When the Enlightenment was criticized, the cultures of those who were perceived as "other" were celebrated as possibly better alternatives to the dominant views of Enlightenment culture. In folklore studies, this included not only North American Native traditions, but also the folk traditions of working-class people in Britain.

As discussed in chapter 5, early anthropologists and folklorists developed a theory of pagan survivals. This was inspired in part by Charles Darwin's theory of evolution, interpreted in terms of cultural evolution. The theory suggested that folklore preserved aspects of previous stages of development, so folk customs were interpreted as remnants of seasonal fertility rituals.[4] All folklore came to be identified with witchcraft. As some Pagans are fond of pointing out, folk traditions such as decorating

Christmas trees and Easter eggs continued after Christianity came to Europe, acquiring a "veneer of Christianity." Magical practices of folk traditions were often largely unchanged when Christian Saints' names replaced the names of pagan deities. There were indeed survivals of folk traditions, but they were as much Catholic as they were pagan: "When Oliver Cromwell and his followers railed against 'the old religion' and forbade the performance of popular year-cycle customs, they were targeting the practice of Catholicism and customs associated with it, not the actual observance of pagan religions. Nevertheless, for the reformers they were practically one and the same. A connection, however ill-conceived, was formed in European, and especially British thought between the practice of folk rituals and customs and 'paganism.'"[5] Protestant reformers interpreted all folk tradition and vernacular magic as "pagan contamination."[6] Many contemporary Pagans later embraced the idea that folk customs are pagan survivals, and they continue to view their own religious practices as being in continuity with pre-Christian traditions.

One of the most important sources of the theory of pagan survivals is James Frazer's *The Golden Bough*. Frazer (1854–1941) was a student of E. B. Tylor, an early anthropologist who originally espoused the idea of pagan survivals. Frazer sought to expose pagan survivals to rational analysis in order to refute them, and religion in general. He wanted to show that European folk traditions were no less irrational than foreign traditions, and thus that all religion is based in nonsense. However, rather than convincing contemporary Pagans that all religion is based on irrational superstition, he laid the basis for the Wiccan seasonal mythic cycle. Frazer presented pagan traditions as fertility cults and argued that rituals involving the idea of a dying and rising god resulted from a universal myth underlying religion everywhere. Pagans later took this supposed universality as proof of the myth's legitimacy.

The Golden Bough was first published in 1890 in two volumes. Frazer later expanded it into twelve volumes and finally abridged it to one volume, which was first published in 1922. In the 1911 third edition, Frazer argues that pagan traditions survive into modern times. He speaks of "spring and midsummer rites which our rude forefathers in Europe probably performed with a full consciousness of their meaning, and which many of their descendants still keep up, though the original intention of the rites has been to a great extent, but by no means altogether, forgotten."[7] Frazer does not identify these with witchcraft or with an organized religion as Margaret Murray later did.

Some aspects of ritual common in Wicca are visible in *The Golden Bough*, and some may be derived from it via later writers who used it as a source. The "cakes and wine" served as refreshments in Wiccan rituals are present, used in a ritual context. However, the ritual itself little resembles what is done in Wiccan circles. Of a Dianic festival, he recounts, "Hunting dogs were crowned and wild beasts were not molested; young people went through a purificatory ceremony in her honour; wine was brought forth, and the feast consisted of a kid, cakes served piping hot on plates of leaves, and apples still hanging in clusters on the boughs."[8]

Frazer's work supports the widespread Pagan notion of conceiving the Goddess as an overarching deity, rather than one goddess among others. He asserts that "Diana was not merely a patroness of wild beasts, a mistress of woods and hills, of lonely glades and sounding rivers; conceived as the moon, and especially, it would seem, as the yellow harvest moon, she filled the farmer's grange with goodly fruits, and heard the prayers of women in travail."[9] Frazer is not referring to a religion of Witchcraft here, but Wiccan readers can easily interpret his work as though he is.

Frazer introduced the idea adopted by Pagans, and Wiccans in particular, of a god who is sacrificed and rises again in a yearly ritual cycle. He describes how this god came to be: "Now on the principle that the goddess of fertility must herself be fertile, it behooved Diana to have a male partner. Her mate, if the testimony of Servius may be trusted, was that Virbius who had his representative, or perhaps rather his embodiment, in the King of the Wood at Nemi. The aim of their union would be to promote the fruitfulness of the earth, of animals, and of mankind; and it might naturally be thought that this object would be more surely attained if the sacred nuptials were celebrated every year, the parts of the divine bride and bridegroom being played either by their images or by living persons."[10] Wiccans call this god who is sacrificed the Horned God, and they celebrate his ritual mating with the Goddess through the Great Rite, which is a ritual sexual union, usually performed symbolically by placing an athame in a chalice of wine.

The New Golden Bough (1959), a later abridgement of the twelve-volume edition, more explicitly identifies the Goddess as a mother-earth figure, a belief supported by many Pagans. Frazer's concept of the Goddess is altered in this edition, taking the emphasis off the Horned God, or the King of the Wood. *The New Golden Bough* presents their relationship thus:

A great Mother Goddess, the personification of all the reproductive energies of nature, was worshipped under different names but with a substantial similarity of myth and ritual by many people of Western Asia; that associated with her was a lover, or rather series of lovers, divine yet mortal, with whom she mated year by year, their commerce being deemed essential to the propagation of animals and plants, each in their several kind; and further, the fabulous union of the divine pair was simulated and, as it were, multiplied on earth by the real, though temporary, union of the human sexes at the sanctuary of the goddess for the sake of thereby ensuring the fruitfulness of the ground and the increase of man and beast.[11]

Despite his intention to dispel belief in religion, Frazer's *Golden Bough* continues to inspire Pagan belief in the dying and rising god who mates with the Goddess in seasonal festivals to secure the fertility of the land.

The influence of Charles Leland's *Aradia* on the development of Wicca is perhaps more immediately obvious than that of Frazer's work. Leland (1824–1903) wrote explicitly of Diana as the Goddess of the witches. Scholars describe Leland variously as an amateur ethnographer or amateur folklorist. Leland produced his work in the late Victorian era, before anthropology formed as a discipline.[12] He was a journalist by trade but studied a number of folk and indigenous cultures in Europe and North America. He attended some classes on folklore in Germany, so he can be called an amateur folklorist.[13]

Like the French historian Jules Michelet, Leland presented witchcraft as a pagan survival and a form of peasant resistance to the Catholic Church and aristocratic power. His book *Aradia: The Gospel of the Witches*, first published in 1899, includes a creation story in which Diana fools Lucifer into fathering Aradia, who becomes the savior of the witches. According to Leland, he met a hereditary witch, Maddelena, in 1886, and "employed her specially to collect among her sisters of the hidden spells in many places all the traditions of the olden time known to them."[14] He says that he drew on other sources in producing his book, but he did

Figure 11. Maddelena (from Doreen Valiente's *Rebirth of Witchcraft*)

obtain a handwritten copy of the "Gospel" from Maddelena.[15] He indicated that he was dealing with a member of the *strega*, "fortune-tellers or witches, who divine by cards, perform strange ceremonies in which spirits are supposed to be invoked, make and sell amulets, and in fact, comport themselves generally as their reputed kind are wont to do, be they Black Voodoos in America or sorceresses anywhere."[16]

Leland argued that while he did not know for certain whether Maddelena obtained her knowledge of *strega* traditions from oral or written sources, he believed it was chiefly from oral sources because magical practitioners rarely make written records of their work.[17] In addition, he suggested that everything a witch wrote would likely have been destroyed by priests or pious Christians, who would fear such documents.[18] Some Pagans similarly argue that there are few written sources documenting the practice of witchcraft because of low literacy levels, and because having written material would have been incriminating during the witch hunts.

Aradia includes charms, invocations, and spells. These generally concern things relevant to daily life: love, luck, and good wine. Many Pagans conduct similar sorts of spells and may find inspiration in those recorded by Leland. Leland indicates that his book is "only the initial chapter of the collection of ceremonies, 'cantrips,' incantations, and traditions current in the fraternity or sisterhood, the whole of which are in the main to be found in [his books] *Etruscan Roman Remains* and *Florentine Legends*."[19] Some contemporary Pagans continue to find inspiration in these books by Leland. More importantly, Leland's work supported the "equation of certain elements of peasant culture—legends, beliefs, divination, and folk medicine—with the practice of witchcraft, so that the presence of the former stood as proof of the existence of the latter."[20] The most significant passage in *Aradia*, regarding the development of Wicca and Paganism, is a section of the text containing the teaching of Aradia, which later (through Gerald Gardner and Doreen Valiente) became the "Charge of the Goddess." It was through this text that Gardnerian Wiccans acquired the habit of meeting at the full moon, the name of the goddess Aradia, and possibly the practice of conducting rituals in the nude. (Gardner and others in the New Forest coven were naturists, or nudists, apart from their activities with Wicca.)

Margaret Murray (1863–1963) built directly on Frazer's description of folk traditions as pagan survivals of fertility cults, but she argued that witchcraft had been an organized religion. She presented witchcraft as a fertility cult of a horned god, persecuted by Christian Inquisitors who wrongly interpreted him as the devil.[21] Murray's work has been used by Gardnerians and other Wiccans, primarily in constructing and substantiating a myth of origin. Murray's *The Witch-Cult in Western Europe*, first published in 1921 but popular in the 1940s when Wicca was first forming as a religion, seemed to give evidence of a surviving witch cult. More recently, Wiccans see her account as part of sacred history or inspirational myth. Her books have been used for inspiration in the writing of myths of origin and in reconstructing Witchcraft from a perspective more sympathetic than that of mainstream history.

Murray contributed to contemporary Paganism the theory that the witchcraft persecuted in the witch hunts was an organized religion. She presented this religion as a peasant or indigenous religion, and as a fertility religion, which was a common view of such religions. It was through her work that Pagans developed the idea that Witchcraft is a tradition that stretches back to the Paleolithic era.[22] Murray linked the "Devil" or Horned God of the trial records with Paleolithic cave paintings in southern France in her *Encyclopedia Britannica* article on witchcraft.[23] According to that encyclopedia article, the religion of witchcraft survived into the eighteenth century in England, and into "the present day" (1929 is the publication date of the article) in France and Italy.[24]

Because most of her evidence is taken from trial confessions, the rituals she describes focus on a male deity, and on "paying homage to the Devil," as she phrases it.[25] She deemphasizes the importance of the god in her later writings on Witchcraft, but in some ways her *God of the Witches* can be seen as a culmination of the cult of Pan in the writings of modern Romantics in England.[26] Rather than the Greco-Roman god name of Pan, Murray preferred to call the Horned God by the Gallic god name Cernunnos. She collected evidence of gods with horns across Europe and the Near East and interpreted them all as aspects of the Horned God, whether he wore stag antlers or ram horns. Subsequently, Wiccans adopted her idea of the Horned God as their primary identification of male deity.

Murray's work also inspired the idea of "The Green Man," later picked up by contemporary Pagans. Murray associated British folk traditions in general with witchcraft, including the stories of Robin Hood, and she linked church carvings with paganism. She interpreted the female figures in medieval churches as pagan goddesses of fertility, which, as previously discussed, inspired Lady Raglan, a fellow member of the Folk-Lore Society, to interpret the foliate heads of fourteenth- and fifteenth-century churches as Frazer's dying and rising vegetation god, which Raglan called "The Green Man."[27]

Murray also linked the word "witch" with the meaning "to know," a false etymology still espoused by some practitioners but not by scholars.[28] In addition, her work gave Pagans the idea of dancing in a circle as a ritual practice for securing fertility (of land and game), and the sense of witchcraft as "Celtic."[29] The practice of dancing in a circle has evolved into the Pagan ritual of the spiral dance. Murray's work mentions "cakes and wine," but she describes the practice as varying from feasts, to homely picnics, to wine and cakes and meat.[30] She also notes that candles were used in ritual,[31] but she does not suggest that they were used at the cardinal points as they are by contemporary Wiccans. In addition, she reports that "the 'fixed number' of coven members among the witches of Great Britain seems to have been thirteen: twelve witches and their officer."[32] Many Pagans reject hierarchical structures and regard covens as optional, but Murray's influence is evident in the often-repeated idea that covens are "traditionally" made up of thirteen members.[33]

In many ways, Murray made the actual practice of witchcraft as a religion possible by making the practices of witches explicit in *The Witch-Cult in Western Europe*. However, Gerald Gardner significantly changed Murray's work and popularized it as a religion that continues into modern times. Gardner seems to have derived many of his ideas about ritual from her work, including the structure of the festival cycle and the habit of calling the festivals "sabbaths" or "sabbats." Initially, Gardner adopted the sabbaths Murray described as the four sabbats of Candlemas, May Eve (Beltain), Lammas, and Samhain. He later added the solar festivals, initially celebrated at the full moon closest to the solstices and equinoxes. Wiccans meet at sabbats and esbats, as Murray describes them, but not necessarily publicly, as she suggests witches did at sabbaths in the past.[34] Some Wiccan groups follow her suggestion that "the Esbat differed from the Sabbath by being primarily for business, whereas the Sabbath was purely religious."[35]

The influence of writings on folklore by Frazer, Leland, and Murray is notable, but the understanding of deities in popular English culture more generally derives from the work of scholars of the late Victorian and Edwardian eras. These scholars' writings on religion focused on primal forces such as Earth, Sky, Corn (Grain), Vegetation, Nature, Mother, and Father. Wicca's sense of tension and polarity between female and male is probably derived from such scholarly writings about religion, since it bears little resemblance to functional pantheons of indigenous peoples as described by modern anthropologists. Some scholars take this as evidence that British Witchcraft is essentially post-Christian rather than pre-Christian.[36]

The influence of English Romantic poetry seems to have tempered the influence of scholarly writings about deities. Poetry, short stories, and novels have influenced the development of Paganism as a religion through writings that, while not necessarily Pagan, approach Paganism in sensibility. The writings of the English Romantic poets John Keats, Percy Bysshe Shelley, and William Butler Yeats are filled with pastoral imagery and images of nature as the greenwood (enchanting, leafy glades inhabited by elves or faeries). The greenwood is also portrayed as being present in single trees, stone circles, burial mounds, cathedrals, grottoes, and pools.[37] The Romantics and some later Victorians developed a playful reenchantment of nature through poetry and stories. They personified natural forces (most of all Pan) but also wrote of other-than-human persons such as faeries, gnomes, goblins, dwarves, trolls, nymphs, mermaids, selkies, dragons, unicorns, elementals, and various gods and goddesses. In poetry and fiction, these are accepted as literary characters, but contemporary Pagans may understand them as real, as imagined, as images, as metaphors, or as **archetypes**.

Pan was relatively unimportant in Britain until he was celebrated in the poetry of English Romantics. He became not just a god of the forest, but the personification and guardian of the English countryside. This idea of the God is distinct from Frazer's idea of a dying and rising vegetation god, although some Pagans later combined the two by splitting the Horned God into the Holly King and the Oak King. Others may speak of the old and new stag, but many do not conceive of the Horned God as split in this manner. The Romantics and Victorians often presented Pan as a god who appeared at twilight playing a set of pipes. Percy Bysshe Shelley (1792–1822), for example, wrote in his "Hymn to Pan,"

> The light of the dying day,
> Speeded by my sweet pipings.
> The Sileni and Sylvans and Fauns,
> And the Nymphs of the woods and waves,
> To the edge of the moist river-lawns,
> And the brink of the dewy caves,
> And all that did then attend and follow,
> Were silent with love, as you now, Apollo,
> With envy of my sweet pipings.[38]

Pan also appears in similar form in a later story by Kenneth Grahame (1859–1932). As mentioned in chapter 1, English writers of poetry and fiction of the time often presented Pan as the personification and guardian of the English countryside as it was imaged by urbanites on holiday: it is always summer, and the agricultural work of peasants or the lower classes is unseen.[39] Pan appears in Grahame's book for children, *The Wind in the Willows*, first published in 1908, in a strange interlude where an unnamed god of the forest appears. Mole and Rat are looking for one of Otter's children, Portly, who is missing. They stay out searching in their boat all night, and near dawn the landscape seems to change: "Their old haunts greeted them in other raiment, as if they had slipped away and put on this pure new apparel and come quietly back, smiling as they shyly waited to see if they would be recognized again under it."[40] They hear someone playing pipes and are overcome by a feeling of awe. Mole sees "the Friend and Helper," described as having "curved horns," "shaggy limbs," and "kindly eyes."[41] Immediately afterward, they find Portly, but they cannot quite remember their encounter with the god of the forest.

The Romantics also wrote of other mythic figures in a way that is inspirational for contemporary Pagans. John Keats (1795–1821) wrote about an enchanting female spirit in his poem "Lamia":

> Upon a time, before the faery broods
> Drove Nymph and Satyr from the prosperous woods,
> Before King Oberon's bright diadem,
> Sceptre, and mantle, clasp'd with dewy gem,
> Frighted away the Dryads and the Fauns
> From rushes green, and brakes, and cowslip'd lawns,
> The ever-smitten Hermes empty left
> His golden throne, bent warm on amorous theft:
> From high Olympus had he stolen light,
> On this side of Jove's clouds, to escape the sight
> Of his great summoner, and made retreat
> Into a forest on the shore of Crete.[42]

Keats based this poem on a folktale of a man who was enchanted by a lamia, a seductive female serpent demon in the original tale.[43]

Rudyard Kipling (1865–1936) wrote stories featuring a romantic view of the English countryside, fitting the then-popular image of "Merrie Olde England" that has subsequently been preserved by some Pagans. Contemporary Pagans continue to enjoy Kipling's *Puck of Pook's Hill* and *Rewards and Fairies*, collections of stories, many of which are set in the Middle Ages. These stories were purportedly written for children but are also enjoyed by adults. Kipling's stories influenced the practice that some Pagans have of swearing by "Oak and Ash and Thorn." The protagonist of many of the stories, a faery named Puck, always swears by these. Verses of "Puck's Song" appear in Gardnerian ritual, quoted in the May Eve and August Eve celebrations in "Ye Bok of ye Art Magical," Gardner's original Book of Shadows,[44] and "A Tree Song" has made its way into Pagan ritual, sometimes without awareness of its origin.[45]

Some other Pagan ideas about the faeries are inspired by the poetry of William Butler Yeats (1865–1939). Yeats wrote "The Stolen Child," a poem that is popular with Pagans and is most familiar to many through the song recorded by Loreena McKennitt.[46] Many Pagans feel a similar pull to the land of faery that Yeats describes in his poem:

> Come away, O human child!
> To the water and the wild
> With a faery, hand in hand,
> For the world's more full of weeping than you can understand.

Where the wave of moonlight glosses
The dim grey sands with light,
Far off by furthest Rosses
We foot it all the night,
Weaving olden dances.[47]

Yeats lived much of his life in Ireland and was influenced by the landscape and folk traditions there, as well as by local myths. He spent a summer with Lady Gregory, who published the *Mabinogion*, a collection of medieval Welsh stories. He had a religious temperament, but his father was a skeptic and did not raise him to have faith. Yeats searched through a variety of esoteric traditions in folklore, theosophy, spiritualism, and Neoplatonism. He eventually became a member of the occult group the Hermetic Order of the Golden Dawn, a group that later influenced the development of Paganism as part of the Western esoteric tradition.[48]

A later member of the Hermetic Order of the Golden Dawn also influenced the development of Paganism: the ceremonial magician Aleister Crowley (1875–1947). Raised in a conservative sect of Christianity called the Plymouth Brethren, Crowley became infamous for flouting the conventions of society and styling himself "the Beast." The Wiccan Rede "An it harm none, do what thou will," appears to be derived from Crowley's statement in *The Book of the Law*: "Do what thou wilt shall be the whole of the law."[49] His definition of magic as "the Science and Art of causing Change to occur in conformity with Will" also influenced Pagan understandings of magic and some Pagans' preference for his spelling of magic as "magick."

It has long been rumored that Crowley wrote part of the ritual texts in Gerald Gardner's original Book of Shadows. Doreen Valiente indicates that the influence of Crowley's *Book of the Law* was visible in the original Book of Shadows, but that she reduced the "Crowleyanity" in it, retaining the spirit of the passage from Leland's *Aradia*, which she recognized as a source text, in rewriting the Charge of Goddess.[50] Crowley and Gardner met in May of 1947 and exchanged a few letters afterward,[51] but Crowley died later that year. Crowley gave Gardner a charter to operate a chapter of the Ordo Templis Orientis, or Order of the Temple of the Orient (OTO).[52] It appears that Gardner consulted with Crowley in creating texts for ritual, or used Crowley's written works. Valiente says that Gardner used Crowley's work to supplement the fragmentary material he received from the New Forest coven, explaining that "he had felt that Crowley's writings, modern though they were, breathed the very spirit of paganism and were expressed in splendid poetry."[53] Valiente suggests that the fact that Gardner paid Crowley for the OTO charter may be the origin of the rumor that Gardner paid Crowley to write the witchcraft rituals. It should be noted that Crowley was a magician rather than a Witch. There is no mention of Wicca as a religion in either his published or his unpublished writings.[54]

Another member of the Hermetic Order of the Golden Dawn has also had a lasting influence on Paganism. Dion Fortune (1891–1946) later founded the Fraternity (now Society) of the Inner Light, and her work together with Crowley's forms the basis of the Western mystery tradition.[55] Dion Fortune was the magical name of Violet Mary Firth, who, like Crowley, was not a Witch but a practitioner of ceremonial magic. The rituals and imagery of her novels *The Sea Priestess*, *The Goat-Foot God*, and *Avalon of the Heart* have inspired Pagans in creating rituals. Pagans continue to recommend her *Psychic Self-Defense* for practical purposes.[56]

Robert Graves (1895–1985) was not explicitly part of the development of Wicca, but he appears to have been a devotee of the Goddess, and he gave Paganism a lasting mythic vision of the relationship between the Goddess and her consort. Graves was a twentieth-century poet, and a good, if eccentric, scholar. He is best known for his theory of myth and poetry presented in his 1948 book, *The White Goddess*. This work was never meant to be academic history but poetic metaphor.[57] *The White Goddess* is not just descriptive, but prescriptive. In it, Graves advocates a return to Goddess worship and matriarchal society to reinvigorate poetry. A return to Goddess worship, he thought, would give poetry force and clear mythic vision.[58] Graves felt that the only true theme, "the Theme," for poetry was the story cycle of the Goddess and her marriage with the Sun God and his sacrifice.

Graves' writing about the Theme is a rich source for the seasonal mythic cycle in Wicca. He explains that "the Theme, briefly, is the antique story, which falls into thirteen chapters and an epilogue, of the birth, life, death and resurrection of the God of the Waxing Year; the central chapters concern the God's losing battle with the God of the Waning Year for love of the capricious and all-powerful Threefold Goddess, their mother, bride and layer-out."[59] Graves wrote of the Theme also in a poem to his son who was born the day before the winter solstice in 1945, "To Juan at the Winter Solstice":

> She in her left hand bears a leafy quince;
> When with her right she crooks a finger, smiling,
> How may the King hold back?
> Royally then he barters life for love . . . .
> Much snow is falling, winds roar hollowly,
> The owl hoots from the elder,
> Fear in your heart cries to the loving-cup:
> Sorrow to sorrow as the sparks fly upward.
> The log groans and confesses:
> There is one story and one story only.[60]

Graves was apparently influenced by Murray. He argues that the Theme was "secretly preserved as religious doctrine in the covens of the anti-Christian witch-cult."[61] Using poetry as evidence, he argues for the survival of ancient goddess religion into later times. For example, he states that "Demeter as a Mare-goddess was widely worshipped under the name of Epona, or 'the Three Eponae,' among the Gallic Celts, and there is a strange account in Giraldus Cambrensis' Topography of Ireland which shows that relics of the same cult survived in Ireland until the twelfth century."[62] Poetic themes do not indicate the existence of a practicing cult, yet Graves' poetry is a fertile source for the myth and symbolism of Wicca.

The White Goddess is still recommended reading for most Pagans, and Graves' theory that the Goddess will return to power as belief in her returns is a common Pagan sentiment.[63] It is from Graves, as well as other literary sources, that Wiccans get their concept of the Goddess as triune. The Goddess had been presented previously in triple form, but Graves was unusual in celebrating not just her mother and maiden forms, but also the Crone. He identified the Crone aspect of the Goddess with Ceridwen, whom he interpreted as a sow goddess who eats her own young.[64] Graves used Frazer as a source for his mythic vision of the Goddess and her consort.[65] He split Frazer's dying and resurrected god into the gods of the waxing and waning year, probably from Welsh stories of annual fights, such as Gwyn ap Nudd and Gwythr in the *Mabinogion*.[66] Graves' understanding of the seasonal relationship between the Goddess and the God became integrated into the Wiccan festival cycle. He constructed a poetic myth that contributed to making Goddess religion explicit in the form of Wicca.

Literary sources continue to be important inspirations in reconstructionist traditions in Paganism. Reconstructionist traditions often use the literature of the cultures whose religion they are reconstructing. Norse reconstructionists, who sometimes identify themselves as Heathen or Asatru, for example, find inspiration in the Icelandic Eddas and the Sagas. Heathens use the Eddas and the Sagas to learn about Norse deities and religious practices. The Poetic or Elder Edda is a collection of poems about the god Odin and other figures in Norse mythology, probably recorded in the thirteenth century. The Icelander Snorri Sturluson composed the Prose or Younger Edda, which is a handbook on Icelandic poetry, in the thirteenth century. The Sagas are epic stories of Viking heroes recorded between the thirteenth and fifteenth centuries. Heathens have developed a shamanistic ritual practice of *seidr* out of a passage from the Saga of Erik the Red.

Seidr is an ecstatic ritual practice in which a practitioner goes into trance (into the underworld or otherland) with the help of her coreligionists and answers questions from other participants in ritual. The Saga from which *seidr* practices are reconstructed gives descriptions of a visiting seeress, a *spákona* or *volva*, including her clothing, shoes, staff, and cloak. She is asked to consider the future of the community, and she eats a ritual meal. The following day, she sits on a "high seat" while others sing a special song to "the powers" so that she can go into trance.[67] In a contemporary reconstruction of this practice,

> the volva sits on the high seat holding onto her staff, surrounded by a circle of singers. The sound carries the volva into an altered state of awareness, in the spirit world. There she meets with spirits, gods and forces, and puts forward her request for help or knowledge. When her main task is complete and the song dies out [the] volva is still "between the worlds" and in this state she can give oracular answers to questions from members of the group.[68]

Such practices derived from the Sagas can be profound experiences for participants. Jenny Blain, a researcher and practitioner, describes her first participation in *seidr*:

> I had been working hard, visualizing the journey and taking mental notes. What I did not expect was the very strong pull, experienced both as a yearning and as a direct physical tug to the pit of my stomach, to follow her. Remembering the instructions, I concentrated on visualizing the gates before me, closed. Diana had said the seeress would remain connected to us, by a silver cord. I felt the cord, an umbilicus between myself and Winifred, felt its tension. Questioners stepped forward, and listening, I felt that attachment, that pull. Some asked of jobs, some of relationships, health, future meetings, relatives. One asked of a severe health problem and the need to face her mortality, and I listened in the half-world of trance, before the gates, profoundly moved. When Winifred left the high seat, I felt my body doing work, drawing her back, lending my own strength.[69]

Greek reconstructionists look to the Homeric hymns and to Hesiod's writings. Some also look to the writings of Sappho. The Homeric hymns include long verses honoring Demeter, Apollo, Hermes, and Aphrodite. Hesiod's *Theogony*, written late in the eighth century BCE, tells a story of the creation of the universe and the god/desses. It is a creative genealogy of the god/desses—he adds god/desses to fill in gaps in Greek mythology, and he possibly invented names for the muses. Hesiod's story begins with the union of Chaos (or the Chasm) and Earth. It tells of their children, the Titans, and the subsequent war of the gods, won by Zeus and his followers. The *Theogony* is a triumphalist celebration of the importance of Zeus. It is the oldest source of some of the best-known Greek myths, including the stories of Prometheus and Pandora.[70]

Egyptian reconstructionists, and some Roman reconstructionists, find inspiration in the novel *The Metamorphoses*, better known as *The Golden Ass*, written by Lucius Apuleius (c. 123–180 CE). *The Golden Ass* tells the story of a man who is cursed by a witch and turned into an ass. He is eventually released by the goddess Isis, and he becomes one of her priests. The novel is from ancient Rome, but it is also used in the reconstruction of Egyptian religion because Isis was an Egyptian goddess. In the time of the Roman Empire, Isis became an overarching goddess figure, and she is presented as such in *The Golden Ass*. The vision the protagonist has of Isis is particularly influential, not only for Egyptian and Roman reconstructionists, but also for Wiccans and other Pagans, as Isis is often understood as the Goddess, rather than as one goddess among others.

Contemporary novels have also influenced Pagan traditions, particularly the fantasy novels of J. R. R. Tolkien, Marion Zimmer Bradley, Robert Heinlein, and, more recently, Terry Pratchett and J. K. Rowling. Paganism has been influenced in a general way by fantasy novels in which magic is commonplace and effective, and in which interaction with other-than-human persons is possible. The most obvious or explicit influence is Robert Heinlein's novel *Stranger in a Strange Land*, first published in 1961. This science-fiction novel inspired the formation of the Church of All Worlds (CAW), modeled on the church of the same name in the novel. Practitioners derived the ritual greeting "Thou art Goddess" or "Thou art God," and a liberal understanding of loving relationships, from the book, which became influential more generally in the Paganism of the late 1960s and early 1970s.

In Heinlein's novel, the Church of All Worlds is a religious organization founded by a man, who was raised by Martians, to help humans overcome their alienation from each other and the natural world. Local groups of the church are called "nests" in the book, and CAW follows that structure. Members share a rite of communion in the nests, a ritual of water sharing derived from the novel. This involves a ritual recognition of the necessity of water for all life, as members speak the words "May you never thirst" in sharing water. It also involves a ritual recognition of the immanence, or indwelling, of the divine in each other, as participants address each other saying "Thou art Goddess" or "Thou art God." The greeting "Thou art God" appears in Heinlein's novel, but CAW practitioners have modified it into female and male statements, and it has passed into common Pagan usage in that form. Some CAW members also practice group marriage, as in the novel, including cofounder of the group Oberon Zell-Ravenheart, along with his longtime partner, Morning Glory Zell-Ravenheart. Morning Glory coined the term "polyamory" to describe open yet committed relationships such as they share.[71] When CAW obtained tax-exempt status in 1970, it became the first officially recognized

Figure 12.   The Ravenhearts (photo provided by Oberon Zell-Ravenheart)

Pagan religious organization in the United States. As part of his activities with CAW, Zell-Ravenheart edited the Pagan magazine *Green Egg*, which was influential on Pagans across North America, from 1968 to 1975 and from 1988 to 1996. Through it, he popularized the terms "Neo-Pagan" and "nature religion" beginning in the 1960s.

Regarding the influence of novels on Paganism, "the influence of J. R. R. Tolkien is, of course, inestimable."[72] Tolkien's work essentially spawned the modern genre of fantasy and gave the language and terms for faeries and other creatures to English culture.[73] His *Lord of the Rings*, first published in one volume in 1968, encapsulates popular aspects of European mythology and folklore. It is through Tolkien's vision of Middle Earth that many practitioners know the mythology and folklore of elves, dwarves, and wizards—if not from reading his work directly, then through its indirect influence on the role-playing game Dungeons & Dragons, which is largely based on Tolkien's universe. Tolkien's influence was renewed in the early twenty-first century through Peter Jackson's trilogy of films based on *The Lord of the Rings*.

Many Pagans find Marion Zimmer Bradley's fantasy novel *The Mists of Avalon* inspirational. It is a retelling of the story of King Arthur from the point of view of the women involved and is set at the time of the initial confrontation between pre-Christian pagan traditions and Christianity in Britain. Its appeal is widespread among Pagans, including practitioners of Goddess religion, Druidry, Wicca, and others. Pagans use *The Mists of Avalon* as an inspiration specifically for initiation rituals and men's mysteries.[74]

Terry Pratchett's fantasy series of Discworld novels, set in a parody of Medieval Europe and populated by trolls, dwarves, wizards, witches, regular humans, and the "lords and ladies" (faeries), describes a worldview familiar to Pagans. Pagans learn about the nature of other-than-human persons and about the use of magic through the novels. Pratchett's presentation of witches' views on deity in the Discworld novels easily applies to Witches in contemporary Paganism.[75] Just as in the novels, Pagans are somewhat ambiguous in their ideas about the existence of the god/desses. While Pagans do not so much believe in the god/desses as develop relationships with them, as in Discworld, the fate of the deities are somehow dependent on the faith of the humans who believe in them. A god without believers dwindles, as illustrated in Pratchett's novel *Small Gods*. As one scholar explains, "Deities are fundamentally products of belief. This may explain why deities do whatever people would like to do if they had the power or the ability. Pratchett shares a view of religion also known to devotees of Monty Python: it becomes dangerous when taken too seriously and is best engaged in or opposed with humour."[76]

The use of magic in Discworld is also similar to Pagan understandings of magic, and some Pagans see Pratchett's novels as a teaching tool for the use of magic. Pratchett's words, "People who used magic without knowing what they were doing usually came to a sticky end. All over the room sometimes,"[77] communicate a Pagan sense of interconnectedness and an understanding that magical actions can have unexpected results. Practitioners need to consider carefully what might happen. Pagans often mention Ursula Le Guin's Earthsea series of novels as a teaching tool for the ethical use of magic, while J. K. Rowling's series of fantasy novels featuring Harry Potter, now a series of feature films, inspires interest in magic and witchcraft more than it influences ritual forms or practices within Paganism.

Literary sources continue to influence Pagan practices and beliefs. The variety of popular books on Paganism and contemporary ready access to the Internet may lead new Pagans in different directions than material on magic and folk traditions did in the 1940s and 1950s, but Pagans often find their way back to the original sources that first inspired the development of Wicca and other Pagan groups.

FURTHER READING

Magliocco, Sabina. *Witching Culture: Folklore and Neo-Paganism in America*. Philadelphia: University of Pennsylvania Press, 2004.
Clifton, Chas S., and Graham Harvey. *The Paganism Reader*. New York: Routledge, 2004.
Harvey, Graham. "Fantasy in the Study of Religions: Paganism as Observed and Enhanced by Terry Pratchett." *Diskus* 6 (2000), Web edition. http://web.uni-marburg.de/religion-swissenschaft/journal/diskus (accessed June 8, 2003).
Hutton, Ronald. *The Triumph of the Moon: A History of Modern Pagan Witchcraft*. Oxford: Oxford University Press, 1999.

NOTES

1. Lewis Spence, "Hermes Trismegistus," *The Encyclopedia of the Occult* (London: Bracken Books, 1988), 208–9.
2. Sabina Magliocco, *Witching Culture: Folklore and Neo-Paganism in America* (Philadelphia: University of Pennsylvania Press, 2004), 4.
3. Magliocco, *Witching Culture*, 37.
4. Magliocco, *Witching Culture*, 5.
5. Magliocco, *Witching Culture*, 32.
6. Magliocco, *Witching Culture*, 32.
7. James George Frazer, *The Golden Bough*, 3rd ed. (London: Macmillan, 1911), 1:xix.
8. Frazer, *Golden Bough*, 1:14.
9. Frazer, *Golden Bough*, 2:128.
10. Frazer, *Golden Bough*, 2:129.
11. James George Frazer, *The New Golden Bough: A New Abridgment of the Classic Work*, edited by Theodor H. Gaster (New York: Criterion Books, 1959), 299.
12. Chas S. Clifton and Graham Harvey, *The Paganism Reader* (New York: Routledge, 2004), 61.
13. Magliocco, *Witching Culture*, 46.
14. Charles G. Leland, *Aradia: Or the Gospel of the Witches* (New York: Samuel Weiser, 1974), vii.
15. Leland, *Aradia*, vii.
16. Leland, *Aradia*, v.
17. Leland, *Aradia*, vii, viii.
18. Leland, *Aradia*, xi, xii.
19. Leland, *Aradia*, 109.
20. Magliocco, *Witching Culture*, 46.
21. Magliocco, *Witching Culture*, 47.
22. Magliocco, *Witching Culture*, 47–48.
23. Clifton and Harvey, *Paganism Reader*, 92.
24. Clifton and Harvey, *Paganism Reader*, 91.
25. Margaret Alice Murray, *The Witch-Cult in Western Europe: A Study in Anthropology* (Oxford: Clarendon [Oxford University Press], 1921), 124.
26. Ronald Hutton, *The Triumph of the Moon: A History of Modern Pagan Witchcraft* (Oxford: Oxford University Press, 1999), 196.
27. Hutton, *Triumph of the Moon*, 198.
28. Clifton and Harvey, *Paganism Reader*, 90.
29. Magliocco, *Witching Culture*, 48.

30. Murray, *Witch-Cult in Western Europe*, 139, 140.

31. Murray, *Witch-Cult in Western Europe*, 144.

32. Murray, *Witch-Cult in Western Europe*, 191.

33. Clifton and Harvey, *Paganism Reader*, 90.

34. Murray, *Witch-Cult in Western Europe*, 97.

35. Murray, *Witch-Cult in Western Europe*, 112.

36. See, for example, Hutton, *Triumph of the Moon*, 130–31.

37. Graham Harvey, *Contemporary Paganism: Listening People, Speaking Earth* (New York: New York University Press, 1997), 164.

38. Percy Bysshe Shelly, *The Oxford Book of English Verse: 1250–1900*, ed. Arthur Quiller-Couch (Oxford: Clarendon Press, 1919), www.bartleby.com/101/605.html (accessed June 8, 2003).

39. Hutton, *Triumph of the Moon*, 44.

40. Kenneth Grahame, *The Wind in the Willows* (London: Puffin Books, 1994), 120.

41. Grahame, *Wind in the Willows*, 124.

42. M. H. Abrams, "John Keats," *Norton Anthology of English Literature*, 5th ed. (New York: W. W. Norton, 1986), 2:827–28.

43. Abrams, "John Keats," 826.

44. Hutton, *Triumph of the Moon*, 233.

45. Clifton and Harvey, *Paganism Reader*, 80.

46. Loreena McKennitt, "Stolen Child," *Elemental* (Stratford, ON: Warner Music Canada, 1994).

47. M. H. Abrams, "William Butler Yeats," *Norton Anthology of English Literature*, 5th ed. (New York: W. W. Norton, 1986), 2:1934.

48. Shelly Rabinovitch and James Lewis, eds., *Encyclopedia of Modern Witchcraft and Neo-Paganism* (New York: Citadel, 2002), 170.

49. Aleister Crowley, *The Book of the Law* (York Beach, ME: Samuel Weiser, 1976), 23.

50. Doreen Valiente, *The Rebirth of Witchcraft* (Custer, WA: Phoenix Publishing, 1989), 61.

51. Hutton, *Triumph of the Moon*, 221.

52. Valiente, *Rebirth of Witchcraft*, 16.

53. Valiente, *Rebirth of Witchcraft*, 57.

54. Hutton, *Triumph of the Moon*, 220.

55. Rabinovitch and Lewis, *Encyclopedia of Modern Witchcraft and Neo-Paganism*, 195.

56. Rabinovitch and Lewis, *Encyclopedia of Modern Witchcraft and Neo-Paganism*, 104–5.

57. Margot Adler, *Drawing Down the Moon: Witches, Druids, Goddess-Worshippers, and Other Pagans in America Today*, revised and expanded ed. (Boston: Beacon Press, 1986), 60.

58. M. H. Abrams, "Robert Graves," *Norton Anthology of English Literature*, 5th ed. (New York: W. W. Norton, 1986), 2:2245.

59. Robert Graves, *The White Goddess: A Historical Grammar of Poetic Myth* (London: Faber & Faber, 1948), 20.

60. See Abrams, "Robert Graves," 2250.

61. Graves, *White Goddess*, 20.

62. Graves, *White Goddess*, 337.

63. Hutton, *Triumph of the Moon*, 190.

64. Hutton, *Triumph of the Moon*, 192.

65. Graves, *White Goddess*, 62.

66. Hutton, *Triumph of the Moon*, 193.

67. Jenny Blain, *Nine Worlds of Seid-Magic: Ecstasy and Neo-Shamanism in North European Paganism* (London: Routledge, 2002), 31.

68. K. Kelly, "Close to Nature: An Interview with Annette Host," *Spirit Talk* 9, quoted in Blain, *Nine Worlds of Seid-Magic*, 44.

69. Blain, *Nine Worlds of Seid-Magic*, 76.

70. See M. L. West's introduction to Hesiod, *Theogony and Works and Days*, trans. M. L. West (Oxford: Oxford University Press, 1988).

71. Shelly Rabinovitch and James Lewis, *Encyclopedia of Modern Witchcraft and Neo-Paganism* (New York: Citadel, 2002), 122.

72. Clifton and Harvey, *Paganism Reader*, 327.

73. Graham Harvey, "Fantasy in the Study of Religions: Paganism as Observed and Enhanced by Terry Pratchett," *Diskus* 6 (2000), Web edition, http://web.uni-marburg.de/religionswissenschaft/journal/diskus (accessed June 8, 2003).

74. Clifton and Harvey, *Paganism Reader*, 326.

75. See Harvey, "Fantasy in the Study of Religions."

76. Harvey, "Fantasy in the Study of Religions."

77. Quoted in Graham Harvey, *Contemporary Paganism: Listening People, Speaking Earth* (New York: New York University Press, 1997), 105.

7

Social and
Charismatic Influences

There is no single founder of Paganism, but a few charismatic figures, popularizers, and authors have had disproportionate influences on the development of Paganism. Characteristically, these individuals have had as much, or more, impact through their published writings than they have had in person. Following the cultural trend of the revival of folk traditions and the popularity of magical techniques from ceremonial magic in Britain, Gerald Gardner, Doreen Valiente, and Raymond Buckland brought Gardnerian Wicca to public attention in Britain and North America. Starhawk and Z. Budapest were key contributors to the development of feminist Witchcraft in California. Isaac Bonewits, Scott Cunningham, and Diana Paxson have been influential in the diversification of Paganism. While this chapter looks at influential individuals and their relations to social movements and cultural trends in the development of Paganism, it is not a complete who's who of Paganism. There are a number of contemporary encyclopedias that can serve that purpose.

Gerald Gardner (1884–1964) is the first great public figure in the history of contemporary Paganism. He popularized Wicca through his writing, by creating covens, and through the Witchcraft museum on the Isle of Man, which he ran with Cecil Williamson. Gardner became the resident Witch, and he used the museum as a publicity tool.[1] If there was a surviving pagan religion in Britain or elsewhere before Gardner began popularizing Wicca, it was well hidden. Some Wiccans argue that although there were no public practitioners prior to Gardner's publication of *Witchcraft Today* in 1954, there were witches who, fearing persecution, remained hidden. These Wiccans refer to the fact that laws against

witchcraft in Britain were not repealed until 1951 as evidence. It is possible that Wiccan groups existed before Gardner's publication of *Witchcraft Today*. However, without any concrete evidence, it is more reason-
able to assume that there were no Wiccan groups preceding the coven
that Gardner formed, or at least not until after the publication of Margaret Murray's *The Witch-Cult in Western Europe* in 1921. There were
practicing magical groups, and there may even have been covens, but
they did not regard themselves as Pagan or Wiccan until after exposure
to Gardnerian Wicca. It appears as though preexisting groups may have
modified their practices under the influence of the Gardnerian Craft,
and later came to identify as Wiccans and Pagans. Victor and Cora Anderson, who developed the Feri, or Faery, tradition, for example, read
Gardner's work in the 1950s. They corresponded with him, and later initiates in the tradition appear to have used his model as something of a
"style guide" for Feri practice, perhaps due to its perceived authenticity
as a survival of the witch cult described by Murray.[2]

Gardner was born in Blundellsands, England, in 1884, and was raised
in a middle-class family with a governess. Due to recurring illnesses as a
child, he received little formal education, but he traveled a great deal, va-
cationing in a variety of warm climates during the winter to calm his
asthma. He became a civil servant, managing tea and rubber plantations
in Borneo, and later he worked as a customs officer in Malaysia. He was
initiated as a **Freemason** in Ceylon and became interested in magic in
Malaysia, and he started reading anthropology and folklore.[3] He retired
from the civil service in 1936 and returned to England with his wife,
Donna. They lived in London for two years and then moved to Highcliffe,
near the New Forest area.[4] Gardner joined a nearby Rosicrucian Theatre
(an amateur theatre group) and began meeting with local occultists. He alleged that within the Rosicrucian Theatre group there was a group called
the Crotona fellowship, through which he met "Old Dorothy," who
headed the New Forest coven.[5] He claimed to have been initiated by Old
Dorothy in September of 1939, and to have worked with her coven into
the late 1940s.[6]

Gardner indicates that in 1946 he received permission from the New
Forest coven to publish some rituals in his novel *High Magic's Aid*, first
published in 1949 under the pseudonym Scire.[7] After the repeal of the
laws against witchcraft in 1951 in Britain, Gardner began to give press interviews to advertise the existence of modern Witches.[8] At this time, he
also belonged to a naturist society, or nudist group.[9] Gardner had apparently long been a nudist, and some Gardnerians continue his practice of
"sky-clad" rituals. In 1954, Gardner's book *Witchcraft Today* came out. In
it, he names "Wica," the religion of the wise. It seems likely that Gardner
invented the word "Wicca" (his spelling was variable) and the religion

around 1950,[10] although he had been involved in various magical practices not known by that name previously.

Gardner's claim to have been initiated into a preexisting coven has been much debated. There is no other first-hand account of the reality of his initiation. Some continue to argue that there was a preexisting coven, but most scholars doubt the existence of the New Forest coven.[11] "Old Dorothy" has been identified as Dorothy Clutterbuck, but Clutterbuck was an upper-class woman in the New Forest region who appears not to have had any occult leanings or any connection to Gardner.[12] Gardner may have named her to deflect attention from his actual initiator, a woman identified by the pseudonym "Dafo," who belonged to the Crotona fellowship and was a **Co-Mason**.[13] She later withdrew from the group, becoming uncomfortable with Gardner's publicity.

Gardner probably created Wicca out of Margaret Murray's account of witchcraft as a fertility religion and organized pre-Christian tradition, and from other readings in anthropology and folklore.[14] Most Wiccan groups have appeared only since 1970, and none before 1950. However, it is inaccurate to say that Gardner completely invented Wicca, because "much of the material in revival Witchcraft was already in place by the early twentieth century."[15] That is, Gardner created and popularized Witchcraft as an explicit religious tradition based on preexisting groups and writings in the Western esoteric tradition and folklore studies. And Gardner did meet people in the New Forest area who were practicing magic, such as Dafo. In addition, although the rituals Gardner used drew on a number of different written materials underlying the ideas of and passages taken from Murray, Leland, Crowley, Kipling, and the *Key of Solomon*, Doreen Valiente suggests that she "found a basic structure" that was not derived from them.[16]

Gardner called the ritual book he used his "Book of Shadows." What appears to be an early version of this book, "Ye Bok of ye Art Magical," was found behind a filing cabinet in Gardner's library. It may be the earliest surviving copy of his Book of Shadows.[17] It was constructed to look like a medieval grimoire, made up of bound blank sheets and then filled in somewhat as a scrapbook. He copied passages from various sources, arranging them thematically, with spaces left for more material. Some of the copied passages came from the *Key of Solomon*, the Bible, the kabbalah (Jewish mysticism), and Aleister Crowley's writings. It also includes rudimentary versions of initiation rituals, with notes added in the margins for stage directions. These marginal notes are not generally included in later copies of the Book of Shadows, which leads some to suggest that "he was commenting on an already existing practice," because "if he had invented the ritual himself, there would have been no need to add commentary and stage directions."[18] However, it seems more likely that Gardner used "Ye

Bok of ye Art Magical" as a magical workbook, as later Witches have tended to use their Book of Shadows. The blank pages may therefore indicate that it was not regarded as complete but as a work in progress. Stage directions sometimes accompany new ritual scripts written by practitioners, so Gardner's marginal notes are just as likely to indicate the newness of the rituals as they are to indicate their age.

Allyn Wolfe, a high priest of the New Wiccan Church of central California, suggests that comparisons between his group's Book of Shadows and Gardner's notebook indicates that both are derived from an earlier source. But even if such a text did exist, it would only indicate that Gardner took some material from a preexisting British occult group, a twentieth-century group rather than a pagan survival. Gardner may have produced "Ye Bok" purely to substantiate his claim that he was copying previous tradition, just as he invented the "Craft Laws," but he could just as easily have believed that he had found an ancient tradition, which was in fact a twentieth-century creation. If Gardner thought he had found a remnant of ancient tradition, and added what he knew from folklore and anthropology, supplementing the materials he found, he would be part of a tradition of folklore reclamation, akin to the Grimm brothers' collection and revisions of folk tales.[19]

Gardner created modern Witchcraft as a religious tradition and is responsible for the initial drive to popularize the Craft. He sought publicity, wrote books on the subject, and initiated people into what he represented as a tradition of Witchcraft continuous with pre-Christian pagan traditions. He introduced most of the core ritual forms of Wicca from other traditions with which he was familiar, such as **Masonry**. The development of most Pagan Witchcraft in the United States can be traced to Gardner's influence, and, as Druid Isaac Bonewits has pithily noted, he took "material from any source that didn't run too fast to get away."[20] Gardner was successful in popularizing Witchcraft in part because it was sustained by cultural trends that supported popular interest in magic and folklore. Margaret Murray's work was popular at the time, and there was interest in occult figures such as Aleister Crowley. As Valiente notes, John Symond's biography of Aleister Crowley, *The Great Beast*, published in 1951, was less sensationalist than previous journalistic accounts of his life, and it renewed public interest in magic.[21]

Doreen Valiente (1922–1999) is largely responsible for developing the version of the Gardnerian Book of Shadows that circulated in the 1960s and 1970s. She has influenced the development of Paganism primarily through her rewriting of Gardner's Book of Shadows in the 1950s. She wrote the original verse form of the Charge of the Goddess based on a passage from Leland's *Aradia*, and the Witches Rune, a liturgy commonly used in Wiccan rituals to raise power and charge magical tools. Her role

Figure 13.   Doreen Valiente (from Doreen Valiente's *Rebirth of Witchcraft*)

in the development of Gardnerian Wicca was largely unknown until the 1970s and 1980s. Verses she wrote have often been reproduced, particularly in North America, as "traditional," without crediting her or the Gardnerian Book of Shadows.

Gardner initiated Valiente in 1953, and they were ritual partners for some time. She became high priestess of his coven but held authority over the coven in name only. Valiente recalls, "We were allowed to call ourselves High Priestesses, Witch Queens and similar fancy titles; but we were still in the position of having men running things and women doing as the men directed. As soon as the women started seeking real power, trouble was brewing."[22] In her book *The Rebirth of Witchcraft*, she discusses the early history of Gardnerian Wicca. She debates the validity of Gardner's claims, as well as the claims of another tradition based on "the Pickingill Material," about which she draws no conclusions due to a lack of evidence. She is very critical of both Gardner and Alex Sanders, a later Witch. Ambivalent about both, she recounts their good points as well as their bad points. Valiente later circled with Robert Cochrane (a pseudonym) and worked with him until he died a few years later, in 1966. Cochrane practiced a shamanic form of Witchcraft, which later informed the practices of the 1734 tradition.[23] ("1734" refers to a mystical number, rather than a year.)

Figure 14.   Alex and Maxine Sanders (photo from Stewart Farrar's *What Witches Do*)

Alex Sanders (1926–1988) proclaimed himself "King of the Witches." With his wife Maxine, styled as "Queen of the Witches," he founded what came to be known as the Alexandrian tradition. The Alexandrian tradition is largely Gardnerian, but with additional elements and emphases from ceremonial magic and spiritualism. In 1965 and 1966, Sanders became a public figure, and his popularity was challenged by prominent Gardnerians, who denounced him as a false Witch who lacked a proper initiatory lineage. He retorted that he had been initiated into the Craft by his grandmother and that it was the lineage of the Gardnerians that was spurious. Sanders and his wife claimed to preside over 127 covens in northern England, and they became famous in the London underground in the 1970s.[24]

Alex Sanders was born in 1926, as Orrell Alexander Carter, into a working-class family. His grandmother, said to be "skilled in the cunning craft," did practice magic, and his mother was interested in spiritualism and introduced Alex to the occult.[25] He sought initiation into Gardnerian Wicca in the early 1960s but was refused. Patricia Crowther reports that he wrote to her in November of 1961 saying that he had always been interested in the occult and had seen her on television, and he wanted to learn from her and her husband, Arnold. They met, but she took a dislike to him and refused to initiate him. He later began circling with Pat Kopanski, who had received first-degree initiation from the Crowther's coven but had developed a dislike for their coven's practice. Sanders may have eventually obtained initiation to the first degree from a Witch with the magical name Medea, but the details of her lineage and Sanders' contact with her are sketchy.[26]

Janet Farrar (b. 1950) and Stewart Farrar (1916–2000) were initiated into Sanders' tradition, which Stewart coined "Alexandrian."[27] They wrote a number of books, notably *A Witches' Bible*, a popular manual in Algard tradition (which blends Alexandrian and Gardnerian Witchcraft). This text virtually replaced the practice of hand copying a coven's Book of Shadows in some groups, as it includes most of that material, as well as commentary on the origins of various parts of the text, including acknowledgment of Valiente's contributions. The Farrar's moved to Ireland in 1975 and added Irish elements to their practice. They became estranged from Sanders by the late 1970s, and allied with Doreen Valiente. Together they analyzed the various versions of the Book of Shadows and concluded that Sanders' tradition was based on Gardner's rather than being inherited from his family.[28] The Algard tradition has been prominent in some parts of Canada, through the Odyssean tradition of the Wiccan Church of Canada.

Raymond Buckland, with his first wife, Rosemary Buckland, brought Gardnerian Wicca to the United States in the early 1960s. They formed a coven in New York and became the official representatives of the

Figure 15.　　Janet and Stewart Farrar (from Farrar and Farrar's *Eight Sabbats for Witches*)

denomination in the United States, until they divorced in the early 1970s. Gardner forwarded queries about joining Wicca from Americans to Ray Buckland, and Buckland ran a Witchcraft museum like Gardner's on Long Island. Buckland initially held that only initiated Witches with a traceable lineage were "real" Witches—that is, that only Gardnerian initiates were "real" Witches, disdaining "do-it-yourself" initiates. He later changed his mind, though, and produced a number of books for popular consumption.[29] His "Big Blue Book," *Buckland's Complete Book of Witchcraft*, introduced many American practitioners to the Craft. It served as a how-to guide for self-initiation, a training guide, and a coven manual for those who could not find an existing coven to train with.

Buckland was born in 1934. His father was a Gypsy, and Buckland studied Gypsy culture and the occult. He read Gardner's work in the 1950s and started corresponding with him, continuing after he moved to the United States. He and Rosemary returned to the United Kingdom to be initiated in 1963.[30] In 1973, shortly after their divorce, Ray created a new denomination, the Seax-Wica tradition, also called "Saxon Wicca."[31] It is less rigid and more democratic than Gardnerian Wicca, and it recognizes self-initiation.[32] It was designed to be accessible and new. It is not directly descended from Saxon origin but is rather newly created, with Saxon folklore included.[33]

Witchcraft also came to the West Coast of the United States in the 1960s and 1970s, but it developed in a different and eventually more influential way in combination with feminist Goddess religion, largely through the teachings of Zsuzsanna Budapest and Starhawk. Zsuzsanna Budapest, commonly called "Z." Budapest, is an American feminist Witch and is largely responsible for the re-creation of "Dianic" Witchcraft, the tradition presented in Leland's *Aradia*. She initially advocated a completely separate practice for women, and she continues to be a lesbian and a priestess of Diana, the goddess in *Aradia*. While some elements of her practice appear to be derived directly from Leland's *Aradia* and the Gardnerian Book of Shadows, she does not cite these works. Diana is an appropriate goddess for Budapest because of her portrayal as an emancipatory force in Leland's *Aradia*, but also because the Roman goddess Diana was known for shunning the company of men.[34] Murray had described Witchcraft as "the Dianic Cult,"[35] but following Budapest, women's-only groups have

Figure 16.   Z. Budapest (photo provided by Z. Budapest)

been called Dianic. Dianic Witchcraft largely became the practice of Witchcraft as "women's religion."[36] However, another group of Dianic Witches, the McFarland Dianics, developed about the same time as Budapest's group. This group includes men, and it recognizes male as well as female divinity.[37]

Budapest was born in 1940 in Hungary, and she immigrated to United States in 1959, initially to Chicago, where she married and had two children. She left what she came to view as the slavery of her domestic role as a wife and moved to Los Angeles, where she began meeting with feminists at women's liberation celebrations. She knew many pagan customs in the secular context of Hungarian folk culture, but in 1970, she started reading other folklore in English and began celebrating the sabbats with other women in a group that became the Susan B. Anthony coven, founded in 1971.[38]

She ran the Feminist Wicca, an occult shop in California, for some time, which Starhawk visited, leading her to participate in her first large all-women ritual, led by Budapest.[39] Budapest has claimed that seven hundred women were initiated into her tradition in the 1970s.[40] She did not initiate all who call themselves Dianic Witches—many had no direct connection to Budapest—but in the 1980s, there were hundreds of Dianic covens operating as women's-only groups.[41] These women were inspired by *Aradia* and Budapest's *The Feminist Book of Light and Shadows*, later published as *The Holy Book of Women's Mysteries*, a how-to book that became a core text for what came to be known as "feminist spirituality," a term coined by Budapest.[42]

The Holy Book of Women's Mysteries has enough in common with Gardnerian material that it appears to be derivative, but Budapest denies having ever read Gardner's work.[43] She indicates that the work of the scholar of classical Greek culture Jane Ellen Harrison was her chief inspiration.[44] She has claimed to be a hereditary witch, following the teachings of her mother, an artist, altar builder, and psychic. She says her mother presented her art and psychic skills as "peasant," and she explains that "peasant" and "pagan" are the same word in Italian. Budapest indicates that she was a Witch before she was a feminist, and that there have been many herbalists and healers in her family, documented back to the year 1270.[45]

Budapest was arrested for fortune-telling in Los Angeles in 1975. She fought the charge on grounds of the right to religious freedom (providing counseling), but lost. Nine years later, after many appeals, the law was defeated and struck down by Rose Bird, then on the California Supreme Court. Traditional Wiccan Witches generally did not support Budapest against the charges, largely because of her feminist politics, but some other Pagans spoke in her defense in letters to the Pagan magazine *Green Egg*.[46] Her trial brought Witchcraft to public attention in California, and drew attention to anti-occult laws. The Los Angeles law forbade fortune-telling, regardless of whether money was charged or not, and was against any practice of magic, including clairvoyance and palmistry.[47]

In 1980, Budapest led a large ritual at the Pan-Pagan Festival in the American Midwest, and for the first time involved men in a ritual, as guardians of the perimeter for women participating in a sky-clad ritual. For most of the women, it was their first ritual in a nonpolarized setting (i.e., it was women and goddess focused, rather than bitheistic with pre-scribed male and female roles). It was a moving experience for the partic-ipants, and "many of these women were forever changed by their experi-ence."[48] Budapest contributed to the development of separate men's and women's mysteries, and to a decline in animosity toward gender-specific events at Pagan festivals. Some Pagans regard separatist Dianic Witch-craft as a necessary stage in the growth of a more balanced view of women and men, and god and goddess, in the Craft, and practitioners de-bate about whether the need for separate men's and women's rituals has past.[49] Budapest herself has mellowed, and conflicts between feminist and mainstream Craft have mostly subsided.

Budapest is somewhat charismatic, and although much of the wider na-tional Pagan community rejected her, she is loved and respected by many in California.[50] She is respected for her creativity, for her ability to inspire and craft new rituals, and for leaving historical questions to the academ-ics. She wrote the classic chant "We All Come From the Goddess,"[51] she hosted a television show in the 1980s, and she has a continuing public presence in Paganism through lecture tours, workshops, articles on the Goddess, and her website.[52]

The Goddess-religion version of Paganism espoused by Budapest and Starhawk attracted many women who had become estranged from or-ganized religion in the second wave of feminism in the late 1960s (the first wave being the suffragist movement, which won women the right to vote). Feminist influences introduced a questioning of sexism and pa-triarchy within Paganism, the idea that "the personal is political," and the consensus decision-making process, as well as a sometimes counter-academic approach to history and myth.[53] Practitioners following Bu-dapest's lead took an attitude of creative inspiration toward myth, his-tory, and tradition. Feminist practitioners often quote a passage from Monique Wittig's novel *Les Guérillières* (*The Wars*): "There was a time when you were not a slave, remember that. . . . Make an effort to re-member. Or, failing that, invent."[54]

Starhawk, an American feminist Witch and an initiate of the Faery tra-dition, is a cofounder of the Reclaiming tradition. Starhawk is an interna-tionally known author and spokesperson for the Craft and for Goddess religion. Her books have been translated into German, Danish, Italian,

Portuguese, and Japanese.[55] She wrote *The Spiral Dance*, one of the most commonly known how-to books introducing practitioners to Paganism. She has been influential in Paganism through embracing feminism while encouraging the participation of men.

Starhawk is also well known for her political activism. She became politically active in protests against the Vietnam War in the 1960s when she was in high school, and she has never stopped. She eventually became a prominent leader and organizer in the peace, antinuclear, and antiglobalization movements. She says that politics and spirituality have always gone together for her,[56] and this combination is integral to the Reclaiming tradition she cocreated. Environmental awareness in particular is inherent to her practice of Witchcraft. She feels that spiritual awareness inspires political action, and she says that the Goddess is not only a symbol but also a living being who "makes demands on us."[57]

Starhawk was born Miriam Simos in 1951, into a Jewish family. She began to have a Pagan view of the world in the summer of 1968, as she hitchhiked and camped along the coast of California. She recalls, "For the first time I lived in direct contact with nature, day and night. I began to feel connected to the world in a new way, to see everything as alive, erotic, engaged in a constant dance of mutual pleasuring, and myself as a special part of it all."[58] In the fall of 1968, she started college at the University of California, Los Angeles (UCLA), and taught a class on Witchcraft with a friend as a project for an anthropology course. They formed a coven and began to improvise rituals. A short while later, she met what she called "real Wiccan Witches" and found "a framework for understanding the experiences [she] had already had" upon hearing the Charge of the Goddess. She underwent some training with those "real Wiccan Witches" but was not inclined at the time to follow their disciplined training program.[59]

Starhawk met Z. Budapest in the early 1970s and learned from her, but she did not become integrated into Budapest's circle. She graduated from UCLA and started writing novels. She moved to New York to try to get published, but she had a series of dreams that led her back to California, where she began a more disciplined religious practice and started writing what was eventually published as *The Spiral Dance*. She taught classes again on ritual and formed the Compost coven out of them. She met Victor and Cora Anderson, who trained her in the Faery tradition, and she gained status in the Pagan community, being elected first officer of the Covenant of the Goddess in 1976.[60]

By 1977, Starhawk developed a desire for a more political religious practice than Compost could provide. She moved to San Francisco and founded Raving, a coven for women only, run on a nonhierarchical basis with no high priestess.[61] In 1979, she started the Reclaiming community, a feminist Witch group, with Diane Baker. Reclaiming began as Goddess religion, conducting emancipatory rituals as a teaching collective on Witchcraft.[62] Out of those first classes, students formed the Holy Terrors coven, and the Wind Hags. Starhawk and others in the Reclaiming community put on the first Spiral Dance ritual at Samhain of 1979, coinciding with the publication of Starhawk's book of the same name. Raving became the Reclaiming Collective in 1980 and continues to present an annual Spiral Dance ritual in the Bay Area.[63]

In 1981, Starhawk was arrested at a demonstration against the opening of a nuclear power plant at Diablo Canyon. She began to support anarchist politics and direct action against environmental destruction, and Reclaiming was opened to male participants. She has been arrested many times since, for demonstrating against clear cutting old-growth forest in Clayoquot Sound, and in Genoa for her participation in antiglobalization protests, among other causes.

Starhawk's influence has been primarily in adding an overtly political tone to Paganism, initially feminism, and later anarchism, direct action, and antinuclear and antiglobalization sentiments. Her outlook might be described as the "California Cosmology" version of Witchcraft, a phrase used to describe the evolution of nineteenth-century American pantheism through Californian writers in the 1970s. They included an eclectic mix of alternative ideas, the common belief "that everything in the cosmos is both sacred and interconnected; that humans in the developed world have become tragically—perhaps fatally—disconnected from the cosmos; and that reconnection is possible given only a change of attitudes."[64]

The Spiral Dance became the best-selling book on Paganism, replacing Gardner's *Witchcraft Today* as the model how-to text, largely because of Starhawk's talent as a writer. Her writing is clear and impassioned, and she is "popularly credited with having inspired the foundation of hundreds of groups of witches all over Europe and North America."[65] Some estimate that *The Spiral Dance* "created a thousand women's covens and spiritual groups," "perhaps more than all the Gardnerians and Alexandrians combined."[66] Some say that although she is an original and talented writer, she is not an original thinker: "Her genius lay in taking ideas from others and combining and applying them in powerful new ways."[67]

While Wicca was spreading into North America from Britain and was being transformed by its encounter with feminist Pagan groups, other American Pagan traditions began to develop. At Carleton College, students formed the Reformed Druids of North America (RDNA) in 1963, in protest of the school's requirements that students attend religious services. Although the requirement was waived a year later, and though RDNA was not initially intended to be a religious group, it grew into one, and into the contemporary Pagan movement through Isaac Bonewits. Bonewits joined RDNA through his roommate at Berkeley, and they

Figure 17.   Isaac Bonewits (photo provided by Isaac Bonewits)

established a grove there as an overtly religious Pagan group. A subsequent schism with more-secular RDNA groups lead to the formation of the New Reformed Druids of North America (NRDNA).[68] Bonewits later founded Ár nDraíocht Féin (ADF), which grew into a much larger organization than RDNA. He has since run ADF as a self-admittedly "benevolent dictatorship,"[69] and has sometimes been a controversial figure in Paganism, leading some to describe him as "extremely opinionated and often difficult, even egotistical," while noting that "he remains one of the most interesting Pagans around."[70]

Born in 1949, Bonewits was religiously inclined from an early age. He went to a high school seminary but was at the same time reading about magic, and he later returned to the public school system. He is perhaps best known for earning a bachelor's degree in magic from Berkeley in 1970 through their independent study program, a feat that the administration subsequently made impossible to repeat. He went on to get a doctorate in anthropology from Berkeley. Publicity from his degree in magic led to the publication of *Real Magic*, which discusses ritual, magic, and psychic phenomena. He has been a public figure in various branches of Paganism ever since, and continues to produce books. He has been initiated into the Gardnerian Craft, NROOGD, and the Order of the Temple of the Orient, among other traditions.[71]

Bonewits has been most influential through his ideas on magic, his discussion of the principles of magic, and his theory of how magic works as discussed in the multiple editions of *Real Magic*. He has also promoted scholarship and general Pagan learning from academic sources on Paganism and Pagan history. He has long been critical of Pagan acceptance of false histories concerning the witch hunts and ancient matriarchies, and he greatly contributed to the growing critical awareness of historical issues in Paganism in the United States by the mid-1970s.[72] He angered many by calling the Wiccan revival myth "the myth of the Unitarian, Universalist, White Witchcult of Western Theosophical Brittany."[73] He has been critical also of Robert Graves, calling him "a sloppy scholar" who "has caused more bad anthropology to occur among Wiccan groups than almost any other work." The problem was not so much in Graves himself, whom Bonewits praises for his inspirational use of metaphor and myth, but in practitioners who treated Graves' and Murray's writings as "sacred scripture."[74]

A number of people find Bonewits' categorization of Pagans into paleopagans, mesopagans, and neopagans useful. Paleopaganism refers to indigenous polytheistic traditions. Mesopaganism refers to reconstructionist traditions that began under the influence of monotheistic and **gnostic** ideas, such as some early forms of Druidism. Neopaganism (also spelled "Neo-Paganism") refers to revivalist and re-creationist groups formed after about 1960, under the influence of modern ideas about inclusivity and equality, that is, with political consciousness.[75] More specifically, Bonewits defines Neo-Paganism as "polytheistic (or conditional monotheistic) nature religions that are based upon the older or Paleopagan religions; concentrating upon an attempt to retain the humanistic, ecological and creative aspects of these old belief systems while discarding their occasional brutal or repressive developments, which are inappropriate."[76]

In the 1980s, Paganism diversified further with the development of reconstructionist traditions drawing from a number of cultures, but Wicca continued to grow in popularity, particularly through the development of solitary practitioners. Scott Cunningham's books, *Wicca: A Guide for the Solitary Practitioner* and *Living Wicca: A Further Guide for the Solitary Practitioner*, made this development possible. Cunningham (1956–1993) was initiated into a number of groups but preferred solitary practice. His writings made the teachings of Wicca widely available, providing access to the religion for practitioners who did not have contact with teaching covens in the United States, or did not want to practice within organized groups. Along with writers such as Heather O'Dell and Marion Green, Cunningham made Wicca accessible to those who were not interested in working in covens.[77]

By making the teachings of Wicca available outside of teaching covens, Cunningham contributed to the growth of eclectic Wicca beyond initiatory traditions.[78] He presented Wicca as a modern religion, newly created and open to possibility, but inspired by past traditions. Indirectly, Cunningham may have contributed to the increased role of festivals in Paganism beginning in the 1980s, since some solitary practitioners attend such festivals in place of regular group practice[79] to gain a periodic sense of belonging.

Cunningham produced more than thirty books on Witchcraft and topics related to the practice of Paganism. He is one of Llewellyn Publications most successful authors,[80] and he is one of the best-selling Pagan authors for a popular audience. More than 400,000 copies of *Wicca: A Guide for the Solitary Practitioner* were sold per year by 2000,[81] and it is now available in Spanish. Perhaps it is in part due to the success of Cunningham's guide that his publisher, Llewellyn Publications, prefers its book titles to include "Wicca" rather than "Witchcraft" or "Paganism," a decision that continues to influence the use of these terms by practitioners. Increasingly, Pagans identify with "Wicca" as a generic term for "Pagan."

A major exception to the tendency toward a preference for the terms "Wicca" and "Wiccan" is in Heathen and Asatru groups, who sometimes even refuse the label "Pagan." One of the more prominent practitioners in this area is Diana Paxson, leader of Hrafnar ("The Ravens"), a Heathen/Asatru reconstructionist group in the United States founded in 1988. She is respected in the Heathen/Asatru community and has exerted an aesthetic influence on Paganism more broadly through the Society for Creative Anachronism (SCA), which she cofounded. The SCA, which began at a party in Paxson's backyard in 1966,[82] revives the clothing and practices of the Middle Ages and the Renaissance, as well as music, herbalism, and medieval cooking. Many practitioners find their way into local Pagan communities through SCA events, and the medieval flavor of their practices permeates Pagan aesthetics.

Paxson was born in 1943 and grew up in California. She earned a master's degree in comparative literature and has had several novels published. She trained as an Episcopal minister at one time, which has led some to jokingly describe some rituals of Fellowship of the Spiral Path, to which she also belongs, as "High Episcopagan."[83] She was first initiated by her sister-in-law, the novelist Marion Zimmer Bradley. She has studied Wicca, neo-shamanism, and other traditions, but her focus is on Asatru,[84] although she remains a member of NROOGD and the kabbalistic group the Fellowship of the Spiral Path.[85]

Paxson's greatest influence has been in the revival of oracular *seidr*, or divination from the high seat, about which she teaches workshops throughout the United States and Europe. Oracular *seidr* "in its present form was first practised within today's **Heathenry** in the US when Diana Paxson went looking for 'something for the women to do' while men were involved in performing 'viking games' and drinking beer, playing out the . . . stereotype of the macho warrior."[86] She has authored a number of novels with Pagan elements, and she contributes regularly to Pagan magazines.[87] She also edits *Idunna*, a journal devoted to Heathenry.

Many other people could be included in a list of those who have made important contributions or played significant roles in the development of Paganism. Ed Fitch, for example, has been credited with creating the "outer court" structure commonly used in Wiccan and other Pagan groups.[88] Gwydion Pendderwen (Tom DeLong) was a prominent bard (musician and storyteller) whose songs became well known and loved beyond his home state of California. Lady Sheba (Jesse Wicker Bell) published the Gardnerian Book of Shadows for the first time. Sybil Leek became known for her claim to be initiated into a tradition other than Gardnerian Wicca. Oberon Zell-Ravenheart (formerly Tim Zell or Otter G'Zell) greatly contributed to the Church of All Worlds and influenced Pagans more generally through his editorship of *Green Egg*. Aiden Kelly became infamous for creating doubt in the authenticity of Gardner's claim to having been initiated into a preexisting religion. Margot Adler became well known to practitioners as well as scholars of Pagan studies through her thoroughly researched and unsurpassed survey of American Paganism, *Drawing Down the Moon*. More recently, Chas Clifton has done much to foster the growth of the field of Pagan studies, moderating the Nature Religion Scholars Network e-list, organizing meetings at the American Academy of Religion, and editing *The Pomegranate: The International Journal of Pagan Studies*. These people, and others, continue to shape the development of Paganism into diverse traditions.

FURTHER READING

Clifton, Chas. *Her Hidden Children*. Lanham, MD: AltaMira Press, 2006.
Hutton, Ronald. *The Triumph of the Moon: A History of Modern Pagan Witchcraft*. Oxford: Oxford University Press, 1999.

NOTES

1. Margot Adler, *Drawing Down the Moon: Witches, Druids, Goddess-Worshippers, and Other Pagans in America Today*, revised and expanded ed. (Boston: Beacon Press, 1986), 62.
2. Cora Anderson indicates that the main "trunk" of the Feri tradition stemming from the Andersons did not rely on Gardnerian material, but that there are branches of the tradition

that are more influenced by Gardnerian practice. Cora Anderson, personal communication, August 23, 2005. See also Chas S. Clifton, *Her Hidden Children* (Lanham, MD: AltaMira, 2006), 132.

3. Sabina Magliocco, *Witching Culture: Folklore and Neo-Paganism in America* (Philadelphia: University of Pennsylvania Press, 2004), 48–49.

4. Ronald Hutton, *The Triumph of the Moon: A History of Modern Pagan Witchcraft* (Oxford: Oxford University Press 1999), 205.

5. Magliocco, *Witching Culture*, 49.

6. Hutton, *Triumph of the Moon*, 206.

7. Adler, *Drawing Down the Moon*, 61.

8. Hutton, *Triumph of the Moon*, 206.

9. Adler, *Drawing Down the Moon*, 61.

10. Clifton, *Her Hidden Children*, 75.

11. Clifton, *Her Hidden Children*, 87.

12. Hutton, *Triumph of the Moon*, 211.

13. Hutton, *Triumph of the Moon*, 212–13.

14. Tanya Luhrmann, *Persuasions of the Witch's Craft* (Cambridge, MA: Harvard University Press, 1989), 42–43.

15. Magliocco, *Witching Culture*, 51.

16. Doreen Valiente, *The Rebirth of Witchcraft* (Custer, WA: Phoenix Publishing, 1989), 63.

17. Magliocco, *Witching Culture*, 51. Magliocco does not state when the book was found, but Hutton, following Aiden Kelly's research, indicates that "Ye Bok of ye Art Magical" precedes the 1953 version of the Book of Shadows. See Hutton, *Triumph of the Moon*, 227. It is held in a collection of Gardner's papers in Toronto by Richard and Tamarra James.

18. Magliocco, *Witching Culture*, 52.

19. Magliocco, *Witching Culture*, 52–54.

20. Quoted in Adler, *Drawing Down the Moon*, 70.

21. Valiente, *Rebirth of Witchcraft*, 17.

22. Valiente, *Rebirth of Witchcraft*, 182.

23. Chas S. Clifton and Graham Harvey, *The Paganism Reader* (New York: Routledge, 2004), 215.

24. Hutton, *Triumph of the Moon*, 326.

25. Hutton, *Triumph of the Moon*, 330–31.

26. Hutton, *Triumph of the Moon*, 320–22.

27. Hutton, *Triumph of the Moon*, 329.

28. Hutton, *Triumph of the Moon*, 338–39.

29. Clifton and Harvey, *Paganism Reader*, 209–10.

30. Shelly Rabinovitch and James Lewis, *Encyclopedia of Modern Witchcraft and Neo-Paganism* (New York: Citadel, 2002), 30.

31. Magliocco, *Witching Culture*, 70.

32. Rabinovitch and Lewis, *Encyclopedia of Modern Witchcraft and Neo-Paganism*, 31.

33. Adler, *Drawing Down the Moon*, 93.

34. Hutton, *Triumph of the Moon*, 344.

35. Adler, *Drawing Down the Moon*, 121.

36. Jone Salomonsen, *Enchanted Feminism: The Reclaiming Witches of San Francisco* (London: Routledge, 2002), 242.

37. Wendy Griffin, "Goddess Spirituality and Wicca," in *Her Voice, Her Faith*, ed. Arvind Sharma and Katherine K. Young (Boulder, CO: Westview Press, 2003).

38. Adler, *Drawing Down the Moon*, 77.

39. Starhawk, *The Spiral Dance: A Rebirth of the Ancient Religion of the Great Goddess*. 10th anniversary ed. (New York: HarperSanFrancisco, 1989), 3.

40. Hutton, *Triumph of the Moon*, 344.
41. Adler, *Drawing Down the Moon*, 121.
42. Rabinovitch and Lewis, *Encyclopedia of Modern Witchcraft and Neo-Paganism*, 32–31. The original publication of *The Feminist Book of Light and Shadows* credits the members of the Susan B. Anthony coven with authorship, but Budapest is listed as the author of *The Holy Book of Women's Mysteries*, although she notes others as contributors.
43. The similarities with Gardnerian material may be due to both traditions using Leland's *Aradia* as a source.
44. Personal communication, July 5, 2005. See also Hutton, *Triumph of the Moon*, 344.
45. Adler, *Drawing Down the Moon*, 76.
46. Clifton, *Her Hidden Children*, 121.
47. Adler, *Drawing Down the Moon*, 187.
48. Adler, *Drawing Down the Moon*, 426.
49. Salomonsen, *Enchanted Feminism*, 242–43.
50. Adler, *Drawing Down the Moon*, 187.
51. Hutton, *Triumph of the Moon*, 360.
52. Personal communication, July 5, 2005. See also Rabinovitch and Lewis, *Encyclopedia of Modern Witchcraft and Neo-Paganism*, 32. Budapest's website can be found at www.zbudapest.com.
53. Clifton, *Her Hidden Children*, 121–22.
54. Monique Wittig, *Les Guérillières* (Boston: Beacon Press, 1985), 89.
55. Rabinovitch and Lewis, *Encyclopedia of Modern Witchcraft and Neo-Paganism*, 250.
56. Starhawk, *Webs of Power: Notes from the Global Uprising* (Gabriola Island, British Columbia: New Society Publishers, 2002), 4.
57. Starhawk, *Dreaming the Dark: Magic, Sex and Politics*, new ed. (London: Mandala [Unwin Paperbacks], 1990), xvi.
58. Starhawk, *Spiral Dance*, 2.
59. Starhawk, *Spiral Dance*, 2–3.
60. Starhawk, *Spiral Dance*, 3–5.
61. Salomonsen, *Enchanted Feminism*, 39.
62. Salomonsen, *Enchanted Feminism*, 1.
63. Salomonsen, *Enchanted Feminism*, 39–40.
64. "The California Cosmology" is a phrase developed by Alston Chase. Ronald Hutton suggests that Starhawk learned this perspective through Carolyn Merchant at Berkeley. Hutton, *Triumph of the Moon*, 350–51.
65. Hutton, *Triumph of the Moon*, 345, 347.
66. Adler, *Drawing Down the Moon*, 228, 418.
67. Hutton, *Triumph of the Moon*, 350.
68. Rabinovitch and Lewis, *Encyclopedia of Modern Witchcraft and Neo-Paganism*, 26.
69. Quoted in Adler, *Drawing Down the Moon*, 327.
70. Adler, *Drawing Down the Moon*, 327.
71. Rabinovitch and Lewis, *Encyclopedia of Modern Witchcraft and Neo-Paganism*, 26.
72. Magliocco, *Witching Culture*, 192–93; Hutton, *Triumph of the Moon*, 369.
73. Adler, *Drawing Down the Moon*, 45.
74. Quoted in Adler, *Drawing Down the Moon*, 59.
75. Isaac Bonewits, "Defining Paganism: Paleo-, Meso-, and Neo- 2.5," Isaac Bonewits' Homepage, 2001, www.neopagan.net/PaganDefs.html (accessed August 6, 2004).
76. Quoted in Adler, *Drawing Down the Moon*, 10.
77. Rabinovitch and Lewis, *Encyclopedia of Modern Witchcraft and Neo-Paganism*, 69.
78. Rabinovitch and Lewis, *Encyclopedia of Modern Witchcraft and Neo-Paganism*, 70.
79. Clifton and Harvey, *Paganism Reader*, 273.

80. Clifton and Harvey, *Paganism Reader*, 273.

81. Rabinovitch and Lewis, *Encyclopedia of Modern Witchcraft and Neo-Paganism*, 70.

82. Clifton, *Her Hidden Children*, 117.

83. Magliocco, *Witching Culture*, 146.

84. Rabinovitch and Lewis, *Encyclopedia of Modern Witchcraft and Neo-Paganism*, 208–9.

85. Magliocco, *Witching Culture*, 81.

86. Jenny Blain, *Nine Worlds of Seid-Magic: Ecstasy and Neo-Shamanism in North European Paganism* (London: Routledge, 2002), 143.

87. Rabinovitch and Lewis, *Encyclopedia of Modern Witchcraft and Neo-Paganism*, 209.

88. Rabinovitch and Lewis, *Encyclopedia of Modern Witchcraft and Neo-Paganism*, 103.

8

Denominations

In discussing the forms and types of Paganism, it is necessary to use a flexible typology, because practitioners do not necessarily fall neatly into distinct categories. There are identifiable denominations in Paganism, named groups or traditions of Pagan practice, but there are also forms of practice that run across the denominations, such as eclectic and solitary practice. There are also overlapping religious movements and types of religious practice that generate cross-denominational forms of Pagan practice, such as shamanism, feminist spirituality, and New Age practices. Shamanism, feminist spirituality and Goddess religion exist as religious traditions in themselves, but they also overlap with Paganism as forms of Pagan practice. Some traditions discussed as denominations can also be seen as forms of practice, such as specific family traditions and reconstructionist traditions. The generally diverse and flexible structure of Paganism makes Pagan traditions difficult to categorize.

The majority of practitioners practice an eclectic form of Paganism. Eclectic forms of Paganism are traditions or practices that draw from multiple traditions, blending them into new forms, either for specific rituals or to create new Pagan denominations. A ritual can be eclectic, an individual's solitary practice can be eclectic, and a tradition can be eclectic but stable over time in an individual's practices or in group practices. An individual or group might, for example, construct a ritual on the basis of what feels right, taking inspiration from a folk practice described in Luisah Teish's *Jambalaya*, using a reproduction of a Cretan goddess figure, and playing Cuban drum music during the ritual, weaving multiple elements into a new synthesis. A solitary practitioner might develop relationships with the goddess Hecate from the Greek pantheon, as well as Brigid from Celtic mythology, and consistently bring together elements of both cultures in all her/his ritual work. Some groups form an eclectic practice that develops into a denomination of Paganism, such as the New Reformed Orthodox Order of the Golden Dawn (discussed with other Witchcraft denominations below), and the Church of All Worlds.

The Church of All Worlds, known as CAW, is a pantheistic, often polytheistic eclectic denomination. Members are not necessarily Pagan, as local groups are completely autonomous, but many are. CAW practitioners share a common recognition of divinity as immanent, or within humans and the rest of nature. As discussed in chapter 7, CAW is modeled after the Church of All Worlds in the novel *Stranger in a Strange Land*, but Zell, Christie, and other early members of CAW also drew on other sources of inspiration. Despite Ayn Rand's antireligious stance, her novels *Atlas Shrugged* and *The Fountainhead* were also important influences in the formation of CAW, particularly in the context of creating an alternative to the strict upbringing that many experienced growing up in the 1950s. Other important sources were emerging research on ecology and ancient cultures, and Abraham Maslow's ideas about self-actualization.[1]

Many Pagans are solitary practitioners, meaning they practice their religion singly rather than in a group. As solitaries, they are not members of any particular group with an identifiable denomination, but they may feel an affinity for a particular tradition. They form a "hidden majority" of Pagans,[2] perhaps constituting up to 70 or 80 percent of practitioners, according to estimates made by an executive of a popular publisher of Pagan books[3] and Witchvox.com cofounder Fritz Jung.[4] Academics report a lower proportion of solitaries, but still more than 50 percent.[5]

Pagans choose solitary practice for a variety of reasons. Some are "in the broom closet" and do not want coworkers or neighbors to know they are Pagan. Others have not found a group to their liking, or are temporarily between groups. Some simply prefer a solitary practice. Solitaries may be in contact with their local Pagan community through friends but not practicing together, or they may have contact with other Pagans through online communities (listservs, chat groups, and web rings) or through regional festivals. Solitaries are more likely than other practitioners to live in rural areas and small towns. They tend to be in their twenties and correspondingly single. They are also more likely than group practitioners to be heterosexual, and, according to at least one study, they are less likely to be politically active than group practitioners.[6]

The general acceptance within Paganism of solitary practice as a legitimate form of practice is perhaps structurally unique to Pagan religion,[7] but it may be less acceptable or common in some denominations of Paganism than in others. Wiccans appear to be more likely to value group practice over solitary practice, with some practitioners viewing coven training as necessary to becoming "a *real* Witch."[8] Practitioners in initiatory traditions in particular are more likely to regard solitary practice as inferior. The individualism of solitaries presents a challenge or resistance to the routinization and institutionalization of Paganism.[9] A solitary Witch can initiate her/himself by whatever means desired, but in an organized tradition like Gardnerian Wicca, a teaching coven must be found, and initiation must be sought through a predetermined and highly structured process. Solitaries do not have to agree with anyone about how to conduct a ritual, and they may have no interest in teaching others or in serving the larger Pagan community, whereas in group practice, practitioners generally learn from elders and develop group norms as a matter of course.

Paganism also takes on a number of forms of practice in its overlap with New Age spirituality, Goddess religion, feminist spirituality, and shamanism. Feminist spirituality can be regarded as a form of practice (feminist Paganism) and a denomination within Paganism, as with Dianic Witchcraft and the Reclaiming tradition, but feminist spirituality and Goddess religion are also movements that extend beyond Paganism. Paganism is interrelated with Goddess religion, feminist spirituality, and women's spirituality more broadly through the common use of metaphors, images of deity as Goddess, and understandings of divinity as immanent in women's bodies and in nature more generally. Practitioners emphasize the equality, and sometimes the superiority, of women.

Feminist spirituality spans a number of religions, including Judaism, Christianity, and others. Rosemary Radford Ruether, for example, is active in Christian feminist spirituality, as is Judith Plaskow in Jewish feminist spirituality. The Fellowship of Isis is an eclectic and pluralist Goddess group practicing feminist spirituality. They were founded in 1976 in Ireland and quickly became an international group. The Fellowship of Isis is not exclusively Pagan, but multifaith.[10] Like some other groups in Goddess religion, it is not restricted to women. Some men participate in Goddess religion and feminist spirituality, but not when it is characterized as "women's spirituality," a term that, ironically, is meant to be inclusive of non-feminist–identified women. Goddess religion is sometimes seen as a type of women's spirituality, because practitioners may or may not identify as feminist. Some practitioners of women's spirituality do not use anthropomorphic metaphors such as "Goddess" for the divine, or do not perceive the Goddess as a person external to themselves. Whether feminist spirituality, Goddess religion, or Paganism is described as a subset of the others is often chosen based on what an author or speaker wants to emphasize.

Feminist spirituality began in the late 1960s and early 1970s in the United States, at about the same time on the east and west coasts. In

California, Z. Budapest coined the term in 1972.[11] In Massachusetts, Mary Daly called on women to form an "exodus community" in her 1971 sermon at Harvard Memorial Church, when she called on feminists to leave the church and create a new community outside patriarchal institutions. The feminist spirituality movement developed in a variety of small groups at about the same time. In some feminist groups, a spiritual dimension evolved over time: some consciousness-raising groups became spirituality groups and began doing ritual as well as holding discussions in circle. Some early Pagan women's spirituality meetings might be described as a cross between Gardnerian ritual and a consciousness-raising group, as women shared their personal experiences sitting in a circle and brought spiritual practice into the group by creating a sense of sacred space.

Various groups using the acronym "WITCH" in the 1970s were originally wholly political in focus, but they picked up on the fact that the witch hunts had targeted women and that modern women were also oppressed, and they began to reclaim the word "witch" through feminist spirituality. Those in the women's movement who desired a spiritual aspect to their politics encouraged each other to form covens and invent new traditions that valued women if they did not like what they found in existing Pagan groups, some of which used to be quite sexist and/or heterosexist. Some Pagans have been critical of practitioners of Goddess religion and feminist spirituality for their use and understanding of mythic history, particularly their ideas about matriarchal prehistory, but liberal feminism has largely permeated Paganism in North America.

Pagans have developed shamanic forms of Witchcraft, Druidry, and Heathenry, creating an overlap between Paganism and neo-shamanism. Pagans create shamanic forms of Wicca and Druidry through the work of writers such as Caitlín and John Matthews. In Heathenry, Jenny Blain, Robert Wallis, and Diana Paxson have developed shamanic forms of practice. "Shamanism" usually refers to indigenous religious practices for relating with spirits, the otherworld, or extraordinary reality. "Neo-shamanism" generally refers to contemporary practices inspired by, but not in continuity with, indigenous practices of shamanism. Shamanism is a category of religion created by academics, initially from reading reports of traders and travelers. Academics first identified shamanism with the Tungus people of Siberia, from whom they took the word "shaman." Subsequently, it came to be associated with similar indigenous practices in other places. Western academics constructed the idea of "shamanism" initially from indigenous groups, and they continue to associate shamanism with indigenousness, although such practices may be universal.[12]

Shamanism shares with Paganism a number of practices and beliefs, such as magic, trance, possession, and raising energy. Practices of both are often directed toward healing, and both involve relationships with other-than-human persons. However, shamans usually undergo an initiation process quite different from that practiced in Pagan groups. For shamans, it is usually a severe experience of confrontation with one's mortality, often through illness or a trance experience of dismemberment. Paganism overlaps with shamanism primarily in the form of neo-shamanism rather than indigenous shamanism. It is labeled "neo" because it is reconstructionist rather than in continuity with indigenous practices.

Neo-shamanism is sometimes called "urban shamanism," usually in the context of universalized versions of shamanic traditions removed from their cultural origins,[13] such as Michael Harner's "core shamanism."[14] Indigenous critics of neo-shamans have called such practitioners "white shamans" and "plastic medicine men."[15] Neo-shamanism is sometimes "dismissed as nostalgic, and challenged as having reduced Shamanism to its lowest common denominators: essentially drumming, vision quests and Otherworld journeys. It is frequently marked by typically modern individualism, vague universalism and woolly psychologization."[16] However, some shamanic practitioners, particularly those who are reconstructionist Pagans, argue that they are practicing their own indigenous traditions in reviving traditions of their Saxon, Celtic, Norse, or Icelandic ancestors. In addition, some practitioners are quite nuanced in their understanding of how they are reconstructing traditions, and are politically aware of issues of appropriation.[17]

Despite the desires of many Pagan practitioners, Paganism also overlaps with New Age spirituality. "New Age" refers to a new era in human consciousness. It is sometimes associated with the "Age of Aquarius" as a post-Christian era. Aquarius is the sign following Pisces, taken in this context to represent Christianity, in the progression of the Zodiac (going backward in relation to the order of the birth signs in astrology). This progression of ages is a reinterpretation of the twelfth-century Joachim de Flores' division of history into the ages of the Father, the Son, and the Holy Spirit, corresponding, respectively, to the ages of the Hebrew Bible, the Christian New Testament, and the Holy Spirit. In the New Age interpretation, the three ages are changed to the ages of Aries (the Father), Pisces (the Son), and the New Age of Aquarius.[18]

New Age spirituality exhibits a tendency toward millenarianism and apocalypticism, or the belief in a coming inevitable cataclysmic change, with the end of the era of Pisces and the beginning of a New Age. This New Age is thought to be an age that will be less corporeal, and in which humans will ascend to a higher consciousness. New Age spirituality tends toward a dualistic understanding of matter and spirit, seeing the natural material world as an illusion or as somehow secondary to the spiritual (ethereal or astral). It tends to have a transcendental outlook, and, being influenced by theosophy, it is more universalistic than Paganism, taking elements from Hinduism, Buddhism, and Christianity.

New Age spirituality is a type of religious outlook that is found in a number of religious traditions, and is often not identified with any religion in particular. There are Buddhist, Christian, and Pagan New Age practitioners, for example. The New Age is not easily delimited because it has no identifiable religious institutions, and practitioners rarely identify themselves as New Agers. Arguably, "New Age" should be understood as an adjective rather than a noun, since it is not so much a movement as a set of tendencies or characteristics found in various religions and movements. Religious traditions can be examined in terms of to what extent or degree they can be described as New Age, rather than by classifying them as part of the New Age movement, which does not exist as a quantifiable entity.[19]

Some researchers present Witchcraft as a subculture of the New Age movement, or use "Witchcraft" and "New Age" interchangeably.[20] In categorizing Paganism with the New Age, some researchers inaccurately present Paganism as "world rejecting."[21] Pagans almost invariably see the divine as immanent within rather than transcendent of the natural world. Few Pagans believe in a radically transcendent deity or godhead.

Pagans often joke about the difference between New Age and Pagan events, saying that it can be summed up in two decimal points: if three dollars admits one to a Pagan workshop, a similar New Age workshop will cost three hundred dollars. Pagans tend to portray New Age practitioners as "fluffy bunnies," superficially playing with belief in angels, channeling, spirit helpers, and animal guides. Pagans suggest that New Agers focus on good, "white" energy, without recognition of the necessary roles and importance of death and darkness. Noting problems with the New Age use of such metaphors of white and light in terms of racism, Pagans tend to present New Agers as more concerned with personal development than Pagans are, at the expense of political and environmental awareness. Pagans suggest that the New Age focus on good energy as white light indicates a lack of depth and a failure to recognize one's shadow side. However, it is possible that Pagans themselves project what they dislike about their coreligionists onto New Agers in their presentation of New Agers as superficial practitioners who draw from too many, too diverse sources without awareness of issues of appropriation. The lack of people who identify as New Age practitioners is conspicuous.

Witchcraft can be seen as a form of practice within Paganism, but also as a group of denominations. Generically, practitioners refer to these traditions as "the Craft," a term that originally referred to Masonry, a Western mystery tradition that influenced some of the early forms of Witchcraft, notably Wicca. Practitioners of the Craft are called "Witches" or "Wiccans." Some of these practitioners wear a pentacle pendant or ring, a five-pointed star inside a circle, as a marker of their religious identification, as some Christians wear a cross, and some Jews the Star of David. Witches form the largest portion of Pagan practitioners, but of these, not all are practitioners of Wicca. Wicca may be the most visible and largest denomination within Paganism, but counting practitioners is confounded by people meaning different things by "Wicca." In Britain, "Wicca" refers exclusively to Gardnerian and Alexandrian traditions, while in the United States it is often conflated with Witchcraft and Paganism more generally. Some call Gardnerian and Alexandrian Wicca "British Traditional Witchcraft," but in Britain this refers to family or hereditary traditions. Some practitioners use the label "Wicca" simply because they prefer it to "Witch."

Some who identify themselves as Wiccans regard initiated Wiccans as the most committed Pagans and suggest that only those trained in a coven are "real" Witches, or that Pagans who do not identify themselves as Witches are simply hiding their identity as Witches. This has led some researchers to report that Witches are more committed to their religion than other Pagans.[22] However, some Pagans see this attitude as domineering. Many reject the labels "Witch" and "Wiccan," to distance themselves either from what they see as the questionable history of Wicca, or from the fabricated association with heretics killed as "witches" in medieval times.

Witchcraft groups are organized into covens. These are usually small local groups with generally less than a dozen members, although outer-court groups may include many more people. Witchcraft has generally followed the basic form and structure of Gardnerian Wicca. Perhaps not all Witchcraft traditions are derived from Gardnerian Wicca, but all seem to be influenced by it in their use of the seasonal festival cycle and in the structure of individual rituals. Other Witchcraft traditions are not necessarily bitheistic, as Wicca generally is.

The Gardnerian and Alexandrian denominations of Wicca are initiatory mystery traditions. Initiates are sworn to secrecy, taking an oath not to reveal the secrets of their initiation. Some Wiccans have criticized others for revealing oath-bound material, particularly for publishing versions of the Book of Shadows. Gardnerians and Alexandrians can be traced back to initiation by Gerald Gardner and Doreen Valiente, or Alex and Maxine Sanders, and sometimes both lineages, as in Algard traditions such as the Farrars' and the Wiccan Church of Canada. Mary Nesnick coined the term "Algard" to describe the tradition she formed through joint initiation in Gardnerian and Alexandrian Wicca.[23] A number of practitioners have been initiated in both traditions.

Gardnerian and Alexandrian groups maintain a hierarchy of status based on levels of initiation, lineage, how many practitioners one has initiated, and how many covens have hived off from one's group. "Hiving off" is the process of forming a "daughter" coven when enough new people have been trained and initiated to require the formation of a separate group. Gardnerian and Alexandrian covens are traditionally said to be made up of between three and thirteen members, but more often they include between five and eight people. Sabbat celebrations open to the public may be much larger. There is no laity within the Gardnerian and Alexandrian traditions, but practitioners make distinctions between neophytes or novices, who are new students; first, second, and third degree initiates; high priests and priestesses (coven leaders); and "witch queens" (high priestesses who have a number of daughter covens).

Through the publication of how-to books on solitary practice and books supporting self-initiation, a variety of traditions have emerged within Wicca. All forms of Wicca, when distinguished from Paganism more generally, with the exception of some Dianic groups that self-identify as Wiccan, tend to be bitheistic, revering a Goddess and a God, sometimes called the "Lady" and the "Lord." Individual covens often use more specific deity names, such as Cernunnos and Ceridwen, or Arianrhod and Lugh. Often the Goddess is elevated in importance, just as the high priestess is elevated in relation to the high priest. Wiccan groups emphasize balance of the sexes and sometimes require the polarity of male and female ritual partners. Wiccans typically meet at the esbats (based on the cycle of the moon, usually at the full moon, but sometimes at the dark of the moon) and at sabbats (the eight seasonal festivals).

Feri (or Faery) Witchcraft is a denomination started by Victor and Cora Anderson in the United States in the 1950s or 1960s, with possible antecedents as early as the 1920s. It began as a mixture of South American folk magic, Kabbalah, Haitian Vodou, and a shamanic interpretation of Hawaiian Huna traditions. There are a number of branches in the Feri tradition, some of which have been more heavily influenced by Gardnerian and Alexandrian Wicca than others. Feri claims a non-Gardnerian origin through Victor Anderson's reported membership in a coven known as the Harpy coven in southern Oregon in the 1920s and 1930s. Anderson also often told a poetic story of his initiation in 1926 by a small African woman who told him he was a Witch.[24] He came upon her sitting nude in circle, surrounded by brass bowls of herbs. She initiated him through sex and told him the secrets of the tradition, and he then had a vision of the Horned God. Anderson indicates that he decided to start a coven many years later after reading Gardner's *Witchcraft Today*.[25] This would have been in the 1950s, according to Cora Anderson's memoir *Fifty Years in the Feri Tradition*, although Victor had initiated Cora by 1944, shortly after they were married.[26] Some of the later versions of the Feri tradition appear to have developed largely in conformity with Gardnerian Wicca, which some scholars suggest Anderson may have initially believed to be an authentic pagan survival, although Cora indicates that Victor thought

Gardner was wrong, even if he did the best he could. In the original branch of Feri, Hawaiian influences were more important than Gardnerian ones. Anderson spoke Hawaiian fluently, having learned the language as a child.[27] He connected the *menehune* of Hawaii with the Fairies of Western Europe, believing both to be a race of little people who spread out of Africa thousands of years ago.[28] Inspired by the Huna belief in three souls, and other religious traditions that support the idea of three souls, as well as Max Freedom Long's writings on the unconscious "Younger Self" and conscious "Talking Self," Feri Witchcraft supports the idea of a third soul, which is the sacred or "Deep Self."[29] This idea has been taken up by many in the Reclaiming tradition, through Starhawk, who studied with the Andersons and was initiated into the Feri tradition, which she, like many, refers to as the "Faery" tradition.

The New Reformed Orthodox Order of the Golden Dawn (NROOGD) is an eclectic denomination of Witchcraft that began in San Francisco, California, in 1967. It is a coven-based initiatory mystery tradition inspired by literary and anthropological sources, particularly Robert Graves' *The White Goddess*. Aiden Kelly is one of the major figures in NROOGD, and his criticisms of Gardner's claim to have been initiated into a preexisting group may be related to NROOGD's pride in being a modernly invented tradition. NROOGD first formed out of a course assignment on designing a ritual. A group of friends performed the ritual a few times, and they were surprised at how much they enjoyed their experience of raising power, so they formed a group in the late 1960s. Other prominent members in NROOGD are Don Frew and Diana Paxson.

NROOGD rituals emphasize poetry and artistry. They are designed to be beautiful and to bypass intellectual skepticism by appealing to the senses aesthetically. NROOGD rituals are often lead by three priestesses and a priest. Practitioners invoke the Goddess in triple form and perform chanting and dancing on the theme of Persephone's descent into, and return from, the underworld.[30] Their rituals often also include spell work and the sharing of food. Like other Witchcraft traditions, NROOGD has eight main festivals, but in place of the fall equinox celebration, they hold an annual ritual based on the ancient Greek Eleusinian mysteries.[31] Like other Pagan groups in the Bay Area of California, NROOGD regularly holds public sabbats in addition to private events within covens.

Dianic Witchcraft is a feminist, Goddess- and women-focused denomination. Some Dianics practice in a separatist fashion, excluding men and any sense of male deity, as in Z. Budapest's early practice. Some practitioners focus on the Goddess in a monotheistic manner as a single overarching deity, but Dianics are often polytheistic, drawing on a variety of goddess figures. Even when practitioners focus on Goddess in the singular, She is apt to be recognized in three forms: maiden, mother, and crone.

Practitioners also often recognize divinity as immanent in themselves, identifying with Artemis, for example, as the "virgin" huntress, who is virgin in the sense of being neither married nor a mother. Most Dianic groups are women's-only groups, and they often practice an eclectic form of Witchcraft in covens.

Reclaiming is also a feminist Witchcraft tradition but is egalitarian in focus, including both men and women. It is a nonhierarchical denomination, and groups within it run on consensus. Reclaiming is distinctive for its blend of politics and spirituality; its activities are oriented toward empowerment and emancipation. Reclaiming is anarchist, organized into largely autonomous cells, but members also practice in covens for ritual work. Initiation is available for those who choose to undertake it, but it is not required for participation. Reclaiming began as a teaching collective in San Francisco, California, offering courses in Witchcraft and Goddess spirituality. The Reclaiming Collective obtained tax-exempt status in 1990 after incorporating.[32] The Reclaiming tradition grew in the Bay Area, but also through intensive weeklong apprenticeship courses in the summer, which came to be known as "Witchcamps."

Reclaiming practitioners practice an eclectic ritual style, summarized as "EIEIO," which stands for ecstatic, improvisational, ensemble, inspired, and organic. In San Francisco, Reclaiming practitioners tend to use the Celtic deity names Brigit and Lugh for the Goddess and God, following the legacy of Starhawk's initiation into the Faery tradition, but the multicultural context of San Francisco also influences Reclaiming practitioners. They celebrate Samhain, for example, in conjunction with the Day of the Dead, through the influence of Mexican American traditions.[33] Reclaiming groups elsewhere are autonomous and take on a variety of different forms depending on the inclination of practitioners and their cultural contexts.

Family traditions, practitioners of which are sometimes called hereditary Witches, constitute a form of practice and a group of denominations. Family tradition groups are founded on the claim of a practitioner to have learned Witchcraft from a family member, stereotypically a grandmother, rather than from books or public groups. They often indicate that they have learned their practices from an oral tradition, and that this is why there are no written records supporting their claims. These traditions are often largely based on the practices of Gardnerian Wicca, but with further inspiration drawn from the culture of the practitioner's ethnic background, as in Leo Louis Martello and Lori Bruno's Italian American Witchcraft (Stregheria). Martello and Bruno formed the Trinacrian Rose Coven in the late 1970s based in part on a family folk-healing tradition. Z. Budapest draws on Hungarian folk traditions in her practice and has described herself as a hereditary Witch. According to some scholars, Victor and Cora Anderson's use of folk magic in the Feri tradition they founded locates the Feri tradition also as a family tradition.[34] The claims of family traditions and ancient mystical heritage have been dismissed by some as a coping mechanism for a lack of substance in such traditions, but embracing folk practices can also be a form of resistance against the leveling process of assimilation into American culture and the secular devaluation of folk traditions.[35]

While some denigrate practitioners such as Raven Grimassi (a pseudonym) for making questionable claims about family traditions, Grimassi's tradition of Italian Witchcraft can be viewed in terms of "folklore reclamation and ethnic identity creation."[36] His folklore-enhanced practices may be interpreted as a form of resistance to the melting pot of dominant American culture. Grimassi claims to have been initiated by his aunt into a family magical tradition of folk healing that included divination and techniques for removing the evil eye.[37] He claims that his Aridian tradition is a North American branch of Tanarra, a version of "the Old Religion" from central Italy, brought to the United States by his relatives. He describes it as a blend of Italian traditions aimed at restoring the Witchcraft tradition given by Aradia. Some scholars suggest that his tradition appears to be created out of Leland's *Aradia* and from generic Wicca, with Etruscan or Tuscan window dressing drawn from folklore, remarking that he does not name his sources, whether written, or his relatives.[38] It is possible that Grimassi's practice of Stregheria as *la Vecchia Religione*, "the Old Religion," is based on a family practice derived from Leland's *Aradia* in a previous generation, but its resemblance to Gardnerian Wicca suggests that the tradition is derived from Gardner's practices as much as from Italian sources. However, this is unlikely to be a problem for Italian American practitioners, especially if they are engaged in folklore reclamation and identity creation.

Reconstructionist Paganism is a form of practice, and a group of denominations, that reconstructs the practices of pre-Christian traditions. Reconstructionist traditions differ from family traditions in that they aim to reconstruct the ancient traditions of a place and culture, for example those of Etruria, rather than using the later folk traditions of Tuscany in a largely Wiccan context, as in Grimassi's tradition. Reconstructionists often explicitly stress that their practices are not derived from the traditions of Wicca, New Age spirituality, or ceremonial magic. Most reconstructionist traditions have a high regard for scholarly knowledge of their traditions, and emphasize historical accuracy in their practices. Practitioners study archaeology and ancient and classical texts, striving to stay current with academic research. They tend to idealize different eras of the past, depending on the time of Christianization in the location of the culture they are reconstructing. Practitioners do not necessarily live in the geographic areas associated with the traditions they are reconstructing. However, some do, and their traditions can be seen to some degree as indigenous movements.

Some Egyptian reconstructionist Pagans call their tradition Kemeticism, from "Kemet," referring to the land of Egypt. Practitioners regard the tradition as an African traditional religion, although most practitioners appear to be English-speaking white Americans. Some Kemetic practitioners focus on Ma'at (truth) and Netjer, understood as the single divine force that is manifested through a number of gods and goddesses. The Kemetic Orthodox tradition describes this interpretation of Netjer as "monolatry," as distinct from monotheism.[39] Some Kemeticists focus on the ancient Egyptian mythology of Isis, Osiris, and Horus. Kemetic practice includes priestly and personal devotions, often through elaborate group rituals, and daily prayer. Practitioners also engage in ancestral devotions, giving offerings so that the ancestors will protect them.

Greek reconstructionists, who refer to their tradition as Hellenismos or Hellenism, revere the Olympic pantheon of gods and goddesses. Votive offerings to the deities are important to their religious practice, as well as hospitality in relation to other humans. "Hellenismos" refers to the religion of ancient Greece that the Roman emperor Julian attempted to revive. Julian was a nephew of the emperor Constantine and became emperor himself in 361, but he was killed just a few years later.[40] The Julian Society, an American group founded in the late 1960s, is not exclusively Hellenist, but is instead a nondenominational Pagan group. Hellenion is an American group that practices Greek reconstructionist Paganism. They obtained tax-exempt status in 2002.[41] Hellenists in general take inspiration from ancient writings such as the Homeric hymns and other works attributed to Homer, as well as those of Hesiod and Julian. They also take inspiration from archaeology.

Reconstructionists of Roman paganism refer to their tradition as Religio-Romana, reviving the name of the pre-Christian religion of Rome. They reconstruct the religion as it was practiced from the founding of Rome in 753 BCE to the beginning of the Christian Roman Empire in 394 CE, but they also take inspiration from pre-Roman Latin and Etruscan culture.[42] Reconstructionist practitioners of Religio-Romana, following ancient practice, value piety, family, community, and the state. Practitioners honor ancestors, *lares* (gods of the gate and household), and *di penates* (gods of the hearth and granary), as well as god/desses such as Iuppiter and Iuno, more familiar to English speakers as Jupiter and Juno. They also revere others in the Roman pantheon such as Minerva, Vesta, Ceres, Diana, Venus, Mars, Mercurius, Neptunus, and Volcanus (the last three more familiar as Mercury, Neptune, and Vulcan), as well as Apollo.

Celtic reconstructionism is popular in Paganism throughout the English-speaking world in the form of Druidry or Druidism. Druidic practices re-

Figure 18.   Contemporary Druid (photo by Wendy Griffin)

construct Celtic culture based on archaeological information about the Celts in Britain and Western Europe, and scant written sources such as Tacitus' incidental comments on the Celts of Europe in *Germania*. Some Druidry is not Pagan; some, which Isaac Bonewits describes as "mesopagan," is monotheistic and is syncretic with Celtic Christianity. The ancient

Druids were a priestly class in Celtic culture made up of learned people who held the lore (stories and genealogies) of the people in their memories, and from whom political leaders were drawn. Roman incursions and Christianization eliminated the Druid class in Britain. A number of Druid groups formed in Britain beginning in the eighteenth and nineteenth centuries for various political and religious reasons. Most members at that time were Christian, but in the 1960s and 1970s, some Druid groups emerged as Pagan. Some Pagan Druids joined existing Druid groups, and others formed new orders.[43]

Druids tend somewhat to resemble the stereotype of bearded men in long white robes conducting ceremonies in oak groves and at Stonehenge. Contemporary Druids are not necessarily bearded, but there are more men than women in Druidry, and they do tend to wear white robes for rituals. They also tend to have a special fondness for trees, and oaks in particular, and have negotiated with Britain's English Heritage department to gain access to Stonehenge to celebrate the summer solstice. Druid groups are organized into groves and orders: groves are local groups, while orders tend to be national or international organizations. Traditionally, the orders are divided into bards, ovates, and druids. The bards are storytellers and poets, the ovates are prophets and seers, and the druids are priests and leaders. Both learning and performance are important in Druidry.

Norse and Germanic reconstructionist traditions are collectively called Heathenry, sometimes referred to as "the Northern Tradition," or "Asatru" based on the Icelandic word meaning dedicated to the Æsir, a group of deities. Heathenry is practiced as an indigenous revival tradition in Iceland, Germany, and the Scandinavian countries. Asatru has been an officially recognized religion in Iceland since 1973. More generally, Heathenry is inspired by northern European traditions, sometimes more so than it is reconstructed, but practitioners see themselves as reviving the indigenous traditions of northern Europe, or Anglo-Saxon and Teutonic culture. Practitioners are not restricted to northern Europe but are found throughout Europe, as well as in North American and Australia. Membership in Heathen groups is not generally restricted by ethnic origin, but some groups are overtly racist and do restrict membership in this way.

Technically, the Æsir are the deities of war, which would imply that the Asatru are dedicated to the deities of war. However, despite this etymology, practitioners of Asatru are not just dedicated to the deities of war, but also to Norse deities more generally, including the Vanir, who are the deities of the land.

Racism and ethnic identity are ongoing issues in Heathen groups, but most mainstream groups try to preserve a sense of openness and inclusivity and are against racist members joining. Heathen groups seem to have an overall tendency toward right-wing politics, expressing conservative views on sex, politics, and history.[44] Because of this, many Heathen groups take an explicitly antiracist stance, although in the United States, Heathen Groups called "Odinists" do not necessarily renounce racism, and some are overtly white supremacists. Such groups take inspiration from the perceived warrior mythos of the Viking era but are rooted in ideas from Nazi Germany. Asatru groups are more likely to look to Iceland for inspiration. Odinism in Britain, for example in Odinic Rite groups, is not associated with Nazism. Heathen groups began to form in England in the early 1970s and in North America in the late 1970s, and the racist/antiracist division originates in that formative period, continuing to be a problem in some groups.[45]

Local Heathen groups are called "kindreds" or "hearths," the structure and organization of which varies.[46] Local groups are most easily found through larger networking organizations such as the Ring of Troth, started by Edred Thorson in Texas, or Hrafnar, started by Diana Paxson in California, both of which are antiracist. The Ring of Troth also exists in Britain, in addition to Odinic Rite groups, and *Hammarens Orden Sällskap* is in Sweden. Some Heathens wear a hammer sign as a symbol of their religious affiliation, either to indicate their dedication to the god Thor or to Heathenry in general.[47]

Heathen groups share a common cosmology of nine worlds, linked through Yggdrasil, the world tree. Midgard, or "Middle Earth," is the realm of humans. There are also the realms of the frost giants, the fire giants, and other giants (Jotnir); that of the Æsir (gods of war) and the Vanir (gods of the land and fertility); and the land of the light elves, the dark elves (dwarves), and the dead. In addition to gods and goddesses, Heathens recognize a variety of other-than-human persons, including spirits of the land, called *landvættir*. "Wight" is a general term for other-than-human persons in Heathenry, indicating sentient beings including gods, local and ancestral spirits, and others.[48] Heathens are more emphatically polytheistic than Pagans in some other traditions, and they are more likely to insist on the ontological existence of the gods and goddesses as actual beings rather than as metaphors or psychological forms.[49]

The most significant Heathen celebrations are Winternights, Yule, and Sigrblot. Winternights is a harvest festival honoring the dead and the beginning of winter. Yule is the winter solstice, celebrated as the New Year, and is a time for oaths. Sigrblot, meaning "victory," is a celebration of the beginning of summer and may originally have been a ritual to ensure "victory" in the coming raiding season.[50] Heathens also hold ritual events called *blots* to exchange gifts with the gods and with ancestors. Contemporary Heathens generally substitute the blood offerings of traditional *blots* with offerings of mead.[51] As discussed in chapter 7, practices such as this and *seidr* are reconstructed based on historical texts, such as the Icelandic Eddas and Sagas.

The development of oracular *seidr* is attracting more women to the denomination, which was initially of interest mostly to male practitioners. Other magical practices of Heathenry include *galdr* and *taufr*. *Galdr* is the chanting of runes, to attune practitioners to the rune and bring them into resonance with it, and can be combined with *seidr*.[52] Heathens may, for example, chant runes to bring themselves into harmony to pursue the common purpose of setting the stage for one among them to go into the deeper trance necessary for *seidr*. Some practitioners describe this as the majority of those participating going as far as to the gate of the underworld, while the one engaging in *seidr* goes through the gate. *Taufr* refers to the practice of making talismans, usually by carving runes onto objects, a practice evident from archaeological remains as well as from stories and poems.

Pre-Christian folk traditions have also been revived in the Baltic countries of Eastern Europe. The revived folk traditions of Lithuania, Estonia, Latvia, and other Eastern European countries are most often practiced by people living in those countries, rather than in a multicultural diaspora context. Baltic reconstructionists tend to identify as Pagans through ethnicity rather than through adherence to other aspects of contemporary Paganism such as polytheism or reverence for nature. The history of these reconstructionist groups includes racism in celebration of ethnicity, but contemporary groups do not practice ethnic exclusivity. In practice, participation is generally restricted to those who know the relevant languages. Music is important in Baltic reconstructionist Paganism, with folk songs—*dainas* in Latvia, and *dainos* in Lithuania—serving as resources for ritual.[53]

Romuva is a reconstructionist group that began at the end of the nineteenth century in Lithuania, with Vyduna (Wilhelm Storosta) reviving folk celebrations in combination with theosophy. This group continued into the 1920s but was halted by the Soviet invasion of Lithuania.[54] It was revived again in the 1960s as a folklore group, which engaged in the collection of folk songs and dances and the re-creation of old festivals, under the name Ramuva. Despite the name change and the ostensible cultural rather than religious focus, it was disbanded again by the Soviets in 1971, only to reemerge during perestroika in 1988. It is now led by Jonas Trikunas, who has been involved with the group since the late 1960s. It became Romuva again in 1991, reviving the earlier name and connection with pre-Christian religion rather than just folklore.[55] Ethnicity and national heritage are important to Romuva members, but also harmony with and respect for nature. Not all members identify as Pagan, but many do.

In Latvia, the group Dievturi practices reconstructionist Baltic Paganism. "Dievturi" refers to "those who hold by the god Dievs," a high god of the sky. Practitioners also recognize Laima, the goddess of fate, and Mara, the goddess of material well-being, but they tend to regard them as helpers of Dievs. Dievturi was founded in 1926 by Ernest Brastins, who was executed by the Soviets in the 1940s. Some members were exiled to the United States during the Soviet persecutions, and they later returned to Latvia. The tradition gradually reemerged with the erosion of Soviet control in late 1980s. Janis Silins and Olger Auns currently lead the group. Under their leadership, Dievturi is not anti-Semitic, but Brastins was, and in his time Dievturi was closely linked with Fascist groups in Latvia such as *Perkunkrusts*, meaning "Thunder Cross."[56] Dievturi's practices are based on *dainas*, or folksongs that give detailed descriptions of ancient beliefs and customs, and which were developed specifically for solstice and equinox rituals.[57]

Pagans in Ukraine prefer to call themselves *yazychnyks* or *ridnovirs*, and their religion *yazychnytstvo* or *ridnovira. Yazychnytstvo* has no exact translation but refers to pre-Christian Slavic and revived Slavic traditions, while *ridnovirs* are practitioners of "native faith." Pagans in Ukraine and elsewhere in Eastern Europe differ from Pagans in English-speaking countries in their preference for thinking of their religion in ethic terms as indigenous religion, and in their treatment of texts such as the *Book of Veles* and Lev Sylenko's *Maha Vira* as scripture. In addition, some Ukrainian Pagan groups, such as RUNVira, which began in the 1960s, are more monotheistic than polytheistic, and are led primarily by men. "RUNVira" is an acronym for *Ridna Ukraïns'ka Natsional'na Vira*, meaning "Native Ukrainian National Faith." Pravoslavia is another Pagan group in Ukraine, whose name refers to "right worship," in contrast to the "right practice" of orthodoxy in Christianity. Pravoslavia was founded in 1993 by Volodymyr Shaian, and it takes the *Book of Veles* as scripture. In contrast to most Pagans in English-speaking countries, Pagans in Ukraine tend to support right-wing politics and ethnic nationalism, sometimes with overt anti-Semitism.[58]

Pagans may joke "that Paganism is now a 'real religion' like other divided and divisive religions,"[59] but Pagan denominations do not often come into conflict over doctrinal issues. Practitioners sometimes come into conflict when they think an individual or group is trying to speak for all Pagans and they feel misrepresented. Other conflicts can arise when practitioners feel that others are judging their religious practices to be inauthentic based on criteria that they do not feel are appropriate. However,

Pagans hold it as an ideal that they are content to let others believe whatever they want and approach divinity however they feel is appropriate.

FURTHER READING

Adler, Margot. *Drawing Down the Moon: Witches, Druids, Goddess-Worshippers, and Other Pagans in America Today*. Revised and expanded ed. Boston: Beacon Press, 1986.
Harvey, Graham. *Contemporary Paganism: Listening People, Speaking Earth*. New York: New York University Press, 1997.

NOTES

1. Margot Adler, *Drawing Down the Moon: Witches, Druids, Goddess-Worshippers, and Other Pagans in America Today* (Boston: Beacon Press, 1986), 287–288, 293.
2. Helen Berger, Evan A. Leach, and Leigh S. Shaffer, *Voices from the Pagan Census: A National Survey of Witches and Neo-Pagans in the United States* (Columbia: University of South Carolina Press, 2003), 238.
3. See Chas S. Clifton and Graham Harvey, *The Paganism Reader* (New York: Routledge, 2004), 273.
4. Shelly Rabinovitch and James Lewis, *Encyclopedia of Modern Witchcraft and Neo-Paganism* (New York: Citadel, 2002), 305.
5. Helen Berger, *A Community of Witches* (Columbia: University of South Carolina Press, 1999), 50, reports that 50.4 percent of practitioners are solitaries.
6. Berger, Leach, and Shaffer, *Voices from the Pagan Census*, 118–21.
7. Rabinovitch and Lewis, *Encyclopedia of Modern Witchcraft and Neo-Paganism*, 252.
8. Berger, *Community of Witches*, 51.
9. Berger, Leach, and Shaffer, *Voices from the Pagan Census*, 230.
10. Rabinovitch and Lewis, *Encyclopedia of Modern Witchcraft and Neo-Paganism*, 97, 100.
11. Rabinovitch and Lewis, *Encyclopedia of Modern Witchcraft and Neo-Paganism*, 97.
12. Graham Harvey, *Shamanism: A Reader* (London: Routledge, 2003), 5–6.
13. Rabinovitch and Lewis, *Encyclopedia of Modern Witchcraft and Neo-Paganism*, 250.
14. See Michael Harner, *The Way of the Shaman* (New York: HarperSanFrancisco, 1990).
15. Rabinovitch and Lewis, *Encyclopedia of Modern Witchcraft and Neo-Paganism*, 186.
16. Graham Harvey, *Contemporary Paganism: Listening People, Speaking Earth* (New York: New York University Press, 1997), 110.
17. See Robert J. Wallis, *Shamans/Neo-Shamans: Ecstasy, Alternative Archaeologies and Contemporary Pagans*. London: Routledge, 2003.
18. Rabinovitch and Lewis, *Encyclopedia of Modern Witchcraft and Neo-Paganism*, 177.
19. Douglas Ezzy, "New Age Witchcraft? Popular Spell Books and the Re-enchantment of Everyday Life," *Culture and Religion* 4 (2003): 49.
20. For examples of those who conflate Witchcraft and the New Age movement, see Tanya M. Luhrmann, *Persuasions of the Witch's Craft* (Cambridge, MA: Harvard University Press, 1989), 30; Wouter J. Hanegraaff, *New Age Religion and Western Culture* (Leiden: Brill, 1996), 79. For discussion of the issue, see Ezzy, "New Age Witchcraft?" 50.
21. Rabinovitch and Lewis, *Encyclopedia of Modern Witchcraft and Neo-Paganism*, 176.
22. See Berger, *Community of Witches*, 10, 51.
23. Rabinovitch and Lewis, *Encyclopedia of Modern Witchcraft and Neo-Paganism*, 6.

24. Cora Anderson, personal communication, August, 23 2005.

25. Margot Adler, *Drawing Down the Moon: Witches, Druids, Goddess-Worshippers, and Other Pagans in America Today,* revised and expanded ed. (Boston: Beacon Press, 1986), 78–79.

26. Cora Anderson, personal communication, August 23, 2005.

27. Cora Anderson, personal communication, August 23, 2005.

28. Chas S. Clifton, *Her Hidden Children* (Lanham, MD: AltaMira, 2006), 130.

29. Sabina Magliocco, *Witching Culture: Folklore and Neo-Paganism in America* (Philadelphia: University of Pennsylvania Press, 2004), 178.

30. Magliocco, *Witching Culture,* 83.

31. Rabinovitch and Lewis, *Encyclopedia of Modern Witchcraft and Neo-Paganism,* 188–89.

32. Rabinovitch and Lewis, *Encyclopedia of Modern Witchcraft and Neo-Paganism,* 219–20.

33. Magliocco, *Witching Culture,* 226.

34. Magliocco, *Witching Culture,* 70.

35. Magliocco, *Witching Culture,* 214.

36. Magliocco, *Witching Culture,* 214.

37. Magliocco, *Witching Culture,* 213.

38. Clifton, *Her Hidden Children,* 125.

39. House of Netjer, "What Is Kemetic Orthodoxy?" Kemetic Orthodoxy website, July 8, 2001, www.kemet.org/kemexp1.html (accessed August 16, 2004).

40. Clifton and Harvey, *Paganism Reader,* 22.

41. Epistates, Hellenion website, 2004, www.hellenion.org (accessed August 16, 2004).

42. *Nova Roma,* "Declaratio Religionis Romanae," *Nova Roma,* 2004, www.novaroma.org/religio_romana/declaration_religio.html (accessed August 16, 2004).

43. Graham Harvey, *Contemporary Paganism: Listening People, Speaking Earth* (New York: New York University Press, 1997), 18–19.

44. Harvey, *Contemporary Paganism,* 65.

45. Jeffrey Kaplan, "The Reconstruction of the Ásatrú and Odinist Traditions," *Magical Religion and Modern Witchcraft,* ed. James R. Lewis (Albany: State University of New York Press, 1996), 200.

46. Rabinovitch and Lewis, *Encyclopedia of Modern Witchcraft and Neo-Paganism,* 127.

47. Harvey, *Contemporary Paganism,* 58–59.

48. Rabinovitch and Lewis, *Encyclopedia of Modern Witchcraft and Neo-Paganism,* 126.

49. Harvey, *Contemporary Paganism,* 67–68.

50. Harvey, *Contemporary Paganism,* 58.

51. Rabinovitch and Lewis, *Encyclopedia of Modern Witchcraft and Neo-Paganism,* 127.

52. Harvey, *Contemporary Paganism,* 61–62.

53. See Michael Strmiska, "The Music of the Past in Modern Baltic Paganism," *Nova Religio: The Journal of Alternative and Emergent Religions* 8 (2005).

54. Rabinovitch and Lewis, *Encyclopedia of Modern Witchcraft and Neo-Paganism,* 180–81.

55. Strmiska, "Music of the Past."

56. Strmiska, "Music of the Past."

57. Rabinovitch and Lewis, *Encyclopedia of Modern Witchcraft and Neo-Paganism,* 182.

58. Adrian Ivakhiv, "In Search of Deeper Identities: Neopaganism and Native Faith in Contemporary Ukraine," *Nova Religio* 8 (2005).

59. Blain, Jenny, Douglas Ezzy, and Graham Harvey. *Researching Paganisms: Religious Experiences and Academic Methodologies* (Walnut Creek, CA: AltaMira Press, 2004), 245.

9

Ethics and Politics

Applying different methods of study to Paganism yields various perspectives on the ethics and politics of the religion and its practitioners. Studying popular spell books and articles in Pagan magazines reveals different concerns than in studying book-length works written by practitioners who approach Paganism with an awareness of scholarly writings on its history, politics, and ethics. Still more perspectives appear from the study of Pagan practitioners through Internet forums, face-to-face interviews, and sociological studies conducted through the use of surveys. One gets a different sense of the popularity of and commitment to certain ethical perspectives such as feminism, environmentalism, and cultural appropriation when one looks at what Pagans say and do in different contexts and forums. Consequently, interdisciplinary study is necessary to gain a nuanced understanding of ethics and politics in Paganism. The study of writings alone will not necessarily give a sense of the politics embedded in the daily lives of Pagans, and the study of Pagan practices will not necessarily yield a sense of Pagan ideals.

Pagan ethics are often critical of mainstream culture, so what Pagans say about ethics often has an active political component. However, ethics also tend to be embedded in Pagans' daily lives, expressed through attitudes toward, and actions in relation to, sexuality, environmental issues, and social justice, more than articulated in rule-based ethics. Pagans have developed formal ethics in the context of magic use and have begun to develop a discourse on environmental ethics. Feminist ethics are often implicit and are thus more evident in actions than in words, while cultural appropriation is a more contentious issue. All political orientations are represented in the Pagan population, but activist and radical stances tend to be more visible than conservative perspectives.

Pagans value experience more than belief or the articulation of it, so Pagans do not tend to produce formal ethics as written arguments. They often prefer to express their ethics through living example, and they tend to be uncomfortable with anything that might be construed as preaching or telling others what to do or what is right. Starhawk, for example, suggests that ethics, as a set of rules and laws, become necessary only when ultimate meaning is projected outside the natural world. Moral integrity, she feels, results from listening to immanent divinity and taking responsibility for oneself.[1] Pagans tend to reject the idea of applying universal principles of ethics, preferring situational ethics that are responsive to contexts, and they often emphasize personal responsibility and the importance of thinking about the consequences of one's actions. More Pagan writings on ethics are appearing as the religion matures, although magical ethics still predominate, as in the recent book on ethics by Shelly Rabinovitch and Meredith MacDonald, *An Ye Harm None: Magical Morality and Modern Ethics*.

The ethic of "do what you will, save you harm none," sometimes called the Wiccan Rede (or "counsel"), is a common ethical principle in contemporary Paganism, particularly among Wiccans and other Witches. As previously noted, it is similar to Aleister Crowley's statement "Do what thou wilt shall be the whole of the law," with the added injunction of harming none. Gerald Gardner may have derived the Rede in part from the Jain idea of *ahimsa*, or nonharming. He appears to have taken the term "sky clad" from the Jains, from his study of them in India. There is a sect of Jains, called the Digambaras, which means "sky clad," who renounce clothing.[2]

Pagans usually understand the Rede as an ethic for magic, as a restriction on what one should do in the context of casting spells. Because magic works through the logic that everything is interconnected, spells and rituals can have unexpected results, and Pagans teach that magical practitioners need to accept responsibility for their actions, including any unintended consequences. Ursula Le Guin's series of Earthsea novels illustrates the ethics of magic use, and is often recommended as a teaching tool. In *A Wizard of Earthsea*, the protagonist, out of pride in response to the taunting of a schoolmate, casts a spell to summon the spirit of a dead woman and accidentally looses a malevolent entity that haunts him for many years.

Pagans often associate the idea of threefold return with the Rede, which indicates that what you do comes back to you threefold. In this, they are influenced by the idea of karma, understood as the "law of returns," although Pagans usually expect the return to occur sooner than the next incarnation. For at least some Pagans, it is consequence that produces the threefold return, not judgment by a deity. Starhawk makes this explicit in her writing,[3] but for others, judgment might be perceived to come from a deity. Some Pagans suggest that consequences to the next seven generations should be considered, an idea derived from Native American traditions.

The adoption of ideas and ritual practices from Native American and other indigenous traditions has lead to accusations of cultural appropriation. Cultural appropriation refers to the borrowing, use, or appropriation of cultural traditions outside of one's ethnic background. Critics of such uses of cultural traditions see it as cultural theft and part of the continuing legacy of colonization. Given that most practitioners of Paganism are eclectic, blending different cultural elements, appropriation is an important issue for the religion. It is probably most problematic in terms of the appropriation of indigenous traditions, but some Gardnerians complain that other Pagan traditions appropriate from their traditions. However, Raven Grimassi says that he developed Stregheria, Italian American Witchcraft, in response to Celtic practitioners who faulted him for the cultural imperialism of his Roman ancestors.[4] Irish practitioners sometimes express anger at the appropriation of Celtic traditions by North American Pagans.

Accusations of cultural appropriation are most familiar in terms of the use of Native American traditions by outsiders. Such practitioners are disparagingly referred to as the "Wannabee Tribe," meaning those who want to be Native American—white people playing at or pretending to be "Indians." This includes "Indian" hobbyists in Europe, and Bear Tribe members in North America, as well as some Pagan and neo-shamanic practitioners. Most Bear Tribe members are white, and the current leader, Wabun Wind, has been referred to as a "whiteshaman." Whiteshamans use a pastiche of "Indian" garb and ritual items, presenting themselves as "real Indians" in contrast to actual Native American persons. Another example familiar to many Pagans is the popular writer Lynn Andrews, who claims to be have been taught by a Native American woman in her book *Medicine Woman* and others, while the tradition she describes is made up of a variety of indigenous practices and beliefs. One might be tempted to think of these practitioners as "jelly donuts": flaky white on the outside, with artificial red flavoring on the inside, in terms opposite to the labeling of assimilated Native Americans as "apples" (meaning red on the outside and white on the inside).

Not all Pagans are aware of issues of appropriation, but many feel conflicted about it. Some of their defenses against accusations of cultural appropriation are emotionally charged because of their conflicted feelings.[5] They are defensive because they feel threatened by having their practices exposed to challenges of inauthenticity. Politically sensitive Pagans have a general sense that practitioners need to seek permission, develop reciprocal relationships, and seek deep rather than superficial knowledge of cultural traditions in borrowing. Some feel that blending is not advisable, while other Pagans are unaware of, or unconcerned with, issues of appropriation.

Some practitioners say that if they find the idioms of other cultures "meaningful and compelling," then their use of such idioms is appropriate.[6] Scott Cunningham, for example, says, "If you feel particularly attracted to other sacred calendars, feel free to adapt them. . . . So long as the rituals are fulfilling and effective, why worry?"[7] Other practitioners are more defensive, such as A. Lizard, who said in an Internet discussion forum, "Use your dream catchers in good health. There are plenty of native Americans using 486 based PCs made in Taiwan right now, and the fact that the i486 chip or a Taiwan assembly plant largely come from non-Native American cultural origins doesn't affect their usefulness to their Native American user base in the least. A tool is a tool is a tool. The question isn't who invented it, it is DOES IT WORK FOR YOU???"[8] Looking at who benefits in each of these cases is useful. Where ritual activities and accoutrements come from matters. Would there not be something offensive about using a crucifix to turn one's compost, even if one regards it as a sacred task?

The sense that it is okay to appropriate the traditions of others to serve one's own needs seems to be a specifically Western idea, based on a conception of knowledge as unrelated to cultural context rather than embodied, encoded, and taught through particular ethical relationships and in specific places. As an outgrowth Western culture, Pagans do emphasize the needs of the self in their defenses of cultural borrowing.[9] Some practitioners suggest that borrowing is a universal practice in religion, as new religions form through syncretism, but this defense can "effectively silence critical voices of those cultures they themselves claim to honor."[10]

Some practitioners have come into dialogue with Native Americans on the issue of Pagan appropriation of Native American traditions. At the 1993 Parliament of World Religions in Chicago, Lakota elders criticized Paganism, among other traditions, for appropriation of "practices of worshipping in circle, invoking the four directions, and purifying with burning incense as imitation of their own practices." Representatives of the Covenant of the Goddess argued that the origins of these practices within Paganism are in European magical traditions, which the elders at the conference accepted. However, Pagans do borrow other aspects of Native American traditions, and Native Americans continue to criticize.[11] Practitioners in New Zealand borrow elements of non-Western traditions, especially from Native American traditions. They use drumming for trance journeys, they employ the practice of acquiring "power animals," and they use smudging for purification.[12] Indigenous scholars have been particularly critical of lucrative New Age uses of Native American traditions of sweat lodges, pipe ceremonies, and medicine wheels.[13]

To be fair, the Pagan adoption of indigenous traditions and the intermixing of other cultural traditions is not necessarily motivated by profit and consumerism, but more often by aesthetics and pragmatism. Pagans are inspired by an eclectic assortment of traditions, and they mix them in their rituals to create beautiful rituals that work. However, Pagans also use cultural traditions outside their own ethnicity because they often see these "other" traditions as spiritually more authentic than mainstream culture. Those who borrow do so because they want to integrate seemingly more authentic traditions into a privileged new culture. However, there is a contradiction between wanting those cultures to be unchanging and pure, fitting their image of ancient indigenous traditions, but also insisting on the flexibility and adaptability of those traditions in their own practices.[14] People are attracted to Native American traditions by their perception of these cultures' respect for nature and their sense of interconnectedness of all things, and the presentation of Native American traditions as a panacea for environmental destruction and other problems in modern culture.[15] Some practitioners continue to see indigenous cultures as repositories of spiritual knowledge lost to Western culture.[16] The problem with such romantic views of indigenous traditions is that they are fed by a desire to escape accountability for racism, genocide, and contemporary problems of substance abuse and sterilization abuse. Romantic appropriators render contemporary indigenous struggles for justice invisible.[17]

Some practitioners suggest that it can be problematic to argue that religion should be ethnically based. While it is easy to sympathize with arguments of Native Americans against cultural appropriation, it becomes less so when Heathens and practitioners of Eastern European Paganisms insist on an ethnic basis for their religious practices. Such Pagan practitioners are immediately presented as racist if they try to restrict their indigenous traditions to those of their own ethnicity. The difference of power in these situations is important, and it should be noted that the balance of power can change over time. Arguments against appropriation present ethnicities as natural, essential, stable categories, but ethnicity is socially constructed. Ethnic and cultural differences are real, but not absolute, and the biological basis of race is questionable.[18]

Pagans are generally described as "white," but they often do not identify as white, citing a variety of European ethnicities in their background.[19] It is not just the culture of the populations of North America, Australia, Brazil, and other places colonized by Europe that are multicultural, but often the individuals themselves. Pagans often describe themselves as "mutts," and Pagan groups, particularly in larger cities, can involve a mix of cultural backgrounds. Is it still appropriation if half the members are of Irish descent, or if two of them are African or Native American? Some Pagans argue that "gods do not respect cultural boundaries," as Gus diZerega says of his experience with **Umbanda**.[20] He does not mix Umbanda and Witchcraft, but he feels called to practice both. Others suggest that because of reincarnation, the ethnicity of one's current incarnation is not all important.[21] Groups like Reclaiming have been accused of cultural appropriation when they have tried to include elements from a variety of cultural backgrounds in efforts to be inclusive, leading to the suggestion that "when it comes to the thorny issues of multiculturalism and respect for other cultural traditions, it seems at times that Witchcraft cannot win for trying."[22]

Respectful participation may be possible when white people develop relationships with Native American communities (rather than individuals) and work in solidarity with Native American groups on social justice issues.[23] Starhawk indicates that borrowing entails responsibility "to participate in the very real struggles being waged for liberation, land, and cultural survival."[24] She suggests that practicing Paganism, as revived European traditions, should obviate the desire to participate in "Wannabee" activities.[25] However, "it cannot be said that the movement

Figure 19.   **North Altar with multicultural elements, Samhain Spiral Dance celebration of the Reclaiming community in San Francisco (photo by M. Macha Nightmare)**

as a whole mobilizes for such causes. . . . Whatever Starhawk says, one senses a mix of romantic nostalgia for the primitive or exotic with cultural ignorance or naivety when Pagans and witches proclaim the potency of, for example, their power animal or dream-catcher."[26] Some practitioners take on a strategy of identifying themselves with Native American critics and distancing themselves from New Agers,[27] seeming to project unethical borrowing practices onto New Age practitioners while defending their own practices.

Appropriation is an unresolved issue in Paganism, especially in relation to identity issues for people of mixed heritage, but also in colonized areas where practitioners engage in practices related to the bioregional idea of rooting in place as an environmentalist strategy. For Pagans who practice their religion as nature religion, it can be important to honor the spirits of the land. Pagans sometimes seek to know these spirits through contact with indigenous sources, whether through individuals, communities, and/or anthropological sources. Borrowing from indigenous traditions is culturally sensitive in New Zealand. Practitioners respect Maori cultural knowledge and spirituality but do not generally try to incorporate it into their practices to any great degree, unlike aspects of Native American spirituality they have adopted. Pagans may, for example, acknowledge and honor local deities and/or local tribes at the beginning of outdoor rituals.[28]

Feminist ethics are more integrated into Pagan practice than ethical sensibility regarding cultural appropriation. The vast majority of American Pagans support gender equity, with 88.1 percent in favor of passing an amendment to enshrine equal rights in the American constitution. Slightly more female than male practitioners support this initiative, but male Pagans are much more likely to support the amendment than the general American public.[29] In Pagan writings and practice, adherence to feminism is often assumed. The Goddess is given priority over male divinity, and priestesses are given priority over priests in Wicca, generally as a compensation for the pervasive patriarchy in mainstream monotheistic traditions. The elevation of the Goddess to the exclusion of the God and men was more pronounced early in the second wave of feminism, although it continues in some women's-only circles. The exclusion of men was explicit in Z. Budapest's *Holy Book of Women's Mysteries*, a manifesto of spiritual politics and radical separatist feminism. Budapest's 1979 book states, "We are committed to winning, to surviving, to struggling against patriarchal oppression," and "we are opposed to teaching our magic and our craft to men until the equality of the sexes is a reality."[30] In the 1989 edition of the book, Budapest adds, "We teach 'Pan' workshops today and work together with men who have changed themselves into brothers."[31]

The equality of the sexes is implicit in Cunningham's *Wicca: A Guide for the Solitary Practitioner*. Complementary of the sexes is often assumed as part of the polarity of male and female in Wicca, but the implementation of the equality of the sexes in practice came to Gardnerian Wicca largely from the United States. Doreen Valiente relates coming to feminist consciousness through reading Starhawk and others.[32] Many attribute the widespread feminist awareness in Paganism to the influence of the sense of empowerment and emancipatory politics of feminist spirituality and Goddess religion in Starhawk's work. The emphasis on the Goddess, and the mass of Paganism books written by women or focused on women's relationship to the Goddess, has more recently led to books aimed at male practitioners, such as *When I See the Wild God*, written by a woman, Ly de Angeles, and other works written by and for men, such as A. J. Drew's *Wicca for Men*.

Practitioners and scholars tend to assume that Paganism, as nature religion, is associated with environmentalism. Pagans are much more likely to support further government spending for environmental protection than the general American population: 92 percent of Pagans versus 55.7 percent of the general American population.[33] There is less agreement about other aspects of how environmental ethics should be practiced, and for some practitioners, environmentalism is not important, even for those who see nature as sacred.

Pagans often espouse the idea that environmental ethics consist in following nature or acting in harmony with nature, an idea that is also common in general writings about environmentalism. Some Pagans, such as Starhawk, feel that ethical action is inspired by the Goddess as incarnated in the living cosmos, or as nature personified. Druids might say that ethical action as action inspired by Awen, the life force of nature. However, nature is not just the "greenwood" where everyone gets along and no one gets eaten. Scientifically minded ecologists indicate that nature is not necessarily harmonious but is unpredictable, even chaotic. According to postmodern thought, the meaning of "nature" is not transparent, and it is necessary to consider with whose idea of nature one should try to be in harmony.[34] Some practitioners see nature as Gaia in James Lovelock's sense of a self-regulating system that, although it preserves life, expresses no favoritism in terms of supporting human life. Some see nature as mother earth, but others express concern that this may have undesirable implications for what women are supposed to be like if they are "natural." Others regard nature in terms of the sublime, something to respect and admire, or even fear, as something more powerful than humans. Less commonly in Paganism, some see nature as fragile and in need of human protection or stewardship. Some Pagans, in common with environmentalists, see nature as something that needs to be preserved apart from humans, sometimes as something pure and pristine, as if we have fallen from a natural state, and natural areas need to be protected from certain kinds of people (sometimes the urban poor, or local poor). Nature is not simply identifiable as something to follow; peoples' ideas of nature and divinity influence how they are inspired to ethical action.

However, to say that all ideas of nature are interpretive need not deny the reality of practitioners' religious experiences of inspiration of ethical action, such as having knowledge or understanding that comes from Awen, or Adrian Harris' argument for somatic knowledge of ecology. Harris, a Wiccan and a founding member of the British Dragon Environmental Group, suggests that Paganism may have a unique role in ecology, providing a revolution in making sense of reality by putting people back in touch with their bodies and the Earth. He argues that somatic (or embodied) knowledge of nature and the body as part of nature can teach people "that all things are ultimately one." He understands somatic knowledge as that which is felt in "good sex" and in "powerful ritual."[35] It is not cerebral knowledge but gut feeling, the result of direct experience. Because it is experienced in the body rather through the intellect, it does not yield a set of ethical principles or program of action. Nonetheless, it motivates environmental actions like the campaigns to save Salisbury Hill and Twyford Down from road building. (The Twyford Down protest was to save three sites, a national park, greenbelt land, and protected land. Despite massive protest, the road was built, to cut twelve minutes of commuter time.) Harris feels that direct experience through participation in ritual can lead to empowerment, which can then result in action toward radical social change.[36]

Written expressions of environmental ethics in contemporary Paganism can also be found in the work of Starhawk and Carol Christ. For Starhawk, environmental awareness is inherent to the practice of Witchcraft. She sees her spirituality as an earth-based tradition, and not only one that is celebratory of nature, but that is also a force for instigating communal change. She suggests that the Pagan recognition that humans live interdependently in community with other animals, plants, and other entities should inspire the desire for social change.[37] Although her sense of ethics is more often implied in her strategies than explicitly stated, she does indicate that true vision inspires political action. For Starhawk, the Goddess is not only a symbol, but a living being who "makes demands on us."[38] She recommends "picking up the garbage that you find in your path," metaphorically and literally, as "an ethical guide for a modern age."[39]

Carol Christ provides more of a theoretical foundation for ethics in Goddess religion in her systematic thealogy, *Rebirth of the Goddess*. Goddess-focused practitioners of Paganism take inspiration from the writings of Christ, but it is unclear to what extent she identifies herself as Pagan. Christ explains how the immanence of the Goddess in humans and the rest of the natural world undergirds a natural sense of ethical relations.

Humans who are in touch with being embodied experience empathy in their relations with others, including nonhumans, and are aware of their dependence on the Earth and of the total interdependence of the web of life. The symbol of the Goddess, through ritual, Christ argues, brings environmental values to consciousness. Rather than lacking a principle of justice, as some critics have claimed,[40] the immanence of the Goddess in nature inspires ethical action. Ethics does not require a basis in transcendence, Christ argues, if nature is "intelligent and loving" rather than "brutal and blind."[41] While cautioning that ethics are necessarily context dependent, she provides a list of principles for Goddess religion:

- Nurture life.
- Walk in love and beauty.
- Trust the knowledge that comes through the body.
- Speak the truth about conflict, pain, and suffering.
- Take only what you need.
- Think about the consequences of your actions for seven generations.
- Approach the taking of life with great restraint.
- Practice great generosity.
- Repair the web.[42]

Although Christ's systematic thealogy is a rare example of highly articulated ethics in Paganism, feminist and environmentalist values are commonly expressed in Paganism through things like their positive attitudes toward the body, sexuality, and nature, and their respect for people who choose to live different lifestyles. Many Pagans describe what they do as a "way of life" rather than a religion.[43] Daily life for Pagans is not mundane or profane as opposed to some more spiritual concern. Pagans integrate spirituality into their daily lives in their work and in their leisure, but this can be a source of tension for Pagans who feel that their jobs entail complicity in systems that go against "nature." Some Pagans undergo a sort of compartmentalization when the ethics of their religious practice are in conflict with their job requirements. Some Pagans are pacifists, but there are Pagans in the military.[44] Other Pagans feel torn between the desire to opt out of Western civilization and the responsibility to engage with it in protest. Pagans' attitudes about conformism and blending into mainstream culture are diverse. Some fear persecution or ridicule, while others feel a need to set themselves apart.

The ethics of the daily practices of conservative Pagans are largely invisible because they blend into the mainstream. Other ethics of daily life embedded in Pagans' lives are visible in their practices around food and their appreciation of the body and sexuality. Some Pagans express their religious values through growing and harvesting their own food. Gardening makes them aware of, and appreciative of, natural cycles, including rain and cold periods of dormancy. Some practitioners see hunting as a sacred task, while others are vegetarian. Pagans generally see sexual expression as natural rather than sinful, and they tend to value all body types, young and old, because of the immanence of divinity in all bodies. Many Pagans also exhibit a preference for natural methods and products, including herbalism and other naturopathic medicine, such as therapeutic massage. Some Pagans leave offerings to landwights and household deities, whether in the city or in rural areas, as a reminder of their dependence on the Earth for food, air, and water. According to some Pagans, their spirituality has made it impossible for them to litter, or not to recycle and compost.

Reverence for nature can inspire political awareness and action integrated into daily life. Some recent work in environmental philosophy points to everyday life for environmental solutions, suggesting that individual complicity in the system of industrial society—the cars we drive, the food we buy, our participation in overconsumption—should be a point of political action. However, others argue that the system does not end by individual action: "picking up litter beside a power station, a chemical factory, a quarry or a motorway is as valuable as putting an Elastoplast on a severed arm."[45] Pagans integrate their politics of everyday life with emancipatory politics.

Pagans are active participants in mainstream politics through voting, but they are skeptical about the integrity of existing social institutions,[46] so they also participate in activities such as political protests and letter-writing campaigns. While Pagan identification with environmental activism increased between 1977 and 1986, it still constituted only a segment of the Pagan movement as a whole. In that period, only about a quarter of Pagans felt that Paganism in general was political.[47] Pagans' self-identification as apolitical may have had more to do with their distrust of mainstream political institutions than their actual levels of political activity through other channels. According to more recent research, the vast majority of Pagans vote, albeit more enthusiastically at the national level than in state or local elections. In addition, about half of all Pagans engage in letter-writing campaigns, about a quarter participate in some sort of local grassroots political activity, and almost half participate in political demonstrations.[48] Social protest may not be a majority position within Paganism, but activism is highly visible amongst practitioners.

Pagans exhibit a wide variety of political orientations.[49] Pagan reverence for nature does not necessarily translate into political action in defense of nature. Celebrating "nature" does not necessarily lead to environmental awareness. One scholar practitioner, for example, reports that at a full-moon trip to Avebury one winter, she found "a collection of ritual litter, primarily candles and wax, that indicated that whatever was foremost in the minds of those who had performed their rituals around specific stones of this great circle the night before, it was not environmental care—at least not in any way that envisaged practitioners' own actions as potentially causing problems."[50] Ribbons, bits of string, and other small offerings might be inoffensive votive offerings for some Pagans, but when left behind, they can become eyesores for others. Despite widespread expressions of reverence for the Earth, researchers have found "a deep split between Pagans whose commitment to ecological principles was strong and practical, and those whose commitment was limited to a religious vision."[51]

Women practitioners are slightly more politically active than male practitioners overall, but they are significantly more likely than males to take part in demonstrations. Pagans in general are much more likely to participate in such events than the general American population.[52] While women are more politically active than male practitioners, especially through their participation in **ecofeminism**, practitioners of the Church of All Worlds and Feraferia also tend to be politically active.[53] Some research indicates that practitioners of women's spirituality may be the most radical Pagans, and that those practicing traditions emerging from British initiatory witchcraft are the least politically active,[54] but it appears that the influence of British initiatory traditions in North America may be more conservative than the development of those same traditions in the United Kingdom. While Gardnerian and Alexandrian groups may be less politically active than eclectic groups in North America, some groups in the United Kingdom, such as the Dragon Environmental Group, are more politically active than many North American groups. In addition, Gardnerians note that the original New Forest coven engaged in political action, conducting a ritual to repel the Nazi invasion of Britain during the Second World War, although some academics suggest that this story may be apocryphal.[55]

Using ritual to achieve political ends is a common Pagan strategy for implementing ethics. Pagans also often mix issues in political rituals, combining ecology and feminism in ecofeminism. Pagans engage in direct action using magic and ritual, as well as conducting these activities as parts of demonstrations and at separate events. Direct action entails a direct refusal to comply with a perceived wrong, and interference with those carrying out such a wrong. It is intended to destabilize systems of control and to undermine the compliance of enforcers, making it expensive to enforce control. It is effective because it creates a crisis of legitimacy as people cease to believe that the system is working.[56] Direct action includes things like ecotage and monkey wrenching (destroying machines like bulldozers at road-building sites), but also other confrontations with political and corporate power through activities like sit-ins and tree sits. Most direct-action protest is nonviolent, despite mainstream

Figure 20. Spontaneous Pagan ritual led by Starhawk at political demonstration against G20 meeting in Ottawa, Canada, 2001 (photo by Barbara Jane Davy)

news coverage that highlights sensationalist violence. It may include civil disobedience, but it is not always illegal.

Some Pagans and environmentalists suggest that direct action has special virtues. The experience of being out in nature, away from the shelter of home at road-building protests, lends an awareness of where water and food comes from and a more immediate sense of human dependence on the natural world. In direct action, one is also forced to confront one's fears of the state, of physical harm, and sometimes of heights (in tree sits) or of being in a state of anarchy. In addition, it often works because it is expensive to evict protestors. This tactic has been particularly successful in the antiroad movement in Britain, in which Pagans participate. However, direct-action campaigns are generally reactive, they focus on single issues, and they can draw media attention away from ongoing long-term campaigning.[57]

Participation in direct action may be less visible in contemporary Pagan discourse than other sorts of environmentalist action because it tends to be something one does rather than writes about. In contrast to Pagan discourse, direct action is highly visible as an activity. Starhawk continues to participate in antiglobalization (or global-justice) protests that use the same sorts of direct-action techniques that she and others developed in antinuclear protests, as do Canadian Pagan groups and others. Starhawk sends out regular updates on her political activities via e-mail and her website, www.starhawk.org.

In Britain, Dragon Environmental Group also participates in direct-action campaigns, as well as other strategies, including regular lobbying and eco-magic. Eco-magic is designed to use ritual to protect the Earth and stop environmental destruction, and it involves contacting the local spirits of place. Dragon runs a course instructing people how to do eco-magic, organizes conservation work, and conducts antiroad and anti-GMO campaigns (against genetically modified organisms). Dragon also offers a bio-magic course that involves the study of woodland ecology, of coming to know trees, and of developing spiritual relationships with them. Membership in Dragon overlaps with that of the radical environmental group Earth First!, which began in the United States, and Dragon camps offer Council of All Beings workshops similar to those in Earth First! groups.

Pagans use magic and ritual to effect political change primarily through changing individual consciousness, and, to a lesser extent, to act directly on local environments or the Earth as a whole. While "navel gazing" may be a stereotype of apolitical mysticism, some Pagans believe that private meditation is directly beneficial to the Earth because everything is connected. Others apply sympathetic magic in Earth-healing rituals. Some practitioners, for example, use homeopathic healing for watersheds by blessing purified water and "inoculating" a body of water. In addition to these direct effects on the natural world, Pagans feel that magic, ritual, and myth can work through changing human consciousness. Even a statement can change consciousness, Starhawk says: "If we call the world alive, we begin to bring her back to life."[58] Ritual can present a richer alternative pattern to mainstream consciousness and challenge cultural patterns of domination.[59] Starhawk argues that since the basic cause of environmental destruction is our estrangement from the natural world, it can be cured by a return to a belief in immanence, which is essentially a change in consciousness.[60] A political ritual of raising the dragon, published by *Moonshine* magazine, was effective in consciousness raising for the antiroad movement in Britain.[61] The dragon subsequently became a symbol of Pagan environmentalism in Britain.

Symbols are an important means of changing consciousness and maintaining alternative worldviews. Carol Christ argues that we cannot just

---

In Council of All Beings rituals, people take on the roles of various animals and speak of their suffering. Some participants in these rituals experience possession by endangered or persecuted animals who call on humans to exercise greater intervention against exploitation.

reject problematic symbols, such as that of a radically transcendent masculine God. "Symbol systems cannot simply be rejected," she says. "They must be replaced. Where there is not any replacement, the mind will revert to familiar structures at times of crisis, bafflement, or defeat."[62] In Pagan ecofeminist practice, the symbol of the Goddess and images of Earth are used to motivate change. Worldviews can be changed through art and myth, particularly through performance art as ritual, because it motivates action. This sort of performance is sometimes called "eco-drama." It can take the form of performances such as Rachel Rosenthal's performance art "Gaia," in which she chastises and appeals to her audience to heal the Earth,[63] as well as more carnivalesque activities and street theatre during political demonstrations and protests. Anti-GMO activists, for example, use a giant "FrankenTony" costume to parody the Tony the Tiger character that Kellogg's uses to market cereals containing genetically modified foods to children. Eco-drama is often used as part of direct-action campaigns, but it tends to have elements of celebration and "info-tainment." It can be educational, entertaining, fun, and political at the same time. Pagan eco-drama often includes dancing, drumming, and singing, and it effectively models a way of life different from that which is protested. Rosenthal's form of eco-drama is somewhat similarly designed to provoke an ethical and political response through aesthetic performance.

Feminism and environmentalism are the most visible political perspectives of Paganism, particularly through the overlap of Paganism with ecofeminism. Feminist ethics are well supported within Paganism, if not currently often voiced. Magical ethics are the most highly developed ethics in Paganism, particularly through oral teaching traditions, and to an extent in written works. Environmental ethics are developing in Paganism through current discourse, and issues in cultural appropriation continue to be debated. Other contentious issues in contemporary Paganism are discussed in chapter 10.

FURTHER READING

Albanese, Catherine L. "Nature Religion and the Turn to Metaphysics." In *Reconsidering Nature Religion*. Harrisburg, PA: Trinity Press International, 2002.
Blain, Jenny. "Contested Meanings: Earth Religion Practitioners and the Everyday." *The Pomegranate: A New Journal of Neopagan Thought* 12 (2000): 15–25.

NOTES

1. Jone Salomonsen, *Enchanted Feminism: The Reclaiming Witches of San Francisco* (London: Routledge, 2002), 81.

2. Christopher Key Chapple, *Jainism and Ecology: Nonviolence in the Web of Life* (Cambridge, MA: Harvard University Press, 2002), xxxii.

3. Starhawk, "Ethics and Justice in Goddess Religion," in *The Politics of Women's Spirituality: Essays on the Rise of Spiritual Power within the Feminist Movement*, ed. Charlene Spretnak (Garden City, NY: Anchor Press [Doubleday], 1982), 417.

4. Sabina Magliocco, *Witching Culture: Folklore and Neo-Paganism in America* (Philadelphia: University of Pennsylvania Press, 2004), 219.

5. Sarah M. Pike, *Earthly Bodies, Magical Selves: Contemporary Pagans and the Search for Community* (Berkeley, CA: University of California Press, 2001), 137.

6. See Pike, *Earthly Bodies, Magical Selves*, 139.

7. Scott Cunningham, *Wicca: A Guide for the Solitary Practitioner* (St. Paul, MN: Llewellyn Publications, 1988), 48.

8. Quoted in Pike, *Earthly Bodies, Magical Selves*, 140.

9. Pike, *Earthly Bodies, Magical Selves*, 137.

10. Pike, *Earthly Bodies, Magical Selves*, 144.

11. Magliocco, *Witching Culture*, 216.

12. Kathryn Rountree, *Embracing the Witch and the Goddess: Feminist Ritual-Makers in New Zealand* (London: Routledge, 2004), 165–66.

13. Andy Smith, "For All Those Who Were Indian in a Former Life," in *Ecofeminism and the Sacred*, ed. Carol J. Adams (New York: Continuum, 1993), 168.

14. Pike, *Earthly Bodies, Magical Selves*, 153.

15. Smith, "For All Those Who Were Indian," 168.

16. See Rountree, *Embracing the Witch and the Goddess*, 166.

17. Smith, "For All Those Who Were Indian," 169.

18. Magliocco, *Witching Culture*, 209.

19. Magliocco, *Witching Culture*, 212.

20. Magliocco, *Witching Culture*, 228.

21. Pike, *Earthly Bodies, Magical Selves*, 139.

22. Magliocco, *Witching Culture*, 220–21.

23. Smith, "For All Those Who Were Indian," 171.

24. Starhawk, *The Spiral Dance: A Rebirth of the Ancient Religion of the Great Goddess*, 10th anniversary ed. (New York: HarperSanFrancisco, 1989), 214.

25. Starhawk, *Spiral Dance*, 214. Starhawk echoes Andy Smith's comments on this issue. See Smith, "For All Those Who Were Indian," 169.

26. Rountree, *Embracing the Witch and the Goddess*, 167.

27. Pike, *Earthly Bodies, Magical Selves*, 145.

28. Rountree, *Embracing the Witch and the Goddess*, 167–68.

29. Helen Berger, Evan A. Leach, and Leigh S. Shaffer, *Voices from the Pagan Census: A National Survey of Witches and Neo-Pagans in the United States* (Columbia: University of South Carolina Press, 2003), 73–74.

30. Zsuzsanna E. Budapest, *The Holy Book of Women's Mysteries, Part 1* (Oakland, CA: Susan B. Anthony Coven No. 1, 1979), 9, 10.

31. Zsuzsanna Budapest, *The Holy Book of Women's Mysteries* (Oakland, CA: Wingbow Press, 1989), 3.

32. Doreen Valiente, *The Rebirth of Witchcraft* (Custer, WA: Phoenix Publishing, 1989), 191.

33. Berger, Leach, and Shaffer, *Voices from the Pagan Census*, 67.

34. Adrian Ivakhiv, "Whose Nature? The Transcendental Signified of an Emerging Field," *The Pomegranate: A New Journal of Neopagan Thought* 8 (1999): 16.

35. Adrian Harris, "Sacred Ecology," *Paganism Today*, ed. Charlotte Hardman and Graham Harvey (London: Thorsons [HarperCollins], 1996), 152.

36. Harris, "Sacred Ecology," 153.

37. Starhawk, *Truth or Dare: Encounters with Power, Authority, and Mystery* (New York: HarperSanFrancisco, 1987), 23.

38. Starhawk, *Dreaming the Dark: Magic, Sex and Politics,* new ed. (London: Mandala [Unwin Paperbacks], 1990), xvi.

39. Starhawk, "Ethics and Justice in Goddess Religion," in *The Politics of Women's Spirituality: Essays on the Rise of Spiritual Power within the Feminist Movement,* ed. Charlene Spretnak (Garden City, NY: Anchor Press [Doubleday], 1982), 422.

40. See Carol Christ, *Rebirth of the Goddess: Finding Meaning in Feminist Spirituality* (Reading, MA: Addison-Wesley Publishing, 1997), 176.

41. Christ, *Rebirth of the Goddess,* 156.

42. Christ, *Rebirth of the Goddess,* 167.

43. Margot Adler, *Drawing Down the Moon: Witches, Druids, Goddess-Worshippers, and Other Pagans in America Today,* revised and expanded ed. (Boston: Beacon Press, 1986), 372.

44. Chas Clifton has discussed the issue of pacifism and Pagans in the military. Chas S. Clifton, "Fort Hood's Wiccans and the Problem of Pacifism" (paper presented at the annual meeting of the American Academy of Religion, Nashville, Tennessee, November 20, 2000).

45. Graham Harvey, *Contemporary Paganism: Listening People, Speaking Earth* (New York: New York University Press, 1997), 140.

46. Berger, Leach, and Shaffer, *Voices from the Pagan Census,* 2003, 88.

47. Adler, *Drawing Down the Moon,* 412, 409.

48. Berger, Leach, and Shaffer, *Voices from the Pagan Census,* 55–57.

49. Adler, *Drawing Down the Moon,* 405, 407; Marion Bowman, "Nature, the Natural, and Pagan Identity," *Diskus* 6 (2000), Web edition, http://web.uni-marburg.de/religionswissenschaft/journal/diskus (accessed May 16, 2001).

50. Jenny Blain, "Contested Meanings: Earth Religion Practitioners and the Everyday," *The Pomegranate: A New Journal of Neopagan Thought* 12 (2000): 25.

51. Adler, *Drawing Down the Moon,* 400.

52. Berger, Leach, and Shaffer, *Voices from the Pagan Census,* 59.

53. Adler, *Drawing Down the Moon,* 403, 414.

54. Adler, *Drawing Down the Moon,* 415.

55. Ronald Hutton, *The Triumph of the Moon: A History of Modern Pagan Witchcraft* (Oxford: Oxford University Press, 1999), 208.

56. Starhawk, *Webs of Power: Notes from the Global Uprising* (Gabriola Island, British Columbia: New Society Publishers, 2002), 228.

57. Andy Letcher, "'Virtual Paganism' or Direct Action? The Implications of Road Protesting for Modern Paganism," *Diskus* 6 (2000), Web edition, http://web.uni-marburg.de/religionswissenschaft/journal/diskus (accessed May 16, 2001).

58. Starhawk, *Truth or Dare,* 8.

59. Starhawk, *Truth or Dare,* 98.

60. Starhawk, *Dreaming the Dark,* 5, 9.

61. Letcher, "'Virtual Paganism' or Direct Action?" 4–5.

62. Quoted in Starhawk, *Webs of Power,* 263.

63. Elinor Gadon, "Gaia Consciousness: Ecological Wisdom for the Renewal of Life on Our Planet," in *The Once and Future Goddess: A Symbol for Our Time* (San Francisco: Harper & Row, 1989), 363.

10

Current Issues

Current issues in Paganism center around the public image of the religion and practitioners' feelings about how Paganism should develop. Some practitioners and denominations want Paganism to grow into an institutionalized religion, while others would prefer that it stay a private and decentralized practice conducted in small groups. Some are concerned that developing institutionalized forms of the religion dulls its countercultural tendencies, but others want to present Paganism as mainstream to gain the legal rights and protections afforded other religions. The basic divide is between those who want Paganism to be an organized religion, and those who do not, either because they want it to be countercultural and do not see how this feature can persist in a bureaucracy, or because they want to preserve it as a private mystery religion. Many Pagans, particularly those who have been involved in the religion for a long time, fear that the contemporary mainstreaming and commercialization of Paganism somehow diminish it. Such practitioners are concerned that the recent popularity of Witchcraft in television programs, movies, and books encourages consumerism and trivializes their religion.

The most contentious issues arise from the desires of some practitioners to flaunt their alternative behavior and exhibit their religion as countercultural on the one hand, and those who are more concerned with fostering mainstream acceptance and pursuing legal rights and protections on the other. This divide becomes particularly obvious at festivals, where Pagans come into conflict over their identity as Pagan and struggle to control how others perceive their religion. However, it is also evident in relations between Pagans and other religions. Some Pagans are confrontational with members of other religions, while others pursue interfaith dialogue and cooperation with Christians and others on common issues such as peace, the environment, and social justice.

The first Pagan umbrella organizations began as antidefamation groups, to try to educate the public and the media about Paganism to prevent religious persecution. Such organizations have tended to present Paganism as being as mainstream as possible, to make it appear harmless so that Pagans will be allowed the same rights and protections as members of other religious groups. Some practitioners prefer to remain hidden to avoid persecution, either as solitaries or as members of groups that are totally private and closed, but some practitioners participate in Pagan pride events, publicizing their religious orientation and forcing it into the mainstream.

Interfaith work encourages mainstream acceptance of Paganism, if not the mainstreaming of Pagan practice. Local interfaith councils are often engaged in community relations, as well as antiracism activities. Some Pagan groups have obtained representation in the Parliament of World Religions, an international interfaith group of scholars and practitioners of the world's religions. The Parliament has met periodically since 1893 and has a mission to foster harmony between religions and to work for peace, justice, and sustainability.[1] Pagan groups that send delegates include Circle Sanctuary, Gaia's Womb, EarthSpirit Community, Covenant of the Goddess, Pagan Federation International, and Reclaiming. The first Pagan elected to the board of trustees of the Parliament was Angie Buchanan in 2003, representing Circle Sanctuary.[2]

Figure 21.   Selena Fox with other members of the Parliament of the World's Religions Assembly of Religious and Spiritual Leaders (photo from *Circle Magazine* 91) (Photo courtesy of Circle Sanctuary, www.circlesanctuary.org, PO Box 9, Barneveld, WI 53507 USA; 608-924-2216.)

Interfaith work is hindered by the hostile attitude of some Pagans toward Christianity. Some practitioners are angry and bitter about their experiences with being raised in Christian families or communities. In some cases, these practitioners identify with those killed in the "Burning Times," conflating the Inquisition, the burning of witches, and contemporary fundamentalism, and they present this image as representative of all Christianity.[3] Other practitioners label this as "Christian bashing," feeling that acceptance of Christianity as a legitimate faith perspective is a sign of maturity. This is a point of conflict on Pagan listservs and newsgroups, and in magazine letters forums.[4] Some Pagans take offence at being wished a "merry Christmas" and decline to attend office Christmas parties, while others delight in explaining the pagan origins of Christian festivals and traditions such as Valentine's Day in the Roman festival of Lupercalia, or Christmas trees and Easter eggs. Pagans who are hostile to Christianity stress the continued animosity of people like Pentecostal televangelist Pat Robertson and his followers, who blame feminists, "pagans," and gays for the ills of American culture. Robertson is the founder of the Christian Coalition and hosts the television show *The 700 Club*. The *Washington Post* has cited him as saying, "The feminist agenda is not about equal rights for women. It is about a socialist, anti-family political movement that encourages women to leave their husbands, kill their children, practice witchcraft, destroy capitalism and become lesbians."[5] Robertson, along with Jerry Falwell, blamed "pagans," feminists, gays, and others for the attacks on the United States on September 11, 2001, on a show aired only a few days later. These are not the views of mainstream Christians.

Some Pagans embrace victim status because it allows them to claim the moral high ground in relating to Christians. In addition, "Persecution stories have more entertainment value than accounts of neighbors cooperating, and they sharpen the boundaries of one's own identity in contrast to the 'other.'"[6] However, stories of persecution are not without basis in fact. Although Pagans do have a number of legal rights to practice their religion without harassment, discrimination, or persecution, they do not have the same rights as practitioners of mainstream religions to perform marriages in all countries, or the same access to tax-exempt status. Educating employers and actively pursuing rights to take religious holidays is necessary, and practitioners are currently struggling to exercise their rights in the military and in correctional institutions. Pagans also experience occasional problems in custody cases, and more serious harassment and persecution do occur.

Some serious maltreatment of Pagans involves accusations of involvement with Satanism, as remnants of misinformation and fear mongering of the Satanic panic of the 1980s. Occasional books, such as William

Schnoebelen's *Wicca: Satan's Little White Lie*, continue to propagate the myth that Wiccans or Pagans more generally practice Satanism. Schnoebelen purports to have practiced as a Wiccan, believing Wicca to be a harmless nature religion when he started, but coming to believe it was Satanist as he advanced through the degrees. This sort of propaganda is produced by evangelical publishers like Chick Publications and is not taken seriously by scholars of religion. Pagan practitioners are quick to point out that Satan is a character of Christian tradition rather than a Pagan god.

An extreme case of persecution occurred in the hate crime committed against a Pagan student of Austin Peay State University, Tennessee. Two men allegedly ran down Brandon Morrison, a Druid, with a pickup truck, bound him, and beat him for almost an hour, cutting him from neck to hip. His assailants quoted the Bible to him, saying, "Thou shalt not suffer a witch to live," and indicated that they would stop only if he repented and accepted God. They left him with a broken rib, tied to a tree. Police are currently investigating this crime.[7]

Less intense, although still troublesome, problems associated with festivals are more common. The owner of a Pagan festival site in New York called Brushwood found a letter in his local paper warning people against the presence of the festival. The author of the letter recounted his supposed former involvement with Satanism, drinking blood, and doing drugs. He claimed to have visited the festival and seen people from his former involvement with Satanism, and he warned people against letting their children get involved with Paganism, saying, "They will brain wash them, turn them into drug addicts, show them all the immoral and deviant things you can dream of. . . . Bet you will not get in during their darkest rituals, but your children might."[8] Circle Sanctuary, in Wisconsin, had to get a restraining order against Reverend Jeff Fenholt, a fundamentalist who was harassing Pagans at their festival site as part of a national campaign against Witchcraft.[9] A ritual site on private property near Atlanta in rural Georgia was systematically desecrated. First there was minor vandalism and the theft of some ritual items, but concerned neighbors later dismantled the site. Footage of this was shown on local television after the neighbors formed a coalition and called a press conference "to stop the Witches."[10]

Festivals are usually held in rural areas, where neighbors are less likely to be friendly or knowledgeable about Pagans and their actual religious beliefs and practices than their neighbors in the urban areas where most Pagans live. Some festivals respond to infiltration of their festivals by uneducated neighbors hoping to catch damning evidence on film by hiring security forces and requiring festival participants to wear plastic tags, although participants are unhappy with this solution. Secrecy and tightening of security for festivals can exacerbate site neighbors' fears, polarizing

Pagans and Christians who each refuse to see or accept that the average practices and beliefs of each are more acceptable to each other than are the radicals on either side.[11]

There seem to be more rumored fears about custody battles than actual cases before the courts, although *Circle Magazine*'s Lady Liberty League notes the difficulties of one couple in adopting their grandchildren after the death of the parents, the opponents of which cited their religious affiliation.[12] In a recent divorce case in Indiana, Judge Cale J. Bradford ruled that a child should not be exposed to Pagan practices over the objections of the parents, who are both Wiccan.[13] Harassment and occasional discrimination seem more common, as in the eviction of Terry and Amanda Riley, members of the Southern Delta Church of Wicca, in Jonesboro, Arkansas, in 1993. Their landlord, accompanied by two evangelical Church of the Nazarene ministers, told them that they needed to vacate their occult bookstore for the protection of children and to preserve the identity of their town as Christian.[14] Wiccan priestess Cynthia Simpson won a federal case in Richmond, Virginia, on November 13, 2003. She was discriminated against by being excluded from serving as clergy in prayer at the opening meetings of the Chesterfield County Board because she was not part of "the Judeo-Christian tradition," thus violating the American First Amendment separation of church and state.[15]

For most Pagans, petty harassment is the most common problem. Loud pestering by a local preacher interrupted a religious meeting conducted at a local park by Lianna Costantino, high priestess of the Sylvian Hearth Pagan Temple near Franklin, North Carolina, leading Costantino to call the local sheriff to remove the protesters. The same preacher denounced her at a town meeting, accusing her of hosting a left-wing website. After a public-education campaign, when he again tried to speak against her at a town meeting, the mayor and city attorney asked him to desist.[16] Pagans also report harassment in their workplaces, such as uninvited religious literature left in their cubicles, jokes at the water cooler about broomsticks, and aggressive proselytism. *New Witch* contributor Michael Samhain suggests that practitioners take proselytism as an opportunity for teaching and dispelling stereotypes. He recommends that practitioners not become aggressive or defensive but remain calm and say that they have chosen their path after considerable thought. He also instructs that it is okay to say that their religion is private and to decline to discuss it, particularly if the person seems incapable of listening.[17] Some Pagans use Hallowe'en as an opportunity for public education, since media people routinely conduct interviews with practicing Witches and other Pagans at that time of year in North America. Practitioners see this as a public-relations opportunity to discuss the stereotyping of witches as hags, and to separate themselves from Satanism in the public mind-set.

An American book, *Pagans and the Law*, by Dana D. Eilers, provides a practical guide for bringing cases involving freedom of religion to court, and indicates what to do about harassment and libel.[18] In Canada, Kerr Cuhulain's *Law Enforcement Guide to Wicca* has long provided a resource for practitioners and police.[19] For the most part, Pagans do have freedom of religion, excepting the right to perform marriages, which is denied in some areas, but they need to use the law to enforce their rights. A number of groups supporting religious freedoms for Pagans are currently active. These include *Circle Magazine*'s Lady Liberty League; the Association of Magical and Earth Religion; and, through providing information, the Ontario Organization for Religious Tolerance and the Pagan Federation/ Fédération Païenne in Canada. The Pagan Unity Campaign was created with the aim of "protecting and furthering Pagan rights," and to "raise political awareness and encourage political participation" in America.[20] They began an "I am" campaign in 2001, encouraging practitioners to send postcards of their local towns and cities to elected officials, with "I am a Pagan ____" on the back. Practitioners were instructed to fill in the blank to say "I am a Pagan mother," or "I am a Pagan professional," or whatever they felt was appropriate, and to include the Pagan Unity slogan: "I am free. We are united." Through this campaign, the group intended to gain political recognition for Pagans as a voting bloc. Across North America, Pagan Pride projects and events, modeled on gay pride, have similar objectives of raising public awareness of their existence.

The United States military has been aware of Wicca, if not Paganism more generally, since the 1970s, when access to chaplains in the military began to be an issue. Conservative lobby groups and members of Congress have protested Fort Hood's Open Circle, and when George W. Bush was running for office in 1999, he said, "I don't think witchcraft is a religion and I wish the military would take another look at this and decide against it," but the military has consistently supported the chaplains' decision to allow the Wiccan group, defending the American First Amendment guarantee of freedom of religion.[21]

Pagan and interdenominational chaplains who are knowledgeable about Paganism are becoming more common at college and university campuses, as well as in the military, but practitioners in correctional institutions continue to have problems accessing religious services and being allowed to practice their religion freely. Practitioners report that their rights to freedom of assembly and to possess religious items have been denied. An inmate in Texas reports that the chaplain at his institution refuses to let his Pagan group meet and refuses to issue a pass for him to wear a pentagram medallion, which he regards as an emblem of religious identification.[22] *Circle Magazine*'s Lady Liberty League reports that a volunteer clergy person, Sarah Rydell, in the Colorado Department of Corrections, has been discriminated against in being denied the right to serve as a volunteer. A policy of the department disallows staff members from also serving as volunteer clergy, and Rydell was ostensibly rejected because she is also a staff member. However, Protestant volunteers who are also staff members have been allowed to continue. The department has initiated an official investigation into this matter. Similarly, the Lady Liberty League reports that a Protestant chaplain at Lee County Correctional Institution in Tennessee is attempting to disband a Pagan group by targeting religious volunteer Laurel Owen, slandering her to the FBI, saying that she was present during a beating in order to have her barred from participation for her own safety. The League concludes that "every case [of religious discrimination] that Pagans have won in California has been followed by an immediate transfer of the participants," effectively disbanding the groups.[23] Within American state prisons, Pagans are effectively being denied the right to assemble to participate in religious services, and there are also a number of pending cases regarding rights to possess religious materials, such as books and pentacles. However, it appears as though the federal system may be more amenable to Pagans, and in the spring of 2005, in the Ohio case of *Cutter v. Wilkinson*, the Supreme Court ruled in favor of allowing prisoners access to alt.religion, an unmoderated public electronic discussion list with content on alternative religious views, including Paganism.[24]

The desire of practitioners for legal protections from harassment, persecution, and discrimination, and the right to practice their religion freely, inevitably leads to increasing levels of organization. When Pagans ask for the same rights and protections as members/adherents of mainstream religions, government, police, and military officials inevitably ask, "Who are your leaders?" and "What are their credentials?" The desire of practitioners for the services of chaplains, and for clergy persons who are legally allowed to perform marriages and funerals, as well as the desire for tax-exempt status for Pagan organizations, drives the bureaucratization of the religion.

Most churches, synagogues, and mosques are run as charitable organizations in the United States, so they do not have to pay taxes and can issue tax receipts for donations. Some Pagan organizations have obtained tax-exempt status in the United States beginning in the early 1970s, but practitioners complain that the rules governing tax-exempt status are designed on the basis of the organization of Christian churches, and that maintaining charitable status encourages the mainstreaming of Pagan traditions on a Christian model. Of particular concern for some groups is the requirement of a membership list.

A clergy class is evolving in Paganism, corresponding to a developing laity that increasingly wants the "pastoral" services offered in other religions. However, some Pagans resist the mainstreaming of the religion in forms that mimic the institutional structures of Christianity, "pastoral" counseling being a particular sore point. (Practitioners who object to the use of this term say that Pagans are not a flock of sheep to be shepherded, as the term in Christian pastoral counseling metaphorically suggests.) As children are increasingly raised in Pagan households, some practitioners in initiatory traditions are concerned about how this is changing their traditions when the religion is something one is born into rather than a path one chooses as an adult.

Some practitioners are happy to become clergy serving a community of laypeople. It may be that some like having the power and status that comes with being a member of the clergy, but some people are just natural organizers and would like to make a living doing what they enjoy and do well. Such practitioners have an interest in the development of institutional structures within Paganism for clergy training and the collection of money. In some denominations of Paganism, payment for ritual services is prohibited. Gardner's Craft Laws, for example, prohibit payment for "the art," or magical work, but allow payment for other services in benefit of the Craft. Gardner felt that payment for "the art" would tempt people to use it for "evil purposes."[25]

Given the cost of maintaining the bureaucratic structures necessary for larger organizations, in terms of time and money, some practitioners question the value of such developments. As discussed in chapter 2, some actively oppose the formation of institutional structures within Paganism. Maintaining an organization often requires that a lot of energy be devoted simply to keeping the institution in place. Committees form to handle fund-raising, someone has to keep minutes, and someone has to make that sure all the other things necessary to maintain a public corporation and/or charitable status are looked after. Even renting a space for a ritual event or public festival requires some organization.

Some practitioners fear that the mystery or "juice" of religious experience is being lost as Paganism is routinized and becomes an organized religion. One Wiccan elder comments, "As its numbers have grown, I fear it has also become, on average, more superficial. I wonder sometimes where the Craft is headed."[26] For some, the mystery of the tradition is threatened by exposing private beliefs about history and origins to public, and academic, scrutiny. Others are more concerned that Paganism will become filled with dead institutions as the focus is shifted from seeking religious experience to maintaining institutions. This leads Chas Clifton to argue that "our model should be the tent rather than the cathedral. Cathedrals are always needing new roofs and plumbing repairs. Tents are packed up and moved to where they are needed next."[27] He asks whether the religion is about maintaining institutional structures or about celebration, meditation, spell casting, and spiritual development. If it is going to happen in community, it will probably have to be about all of these things. Not all Pagans see themselves as part of a mystery religion. Like most religions, Paganism has aspects of both celebration and initiation, allowing room for family participation and community work as well as personal development.

For some practitioners, Paganism will always be about the mystery, the juice of alternative behavior, and countercultural politics. Some will want their religion to be private rather than a publicly practiced religion, while others enjoy how their religious practices challenge the mainstream through the concepts of female deity, ritual nudity, ritual sex, entheogen use, recreational drugs, or anarchist politics. Such practitioners want social change more than social acceptance, to challenge the mainstream rather than join it. Others want for their religion to be publicly recognized as legitimate, and for being Pagan to be as unremarkable as being Baptist. Such basic differences of opinion regarding Pagan identity often become apparent at public festivals. Festival participants have high expectations about finding an ideal sense of community at festivals—that the community will be unified and that the festival will be a time of self-definition and expression. Conflicts arise at festivals in particular because, while Paganism is quite diverse, festivals symbolize the entire community.[28]

Most conflicts at festivals are about representation and identity, or how Pagans understand themselves and present themselves to each other and to the public.[29] The organizers of festivals often present the festivals in terms as mainstream as possible to ease relations with the surrounding community by presenting themselves as normal and friendly. However, some participants want to be able to express themselves at festivals in ways that are not possible in other contexts, for example, through costumes and behavior. Some want festivals to be a countercultural Pagan party zone.[30] Some participants like to show all their tattoos and smoke marijuana freely at festivals, but others are offended by such behavior.[31]

Struggles over meaning arise in ritual spaces at festivals, particularly in the main ritual area, which is shared by the greatest number of people. Practitioners come into disagreement over proper uses of space, and keeping it sacred. Festival participants exhibit diverse attitudes about how to do this and what constitutes keeping it sacred. Complaints about how to keep a fire pit sacred center around drinking alcohol (and leaving beer cans) and smoking (and leaving butts).[32] Some participants complain about loud drumming that goes on all night, but others, such as chaos magician Maddog, assert that loud drumming is how they contact the divine.[33] Festival organizers have additional concerns about drumming when it disturbs nonparticipants of the festival at neighboring sites or in surrounding areas. These sorts of conflicts are aired in newsletters, such as a Ms. Manners column in the *Elven Chronicle*, which offers an opinion about disputes concerning the fire pit at ELFfest. The author writes against "loud, show-off blasts on congas; drying wet sox (etc.); cooking hot dogs over the ritual fire (unless it is Friday) . . . overt sexual grabbing; drinking songs; exaltations of how late it is and isn't it great to be part of third shift [i.e., up late]; getting falling down drunk; suggesting women have no right to drum and should let the MEN do it; and lover's quarrels."[34]

Festival rules generally prohibit the use of illegal drugs, but such policies are typically not enforced, and there is no consensus within the festival communities about illegal drug use. The use of illegal drugs at festivals is not widespread and is no more serious than what is typical at rock concerts.[35] Pagans often have an attitude of openness toward hallucinogens, sometimes called entheogens (meaning substances used to make contact with divinity), some of which are illegal, but some Pagans are against all nontherapeutic drug use. Workshops on entheogens are offered at some festivals, but some practitioners complain that this sort of thing can encourage the wrong impression about Paganism. A letter to *Green Egg* comments on an episode where a child of a visiting non-Pagan friend found a copy of the magazine with an article on drug use in a religious context and said, "Hey, man, these Pagans are sex fiends and drug addicts!"[36]

Paganism is generally a sex-positive religion, and the festival atmosphere in particular is permissive, but some practitioners feel that festivals should be a "safe space."[37] As in any other segment of the population, sexual predation can occur in Paganism, and Pagans have expressed concerns over teachers and elders in the Pagan community who imply or require sexual access as part of initiation or mentoring relationships. However, most concerns about sex are related to harassment at festivals, perhaps because some participants experience them as "temporary autonomous zones" and expect a carnivalesque atmosphere.[38] Festival organizers have created guidelines for dealing with sexual harassment because of occasional incidents. For everyone to feel safe, rules, and their enforcement, are necessary, but this conflicts with many participants' ideals of individualism and self-expression.[39]

Festivalgoers also come into conflict about how much sexual activity it is appropriate to display at festivals. Nudity is commonplace at festivals and unremarkable, but some practitioners exhibit BDSM behavior. Some Pagans object to seeing these practices on display at festivals, particularly when children are present, but others contend that their sexuality is part of their spirituality. Again, these activities generally do not involve anything more extreme than is apparent as rock concerts.[40] One Pagan group circulates a pamphlet for teenagers interested in the occult and concerned parents that indicates that "a teenager seeking sex, drugs and rock and roll in an occult group is more likely to find hugs, home cooking and new age music."[41] A recent trend is the development of "family-positive" festivals, such as Awakening Isis, held between Ottawa and Montreal, Canada, as an alternative to other Pagan events, which is designed to be inoffensive, safe for children, and interfaith friendly.

Identity conflicts within Pagan communities also arise through personal and local disagreements that can escalate into Witch wars. The distinguishing features of Witch wars are that the conflict is publicly aired in the community, and the effects of the conflict are so pervasive that practitioners feel compelled to choose sides or withdraw from the community until the conflict is resolved. Witch wars are largely the result of "competing visions of Witchcraft, in situations that are perceived to involve authority or legitimacy."[42] Structural, personal, and ideological differences can all be factors in the development of Witch wars. The structural organization of Witchcraft, with individual practice, covens, and networking organizations, leads to different views of what Witchcraft practice is. The media tends to contact larger organizations and present their views as representative of all Witchcraft or Paganism, which can polarize communities.[43] Witch wars are often the result of an escalation of a personal conflict "triggered by some perception that an individual or group is attempting to impose their particular vision of the Craft hegemonically," claiming to speak for all practitioners.[44]

Witch wars can develop from interpersonal issues of ego, deception, and rivalry, as well as from disagreements about what is the right way to do Witchcraft. Witch wars usually begin with local gossip that becomes venomous, leading to the label "Bitchcraft" or "Bicca." Such conflicts can be sustained by the desires of individuals for power, money, or sex.[45] Participants in Witch wars often level accusations of requirements for sex for initiation, money for training, or the obeisance of members to one another, or rumors are spread that other individuals in the disagreement require these.

A long-running disagreement that might be described as a Witch war exists between supporters and detractors of Gavin and Yvonne Frost's tradition of Witchcraft. The Frosts gave a workshop on "Heretical Witchcraft" at the 2004 Starwood Festival, in which they claimed that they "were put on trial" by the community; that Llewellyn, a publisher of popular Pagan books, refused to allow any mention of them; and that they were excluded from encyclopedias on Witchcraft. Llewellyn did exclude them in the past for being too "controversial," but current encyclopedias mention them and their Church of Wicca. The initial conflict was over their seeming monotheism (expressed as belief in God) and their attitudes toward sex. Particularly contentious were their recommendations regarding the use of a "*Baton de Commandment*" for sexually initiating girls into Witchcraft at the age of fourteen, and other practices related to removing the "virgin" status of children as early as possible, through circumcision or breaking the hymen. These recommendations initially appeared in the Frost's 1972 book *The Witch's Bible*, in the midst of sensationalist news coverage of Satanic abuse. Some Pagans also found the Frosts' advertisements in tabloids for the "Magic Power of Witchcraft" distasteful. As a result of these differences, in some cases Pagans have been denied access to groups if they were associated with the Frosts. While many people concur that the Frosts are "nice people" and personable, their attitudes toward sex and public relations continue to occasion dissent.[46] Reviews on Amazon.com indicate that not all material on using dildos with young girls has been removed in the new version of the Frosts' book, published as *Good Witch's Bible*.

Local disagreements are often due to personality conflicts, but some splits are caused by denominational or sectarian differences that are the result of differing ideologies. The original conflict between Alex Sanders and practitioners of Gardnerian Wicca began as a personal conflict but generated a new sect. The Gardnerian priestess Patricia Crowther disliked Sanders and refused to initiate him,[47] and he in turn denounced Gardnerian Wicca as inauthentic and created what came to be known as the Alexandrian tradition. Later rivalries between Gardnerian and eclectic traditions are more the result of ideological differences. Traditional practitioners emphasize learning mysticism and esoteric teaching from received tradition, while eclectics focus on creativity and celebratory aspects of the religion. Eclectic practitioners tend to see more traditional practitioners as "hidebound, hierarchical, and slavishly adhering to received material, while traditionals view eclectics as fundamentally missing the point of the entire practice, diluting the mystery tradition to the point of unrecognizability with 'surface' rituals."[48]

Related ideological differences that can contribute to the development of Witch wars are attitudes toward hierarchy and initiation. Eclectic Paganism is generally less hierarchical than traditional initiatory Wicca. Sometimes a hidden hierarchy exists in eclectic groups, where some members defer to one person, or a group of people forming an inner circle in the group, but others express dislike of covert leadership. This has been a problem in the Reclaiming tradition, which is intended to run on consensus, with equal input from all members, but some perceive it to be controlled by the reputation of Starhawk.[49] Such instances of covert leadership can be as much the result of members deferring to those in a perceived position of authority as an attempt to wield power on the part of those in the inner circle. Disagreements about hierarchy and leadership can be intensified when money is involved, as in the purchase of land for holding festivals. This was an issue for the EarthSpirit community, in part because of past conflicts in the purchase of land for Circle Sanctuary.[50]

Belief in the necessity, or not, of initiation is still an debated issue among Pagans. As discussed in *PanGaia*'s "Toe-to-Toe" column, some practitioners feel that initiation creates hierarchy and breeds elitism, while others argue that hierarchy is not necessarily elitist, saying that the degree system in initiatory traditions is merit based. Some support self-initiation, while others argue that it must be conferred by another. Some feel that self-initiation involves direct contact with the Goddess and does not require the sanctioning of an organized group. Others would distinguish between self-initiation and divinity-originated transformative experiences that do qualify as proper initiations. Some detractors of initiation point to the dangers of power-hungry practitioners in positions of power over initiates, citing pressures to have sex, give money, and/or idolize the high priest/ess. However, defenders of initiation into lineages liken coven relations to family relations, saying that they are not authoritarian based, but loving relations. Some initiates regard noninitiates as lazy or undisciplined, or as uncommitted to the religion, while others see initiation as too often providing nothing but empty titles, allowing initiates to elevate themselves over others.[51]

Witch wars arising from ideological differences seem to particularly disturb Pagans, because practitioners espouse an ideal of tolerance for difference. Practitioners can come into conflict when confronted with the actual diversity of practice in the religion. Although Pagans idealize diversity, norms develop within groups, and personalities come into conflict when people with different practices come together, as at local community events and regional festivals.[52] Some Pagans see the "petty bickering" of Witch wars as an obstacle to mainstream acceptance. They criticize practitioners' tendency to nitpick any statements that claim to speak for the Pagan community as a whole, or statements that seem to try to do this. One practitioner, for example, laments, "In public we present ourselves as a disorganized bunch of backbiters and cranks, more interested in trading insults than in working for the common good."[53] Others might wonder who defines the common good, since not all Pagans are interested in seeking mainstream acceptance.

Another source of dissent about what Paganism is and should become arises from political views. According to some practitioners, Paganism is a private matter and has nothing to do with politics, but for some groups, such as those in the Reclaiming tradition, politics and spirituality are closely entwined. Some say religion should be about personal spiritual development, but for others, social justice is inherent to religion. Conflicting views about topics such as this are regularly aired in letters forums in popular Pagan and feminist spirituality magazines. *Sage Woman*, for example, has a regular column, "The Rattle: Our Readers Speak," for practitioners to express differing views in a respectful context. "The Rattle" in issue sixty-five of *Sage Woman* discusses mixing politics and spirituality or magic. Issues around mixing politics and spirituality are not new to women's spirituality and Paganism. Academics and practitioners debated it extensively in the late 1970s and into the 1980s.[54] Researchers have noted a political/apolitical division between "radical" and "traditionalist" practitioners.[55] All the letters in "The Rattle" column in *Sage Woman* 65 support mixing politics and spirituality, but different attitudes about mixing politics and spirituality continue in Paganism. Some take offense at political content in rituals, and others are disappointed with a lack of political content, seeing such rituals as without substance, "airy-fairy," out of touch with real life, and ungrounded. Some practitioners who dislike political content point to serious conflicts involving religion and politics in Ireland and the Middle East.[56]

Pagans also have mixed opinions regarding the image of their religion that is being presented in popular media. Witches and other magical practitioners are increasingly visible in popular culture, appearing as characters on television shows such as *Buffy the Vampire Slayer*, *Charmed*, movies such as *The Craft*, and novels such as J. K. Rowling's Harry Potter series. Some Pagans see this trend as positive. In a *New Witch* editorial, Dagonet Dewr says, "When a neat 'underground' thing becomes mainstream, it's not a defeat for our side, it's a victory. Yes, it can be a bummer to lose our 'outsider' status, but when the causes and lifestyles we believe in and espouse become mainstream they can't be persecuted, ignored, and slandered so easily."[57] Others are displeased with people adopting a "Witch" identity because it is trendy, and feel that the religion is cheapened by the superficial adoption of Witchcraft as a style. They suggest that treating Witchcraft and magic as a style reduces it to something that can be bought and sold. Such practitioners are disturbed by the commercialism and consumerism of "Witchcraft" as a commodity, but others embrace images of Witchcraft in popular culture, and some even construct pop culture altars.

Some Pagans complain about practitioners calling non-Pagans "muggles," after the use of the term for non-magical practitioners in the Harry Potter novels. In a letter to *New Witch*, Peter White says that the adoption of such trendy slang "cheapens our faith." Other see it as fun, or, alternatively, as juvenile. In the same column, Paanntherr indicates that "muggle" is a fictional name for the existing term "cowan" for non-magical practitioners.[58] "Muggles" easily conflates with "mundanes," another term in usage among Pagans in overlap with the Society for Creative Anachronism community.

Many Pagans were angered by the recruiting of a Witch for the reality television game show *Mad, Mad House*, and by the agreement of the well-known Australian Witch Fiona Horne to appear on the show. Pagans were disturbed that the producers sought someone who was a "full time witch, not a lawyer by day, witch by night." They were looking for someone unusual, "alternative," to create a contrast between the "alts" and the "normals," who were the contestants on the show. It was designed as a game show, so that one person would be voted out of the house each episode. Critics of Horne's participation said she treated Paganism as a lifestyle rather than as a religion, even attributing those words to her. After viewing the edited show, Horne says she has "no regrets" regarding her participation, although later episodes were "edited in such a way as to not reflect the true nature of the individuals involved."[59]

Paganism started to become commodified as it emerged from the secrecy of initiatory traditions. Increased public acceptance of the religion led to glossy magazines, Witch characters on television shows, and training courses that charge fees. Participation in Paganism became more easily available through commercial channels than through traditional coven or apprenticeship instruction, since it is easier to buy how-to books and accessories than to find a teacher. Commodified teaching can be differentiated from traditional teaching on the basis of fee payment, reflecting the belief that traditional teaching is a gift and not for sale. Practitioners feel that consumerism encourages superficial participation in the religion and self-indulgence rather than personal growth or mature cultural criticism. In addition, consumerist varieties of Paganism cultivate a sense of lack, encouraging practitioners to consume products in the hope that they can become happy, less lonely or anxious, or better Pagans. As in consumerism in general, consumption creates the desire to consume more. In addition, consumerist varieties of Paganism create the illusion that buying certain products or brands (or things associated with particular people, such as the popular Australian figure Deborah Gray) is the only means of access to their tradition.[60]

Trendy spell books also play a role in the popularization and commodification of Witchcraft. Popular spell books encourage superficial participation in Witchcraft, and "the wide distribution of spell books and the popularity of Witchcraft television shows and movies suggests that New Age Witchcraft is much more common than traditional Witchcraft."[61] Some practitioners see the wide availability of recent spell books as positive, because it provides a safe environment for experimentation, but popular spell books do not encourage learning from other sources. Popular spell books such as Athena Starwoman and Deborah Gray's *How to Turn Your Ex-Boyfriend into a Toad and Other Spells for Love, Wealth, Beauty and Revenge*, Titania Hardie's *Hocus Pocus: Titania's Book of Spells*, and Antonia Beattie's *The Girl's Handbook of Spells: Charm your Way to Popularity and Power* tend to be weak on ethics and encourage practitioners to hold self-centered views.

Spell books aimed at teenage girls can encourage a positive self-image and healthy self-esteem and can contribute to the reenchantment of everyday life. However, some reinforce idealistic images of female beauty, and they generally assume a posture of heterosexism. These books do not encourage cultural change through countercultural living, but they can foster it through personal empowerment.[62]

Not only scholars and Pagan elders are critical of popular spell books and other aspects of commodified practice; youth are also "frustrated by the rabid marketing of diluted and sugar-coated versions of [their] religion to teens."[63] Mattel's attempt to cash in on the popularity of magic with "Secret Spells Barbie" backfired. They removed the product from shelves in the United States due to Christian protests against the marketing of Witchcraft to children. It was not only Christians who were disturbed by the marketing of Secret Spells Barbie; Pagans were also troubled by the presentation of spell crafting to young children in the commercials promoting the doll. The advertisements presented love spells as successful, but without any sense of ethics.[64] The product remains available in Canada, and demand for it may increase from collectors because of its being withdrawn from the American market.

While some Pagans express chagrin at those who find such toys appealing, more often practitioners express embarrassment over people who buy such products or consumerist spell books and treat them like authoritative sources in Paganism. Some Pagans see consumerist Paganism as "flaky" and disdain it as "New Age." They express embarrassment with "newbie," "New Agey," or uninformed coreligionists who express beliefs such as the idea that having a blue tattoo of a crescent moon between one's eyebrows is an ancient practice of Goddess practitioners, when it is derived from Marion Zimmer Bradley's novel *The Mists of Avalon.* Some are embarrassed by SCA-inspired clothing or ostentatious accessories and ritual tools, but others identify such pursuit of intellectual seriousness with "holier than thou" attitudes.[65]

Some practitioners react to the perceived flakiness of consumerist trends with avowals of "Dark Paganism." Dark Paganism includes those who identify with the "Left Hand Path" and the practice of "magick" in a nonconformist manner to "light" or "white" Witchcraft. They indicate that they do not practice black magic in the sense of malevolence or evil, but they feel that a dark version of Paganism is a necessary balance to the "whitewashed" and "sugarcoated" practices of mainstream Wicca. One form of Dark Paganism is Goth Paganism, such as that espoused by John J. Coughlin in his book *Out of The Shadows: An Exploration of Dark Paganism and Magick*, which was one of the first meldings of Goth and Pagan culture. Goth subculture started with ambient, industrial, and some pop music of the early 1980s that explored themes of taboo emotions, such as feelings about death and tragic love.[66] Some practitioners see Goth or Dark Paganism as simply another species of flakiness, equally embarrassing as the "fluffy-bunny," "sweetness and light" variety espoused by New Agey Pagans and marketed to teens.

While some practitioners want Paganism to be a creative alternative to the mainstream, and enjoy disrupting expectations of normal behavior, others feel that mainstream acceptance is important for protecting their rights to religious freedom. One tactic for preserving the alternative nature of Paganism while seeking tolerance and equality in mainstream institutions is to seek "respect, not respectability."[67] Practitioners of contemporary Paganism are diverse in their attitudes, beliefs, and practices, as well as in their feelings about how, or if, Paganism should become an organized religion. As the religion matures, practitioners are seeking equal rights to practice their religion freely, without discrimination, harassment, or persecution, while struggling to preserve the impulses that led them to the religion. Although they remain a minority religion, and practitioners differ in their methods, and sometimes their goals regarding mainstream acceptance, they are claiming a place among the world's religions.

FURTHER READING

Eilers, Dana D. *Pagans and the Law: Understand Your Rights*. Franklin Lakes, NJ: New Page Books, 2003.

Lady Liberty League. Circle Sanctuary. www.circlesanctuary.org/liberty.

New Witch. "Rant & Rave." Regular column in *New Witch* magazine.

Ontario Consultants on Religious Tolerance. www.religioustolerance.com.

Pagan Federation/Fédération Païenne Canada. www.pfpc.ca.

Pagan Pride. www.paganpride.org.

PanGaia. "Feedback Loop: Letters from our Readers," and "Toe-to-Toe: A Forum for Controversy and Opinion." Regular columns in *PanGaia* magazine.

Pike, Sarah M. *Earthly Bodies, Magical Selves: Contemporary Pagans and the Search for Community*. Berkeley: University of California Press, 2001.

Sage Woman. "The Rattle: Our Readers Speak." Regular column in *Sage Woman* magazine.

The Witches' Voice. www.witchvox.com.

NOTES

1. *Council for a Parliament of the World's Religions*, 2002, www.cpwr.org (accessed September 28, 2004).

2. Selena Fox, "Bridges: Pagans at the Parliament," *Circle Magazine* 91 (2004): 34.

3. Sarah M. Pike, *Earthly Bodies, Magical Selves: Contemporary Pagans and the Search for Community* (Berkeley: University of California Press, 2001), 108–9.

4. Pike, *Earthly Bodies, Magical Selves*, 111.

5. *Washington Post*, August 23, 1993.

6. Pike, *Earthly Bodies, Magical Selves*, 120.

7. *Circle Magazine*, "Lady Liberty League Report," *Circle Magazine* 88, 89 (2003), www.circlesanctuary.org/liberty/report (accessed September 24, 2004).

8. Quoted in Pike, *Earthly Bodies, Magical Selves*, 99.

9. Pike, *Earthly Bodies, Magical Selves*, 99–100.

10. Pike, *Earthly Bodies, Magical Selves*, 102–3.

11. Pike, *Earthly Bodies, Magical Selves*, 100, 104–6.

12. *Circle Magazine*, "Lady Liberty League Report," *Circle Magazine* 90 (2003), www.circlesanctuary.org/liberty/report (accessed September 24, 2004).

13. Kevin Corcoran, "Judge: Parents Can't Teach Pagan Beliefs," *Indystar.com*: the online edition of the *Indianapolis Star*, May 26, 2005. This ruling was subsequently overturned. Brendan Coyne, "Court Approves Wicca for Kids, Dodges Constitutional Issue," *New Standard*, August 19, 2005, http://newstandardnews.net/content/?action=show_item&itemid=2250&x=x (accessed August 31, 2005.)

14. Pike, *Earthly Bodies, Magical Selves*, xi–xii.

15. *Circle Magazine*, "Lady Liberty League Report," *Circle Magazine* 90.

16. *Circle Magazine*, "Lady Liberty League Report," *Circle Magazine* 90.

17. Michael Samhain, "Defending the Craft," *New Witch* 6 (2004), www.newwitch.com/archives/06/read/defending.html (accessed September 24, 2004).

18. Dana D. Eilers, *Pagans and the Law: Understand Your Rights* (Franklin Lakes, NJ: New Page Books, 2003).

19. Kerr Cuhulain, *Law Enforcement Guide to Wicca* (Victoria, British Columbia: Horned Owl Publishing, 1989).

20. *Pagan Unity Campaign*, 2004, www.paganunitycampaign.org (accessed September 28, 2004).

21. Chas S. Clifton, "Fort Hood's Wiccans and the Problem of Pacifism" (paper presented at the annual meeting of the American Academy of Religion, Nashville, Tennessee, November 20, 2000).

22. Tom Doyle Jr., "More from Pagans in Prison," letter to the editor published in *PanGaia* 39 (2004): 9.

23. Windwalker, "Lady Liberty League Report," *Circle Magazine* 91 (2004): 54.

24. CNN (Time Warner), "Supreme Court: Prisons Must Accommodate Religions," May 31, 2005, www.cnn.com/2005/LAW/05/31/scotus.prison.religion (accessed September 5, 2005).

25. Chas S. Clifton, "Tents, Not Cathedrals: An Argument against Paid Clergy," *The View from Hardscrabble Creek* 2 (March 1993).

26. Frederic Lammond, "Memories of Gerald Gardner," in *Celebrating the Pagan Soul: Our Own Stories of Inspiration and Community*, ed. Laura A. Wildman (New York: Citadel Press, 2005), 94.

27. Clifton, "Tents, Not Cathedrals."

28. Pike, *Earthly Bodies, Magical Selves*, 53, 116.

29. Pike, *Earthly Bodies, Magical Selves*, xix.

30. Pike, *Earthly Bodies, Magical Selves*, 116–18.

31. Archer, "Bumps along the Pagan Path," *PanGaia* 39 (2004): 22.

32. Pike, *Earthly Bodies, Magical Selves*, 53–54.

33. Pike, *Earthly Bodies, Magical Selves*, 213.

34. Quoted in Pike, *Earthly Bodies, Magical Selves*, 212.

35. Pike, *Earthly Bodies, Magical Selves*, 118, 101.

36. See Pike, *Earthly Bodies, Magical Selves*, 119.

37. Pike, *Earthly Bodies, Magical Selves*, 209.

38. Chas Clifton, NatRel (electronic discussion group of the Nature Religions Scholars Network), September 2004.

39. Pike, *Earthly Bodies, Magical Selves*, 209, 217.

40. Pike, *Earthly Bodies, Magical Selves*, 101.

41. Quoted in Pike, *Earthly Bodies, Magical Selves*, 102.

42. Síân Reid, "Witch Wars: Factors Contributing to Conflict in Canadian Neopagan Communities," *The Pomegranate: A New Journal of Neopagan Thought* 11 (2000): 11.

43. Reid, "Witch Wars," 12.

44. Reid, "Witch Wars," 17.

45. Fritz Jung, "What Is a Witch War?" *The Witches' Voice*, January 4, 1998, www.witchvox.com/wars/ww_whatis.html (accessed September 20, 2004).

46. NatRel, 2004.

47. Ronald Hutton, *The Triumph of the Moon: A History of Modern Pagan Witchcraft* (Oxford: Oxford University Press, 1999), 320.

48. Reid, "Witch Wars," 18.

49. See Jone Salomonsen, *Enchanted Feminism: The Reclaiming Witches of San Francisco* (London: Routledge, 2002).

50. Helen Berger, *A Community of Witches* (Columbia: University of South Carolina Press, 1999), 110.

51. *PanGaia*, "Toe-to-Toe: A Forum for Controversy and Opinion," *PanGaia* 39 (2004): 13–16.

52. Reid, "Witch Wars," 13.

53. Lauryl Stone, "Rant and Rave," *New Witch* 5 (2004): 5.

54. See, in particular, Charlene Spretnak, ed., *The Politics of Women's Spirituality* (Garden City, NY: Anchor Books [Doubleday], 1982).

55. See, for example, Kevin Marron, *Witches, Pagans & Magic in the New Age* (Toronto: Seal Books [McClelland-Bantam], 1989).

56. Archer, "Bumps along the Path," 22, 25.

57. Dagonet Dewr, "The Vibe," (editorial) *New Witch* 7 (2004): 1.

58. *New Witch*, "Rant and Rave," *New Witch* 7 (2004): 5–13.

59. See *New Witch*, "Rant and Rave," *New Witch* 7 (2004): 7–9.

60. This analysis is drawn from Douglas Ezzy, "The Commodification of Witchcraft," *Australian Religion Studies Review* 14 (2001): 31–44.

61. Douglas Ezzy, "New Age Witchcraft? Popular Spell Books and the Re-enchantment of Everyday Life," *Culture and Religion* 4 (2003): 61.

62. This analysis is drawn from Ezzy, "New Age Witchcraft?"

63. See "The Rattle: Our Readers Speak," *Sage Woman* 65 (2004): 89.

64. Phil Brucato, "Chalice & Keyboard," *New Witch* 7 (2004): 30.

65. Archer, "Bumps along the Path," 26.

66. Jason Pitzl-Waters and Jacqueline Enstrom-Waters, "Dark Paganism with John Coughlin," *New Witch* 6 (2004), www.newwitch.com/archives/06/read/dark.html (accessed September 29, 2004).

67. Macha Nightmare, NatRel (electronic discussion group of the Nature Religions Scholars Network), September 2004.

11

Research in Pagan Studies

Research on Paganism was initially conducted in terms of studying a new religious movement, and eventually it developed into the field of Pagan studies as Paganism came to be recognized as a religion. Early sensationalist accounts in the 1960s, most often reported by journalists rather than academics, tended to conflate Paganism with Satanism. Shortly thereafter, scholars began to study Paganism as a cult (a new religious movement). More journalistic surveys appeared in the following decades, and scholarly analysis of trial records began. Other historical studies of the origins of modern Witchcraft have now been conducted, as well as sociological studies and focused ethnographic studies. Pagan studies scholars frequently use interdisciplinary methods drawing on folklore, anthropology, sociology, psychology, and other fields, rather than restricting their inquiries to either text-based research or interviews and surveys. Researchers are developing new methodologies to address the fact that most scholars who study Paganism are also practitioners, elaborating on the method of participant observation. Their work is at the leading edge of engaged, reflexive research in the study of religion.

In addition to giving a brief discussion of the methods used to study Paganism, this section functions somewhat as a review of Pagan studies and is intended to give enough information on sources for instructors to guide students in further research, even if Pagan studies is not their primary area of expertise. It also illustrates the maturation of Pagan studies beyond the study of Paganism as a new religious movement, to a formal area of study within the study of religion, particularly evident in the development of advanced ethnographic and historical studies.

"How-to" books by practitioners of Paganism began to appear in the 1960s, following the popularization of Wicca in Britain and the United States. Shortly afterward, encyclopedic overviews of religion began to include Paganism, listing it as a new religious movement. For example, Robert Ellwood's *Religious and Spiritual Groups in Modern America* (1973) and Gordon Melton's *Encyclopedia of American Religions* (2002), first published in the seventies, discuss Paganism as a new religious movement. Until the late 1980s and early 1990s, Paganism was almost exclusively treated together with "cults" and the New Age movement in academic writings. In his *Encyclopedic Handbook of Cults in America* (1984), Melton treats Paganism as a new "cult" in nonprejudicial terms—evangelicals tend to regard Melton as a cult apologist. More recent discussions of Paganism have appeared in chapters in books on the New Age movement such as Paul Heelas' *The New Age Movement* (1996) and Wouter J. Hanegraaff's *New Age Religion and Western Culture* (1997). Michael York's *The Emerging Network: A Sociology of the New Age and Neo-Pagan Movements* (1995) and Sarah Pike's *New Age and Neopagan Religions in America* (2004) discuss Paganism and the New Age together but differentiate them.

Before encyclopedic studies began to appear, discussions of Paganism surfaced in popular writings by journalists. These accounts were generally sensationalistic and conflated Paganism with the New Age, "the occult," or Satanism. In the United States, such books were produced by Hans Holzer, Susan Roberts, and Brad Steiger. In Britain, Stewart Farrar and June Johns wrote similar volumes, as did Kevin Marron a few decades later in Canada. Holzer produced a number of titles, including *The Truth about Witchcraft* (1969), *The New Pagans* (1972), *The Witchcraft Report* (1973), and *Confessions of a Witch* (1975). Holzer was a popular writer on parapsychology and magical religion who "created a Gardnerian *Cosmo* Girl in 'Heather P.,'" the protagonist of *Confessions of a Witch*, which was presented as nonfiction but is unverified. Overviews by outsiders, such as Steiger's *Sex and Satanism* (1969), Roberts' *Witches U.S.A.* (1971), Martin Ebon's *Witchcraft Today* (1963), Marika Kriss' *Witchcraft: Past and Present* (1970), and Alan Landsburg's *In Search of Magic and Witchcraft* (1977), typically take a broad and shallow "cafeteria approach," providing a sampling of magical religion. These texts follow a basic pattern of giving a brief history of Witchcraft and then recounting the experiences of an attractive young woman who is involved in "the occult," rounded out by interviews with a few prominent personages, and finishing by claiming to know many witches and saying that they are everywhere. There appears to have been something of a circuit of people that journalists interviewed for researching such texts. People on the circuit included Raymond and Rosemary Buckland, who brought Gardnerian Wicca to the United States, and Mary Nesnick, who founded the "Algard" tradition; perhaps some other occult sources; and often Church of Satan founder Anton LaVey. Most of the people on this circuit were published authors at the time.[1]

Kevin Marron produced a similar general account of occult practices in Canada, with his *Witches, Pagans, & Magic in the New Age* (1989). The back cover of the book claims that it is both written with "a journalist's objectivity" and is a "fascinating exposé." He began his research with the intent of getting "a better perspective on Satanism," and his expectation of spectacle led him to express disappointment with the rituals of the Wiccan Church of Canada.[2] Rather than giving a scholarly analysis of Paganism, Marron gives a mass of generalized material without citing sources, giving the impression that what he wrote is just the lasting impression he had of the people he talked with over a few months or years, without any systematic field study.

A number of overviews by practitioners were also produced in the late 1960s and early 1970s. Sybil Leek authored several titles, including *Diary of a Witch* (1968) and *Complete Art of Witchcraft* (1973). Leo Louis Martello's *Weird Ways of Witchcraft* appeared in 1969. Raymond Buckland produced a number of such works, beginning with *Ancient and Modern Witchcraft* (1970) and *Witchcraft from the Inside* (1971).[3] Vivianne Crowley's *Wicca: The Old Religion in the New Age* (1989) was similarly aimed at practitioners but includes scholarly analysis of the religion. She looks at Wicca in relation to Jungian psychology, giving more theoretical than liturgical content, but this text has served as an introduction for many practitioners.

The first significant survey of Pagans was by a journalist, but one who knew Paganism from the inside. Margot Adler's *Drawing Down the Moon* (1986), first published in 1979, gives a detailed and comprehensive overview of contemporary Paganism in North America. For her initial study, she traveled for three months collecting information from groves and covens in the United States and Britain. She conducted a survey distributed nationally in the United States through the periodical *Green Egg*, and she taped more than a hundred hours of interviews. The survey for the second edition of her book was distributed in 1985 through *Panegyria* and at three festivals. Her study was also enriched by background research from libraries and archives in New York.[4] Although her research was restricted largely to the United States, her book remains the most comprehensive discussion of the varieties of contemporary Paganism in print and is notable for being the most commonly cited text among practitioners and scholars of Pagan studies. Adler is currently preparing a revised edition.

Text-based studies of Paganism did not have much to work with initially, since there is no sacred text or scripture that is accepted as authoritative, and scant theological writing was available in Paganism.[5] This lack of written sources initially led most scholars to regard Paganism as "primitive," because academic work focuses on written documents, and modern religions that do not focus on texts were thought to be "uncivilized."[6] Some book-length studies in theology are beginning to appear, such as religion scholar Michael York's ambitious *Pagan Theology: Paganism as a World Religion* (2003), in which he argues that paganism is at once the root of all religion and is worthy of study as a world religion. Carol Christ's *Rebirth of the Goddess: Finding Meaning in Feminist Spirituality* (1997) is a systematic thealogy, and her *She Who Changes: Re-imagining the Divine in the World* (2004) provides a process thealogy, building on the work of the Christian theologians Alfred North Whitehead and Charles Hartshorn. Melissa Raphael also develops a thealogy in her *Thealogy and Embodiment* (1997). Aiden Kelly's polemical denunciation of Gerald Gardner and celebration of Wicca as a new religion in *Crafting the Art of Magic* (1991) and Philip Heselton's counterresponses (2000, 2003) might be considered to constitute a developing theological discourse in Wicca.[7]

Some of the first scholarly written sources relevant to Pagan studies are analyses of trial records and theories about why the witch hunts occurred. Two of the earliest of these are Eliot Rose's *A Razor for a Goat: A Discussion of Certain Problems in the History of Witchcraft and Diabolism* (1962) and Norman Cohn's *Europe's Inner Demons: An Enquiry Inspired by the Great Witch-Hunt* (1975), which counter the theories of witchcraft survivals supported by Margaret Murray and Jules Michelet. Cohn discusses the scapegoating of "witches" as a projection of fantasies, noting that the same accusations were leveled at the early Christians. Christina Larner's *Enemies of God: The Witch-Hunt in Scotland* (1981) provides a social history, explaining the cultural context of how witchcraft was understood in the late Renaissance. Carlo Ginzburg's *Ecstasies: Deciphering the Witches' Sabbath* (1991) is a meticulously researched microhistory, but his conclusions about the connections between shamanism and stories in the Western Alps of attending witches' Sabbath meetings may not apply more generally across Europe.

A number of feminist studies of the witch hunts have appeared, some to greater academic acceptance than others. Barbara Ehrenreich and Deidre English's *Witches, Midwives, and Nurses* (1973) argues that most witches were female healers or midwives, but does not provide a systematic study of the witch hunts and is instead based on anecdotal evidence and a few atypical trials. Donna Read's film *The Burning Times* (1990) details the erosion of women's power in medieval Europe and discusses survivals of images of female divinity in the veneration of Mary. This documentary supports the idea that the church used the witch hunts to suppress women's power, and includes reference to the notoriously exaggerated number of nine million women killed in the witch hunts as a "high estimate." Anne Llewellyn Barstow's "deeply flawed" *Witchcraze: A*

New History of the European Witch Hunts (1994) is more often found in Pagan bookstores than the more reputable Brian Levack's *The Witch Hunt in Early Modern Europe* (1987).[8] Barstow supports the theory that misogyny was the principle cause of the witch hunts, but she ignores evidence that does not fit her theory. Diane Purkiss' *The Witch in History* (1996) explains that midwives may have been more likely to help witch hunters and blame witches than themselves become victims.

More recent textual studies in Paganism offer analysis of how-to texts and other primary sources in Paganism. Douglas Ezzy's study of the commodification of Witchcraft in popular spell books (2001), and Chris Klassen's study of the significance of speculative fiction for feminist Witches (2006) are two notable examples. A whole other bibliography would be necessary to describe the development of the study of feminist spirituality in textual and sociological studies. Wendy Griffin's anthology, *Daughters of the Goddess* (2000), is a good place to start.

Histories of the development of Paganism and subgroups within it began to appear in the late 1980s, first with Aiden Kelly's *Hippie Commie Beatnik Witches: A History of the Craft in California, 1967–1977* (1993), which is a personal memoir of the formation of the New Reformed Orthodox Order of the Golden Dawn (commonly known as NROOGD) and other groups in California in the 1960s. Doreen Valiente's *The Rebirth of Witchcraft* (1989) is similarly valuable as a personal memoir of her experiences in the early development of Wicca in Britain, since she recounts first-hand knowledge of Gerald Gardner and was a member of his coven. She also discusses other important figures in the genesis of contemporary Paganism in Britain. It would be hard to find a more respected figure in Pagan studies than historian Ronald Hutton, who produced a comprehensive history of the development of modern Witchcraft and Paganism in Britain out of folklore and literary sources, published as *The Triumph of the Moon* (1999). He combines thorough research and scholarly methods with a sympathetic attitude toward his subject matter. Hutton's British history is rounded out by Chas Clifton's history of Paganism in America, *Her Hidden Children* (2006), which describes the convergence of multiple strands of magical religion into the Gardnerian template, along with the influences of American environmentalism on the religion.

The field of Pagan studies emerged through the development of these histories, as well as through anthologies of conference papers, and the sociological and ethnographic studies that began to appear following American anthropologist Tanya Luhrmann's study on the practice of magic in contemporary British occultism, *Persuasions of the Witch's Craft* (1989). A few years after Luhrmann's study appeared, two conferences on contemporary Paganism in the United Kingdom produced anthologies of academic papers. The first international conference on contemporary Pagan studies was in 1993, at the University of Newcastle-upon-Tyne, which resulted in the publication of *Paganism Today* (1996), edited by Charlotte Hardman and Graham Harvey. A 1996 international conference at the University of Lancaster resulted in the anthology *Nature Religion Today* (1998), edited by Joanne Pearson, Richard H. Roberts, and Geoffrey Samuel. These conferences included presentations by a number of people who were then conducting studies on Pagans as part of their doctoral degrees. Over the same period, the Nature Religion Scholars Network formed, initially as an e-mail discussion group in 1996, and has grown into an international community of scholars engaged in Pagan studies, to become a program unit of the American Academy of Religion in 2005. James Lewis' anthology *Magical Religion and Modern Witchcraft* (1996) also appeared in the 1990s, collecting a mix of scholarly and practitioner-authored essays. *Belief beyond Boundaries: Wicca, Celtic Spirituality and the New Age* (2002), another anthology, edited by Joanne Pearson, which was designed as a textbook for a course on alternative spiritualities at the Open University, Milton Keynes, England, would make a good companion text to this one, although it can be expensive and difficult to obtain outside Britain. Another notable development is *The Pomegranate*, initially edited by Fritz Muntean, and now a refereed journal edited by Chas Clifton.

Sociological and anthropological studies of Pagan practitioners have been markedly interdisciplinary. Researchers approach Pagan studies from a variety of disciplinary backgrounds, not just sociology and anthropology, but also religious studies, women's studies, cultural studies, history, nature writing, political studies, philosophy, theology, folklore, archaeology, and psychology. In addition, each researcher reads background sources authored by other scholars as well as practitioners, including such diverse research sources as overviews, histories, how-to books, theological works, web pages, and listserv postings, while also collecting additional data directly from current practitioners. The growth of the Internet has increased the ease of collecting data and distributing surveys through electronic discussion lists and websites. However, it also creates a new source of bias because electronically distributed surveys can favor the computer-literate portion of the population and possibly overrepresent practitioners with higher incomes and education levels. Data analysis can be simplified with new technologies, but the trend in Pagan studies research is as much toward the collection of focused ethnographies through self-reflexive studies of small groups as it is toward the sort of quantitative research facilitated by new technologies.

Research on religious groups is usually conducted through some form of participant observation. The aim of this method is to study a population "horizontally," in solidarity with indigenous points of view, rather than "vertically," from externally generated categories. In practice, this method often generates conflict between inductive empirical approaches and a fear of "going native" and losing one's objectivity.[9] The participation of researchers in religious activities of Pagan practitioners varies from striving to maintain scholarly distance to engaging in reflective insider scholarship. A tension between participation and observation is evident in most studies of Paganism, regardless of where the scholar begins in relation to practitioners. Religion scholar Graham Harvey, for example, did fieldwork in preparation for his overview of Paganism, *Contemporary Paganism: Listening People, Speaking Earth* (1997), including interviews and participant observation,[10] but this methodology is not transparent. Despite his intent to describe what Pagans do rather than what they ought to do,[11] he appears to describe Paganism more as he would like it to be than as it actually is, glossing over troubling aspects like racism in Heathenry and making Paganism appear more uniformly environmentalist than it is.[12]

Anthropologist Lynn Hume's *Witchcraft and Paganism in Australia* (1997), produced in the same year as Harvey's work, is unfortunately now out of print. Sociologist Helen Berger's *A Community of Witches* (1999) is the result of ten years of participant observation in a community of Witches in the eastern United States. She also conducted a national survey of Pagans for *Voices from the Pagan Census: A National Survey of Witches and Neo-Pagans in the United States* (2003), with Evan A. Leach and Leigh S. Shaffer. The latter text, in particular, maintains scholarly distance from Paganism through sociological analysis. Síân Reid has also produced a national sociological survey of Pagans in Canada with her doctoral thesis *Disorganized Religion: An Exploration of the Neopagan Craft in Canada* (2001). She distributed her survey through a national Pagan magazine, *Hecate's Loom* (now defunct), and conducted interviews with some respondents. She compares demographics of the Pagan population with the general Canadian population, examines contemporary Paganism in the context of religion in Canada, and explores how practitioners construct their identities and communities in late modernity.

Ethnographic studies of Pagans include those of Sarah Pike, Jone Salomonsen, Kathryn Rountree, Sabina Magliocco, Jenny Blain, and Robert Wallis. Religion scholar Sarah Pike's *Earthly Bodies, Magical Selves: Contemporary Pagans and the Search for Community* (2001), a five-year ethnographic study of Pagan festival participants, is sympathetic yet critical. Theologian Jone Salomonsen's study of Reclaiming Witches in San Francisco, *Enchanted Feminism* (2002), is a ten-year ethnographic and theological study conducted between 1984 and 1994 on the original Reclaiming Community. Salomonsen became initiated as part of her research but did not become Pagan. Anthropologist Kathryn Rountree produced an ethnographic study of feminist Witches in New Zealand, *Embracing the Witch and the Goddess* (2004). She gathered primary research for the study during three years of doctoral research and continued her studies over the next ten years. Following feminist scholar Mary Daly, Rountree aims to give "a hag-identified vision" of feminist witchcraft. While she was not a practitioner when she began her studies, and found its ritual trappings "rather outlandish at first," she discovered that the worldview of feminist witchcraft was not far from her own.[13]

In *Witching Culture: Folklore and Neo-Paganism in America* (2004), Sabina Magliocco presents an ethnography of one of the oldest Pagan communities in North America, in Northern California. Magliocco conducted research in Berkeley and around the Bay Area of San Francisco in the mid- to late 1990s, and her ethnography focuses on the role of anthropology and folklore in the development of Paganism. Although she became initiated into a Gardnerian group, the Coven Trismegiston, and into the Reclaiming tradition, she regards herself as "neither and both" an insider and an outsider. She compares the question of emic versus etic (insider versus outsider) perspectives to people asking her if she is really American or Italian, indicating that there is a problem with essentialist categories that insist on an either/or dichotomy and reduce actual differences and ambiguities to fit the categories of study.[14]

Jenny Blain and Robert Wallis have produced critical self-reflexive ethnographies of Pagan groups. These ethnographies are politically conscious works in experiential anthropology written from insider perspectives. Blain's *Nine Worlds of Seid-Magic: Ecstasy and Neo-Shamanism in North European Paganism* (2002) is an insightfully autobiographical ethnography of reconstructionist practices of oracular *seidr*. Wallis' *Shamans/Neo-Shamans: Ecstasy, Alternative Archaeologies and Contemporary Pagans* (2003) is what he calls "autoarchaeology," ethnography that is self-reflexive and politically aware. His work is particularly postmodern; and, being complex, nuanced, and intentionally nonnormative, it is suitable only for advanced-level study.

Blain, Ezzy, and Harvey's *Researching Paganisms* (2004) is an excellent collection of writings on the development of methods rooted in, but going beyond, participant observation. A number of the contributors build on what anthropologists David Young and Jean-Guy Goulet (1994) call experiential ethnography—research that treats one's own experiences as data. Experiential ethnography developed to deal with the need to take informants seriously when they talk about what Young and Goulet call "extraordinary experiences." Experiential anthropology develops the method of participant observation, adding specifications of the level and type of participation necessary for study of religious groups, and recognizes the importance of interpretation in all observation. The contributors to *Researching Paganisms* are academics and practitioners, which are not necessarily exclusive categories, and their essays discuss insider/outsider complications in research, such as accusations and fears about "going native" and how conducting fieldwork can influence those researched and also change the researcher.

Serious participation in religious activities by researchers can change their perceptions despite their desires to retain objectivity, and can help them appreciate practitioners' experiences more deeply. Sarah Pike relates, "At times during my fieldwork, I 'went native' and felt like I was truly a Pagan too, but I always returned to my intellectual roots and my desire as a scholar to tell others' stories. In some sense I was a Pagan and still am, because there is no going back to who I was before my research began."[15] Magliocco had an extraordinary experience during ritual, which led her to study the role of ecstasy in depth.[16] Both Pike and Magliocco note the importance of bodily experiences in ritual. Pike says she gained knowledge of emotional, sensual, erotic, and embodied aspects of Pagan ritual through participation, and learned things she would not have by simply asking questions about it and observing.[17]

Serious participation can help researchers enter more deeply into the worldview of practitioners, but there are complications with being one's own informant. Síân Reid found it untenable to do ethnographic research because she was already embedded in the population she wished to study for her doctorate. The experience of socialization into the group could not be freshly approached as a researcher, because she was already socialized. As an insider in the religion, one needs to avoid assuming that one understands the meaning of things in the same way other practitioners do, and one cannot assume that one's own practices are normative.[18] Since Reid could not see a way to sufficiently problematize her worldview and become aware of her preconceptions, she chose to conduct sociological research exclusively through surveys and interviews rather than participant observation, withdrawing from community practice during the course of her research.[19]

Jenny Blain chose another path in addressing the need to problematize one's worldview as a researcher/practitioner, seeking to "render the familiar unfamiliar" in autoethnography through considering the process of becoming conscious of her involvement.[20] Blain's work is somewhat autobiographical, but reflectively and insightfully so. She describes how she participates in ritual but never completely belongs as an academic, a practitioner, and one who walks in other worlds.[21] She sees her work as a process of brokering, enabling conversation between the academic world and the practitioner world, and she notes that such work requires the development of specialized research ethics. She feels obligated to ensure that her research findings are accessible to other practitioners, and a sense of responsibility regarding the effects of her research on practitioners and the sites they regard as sacred.[22]

Some researchers regard autoethnography as inauthentic, believing that outsider research is "objective" in contrast to biased insider research. Insider researchers are faulted for lacking critical reflection and for being too close to practitioners and the topics of study. Scholar practitioners point out that no research position is without bias, and indicate that desires for unbiased objectivity are "remnants of positivism."[23] Robert Wallis regards his position as a researcher as a "double insider," both a scholar and a practitioner. Even researchers who attempt to maintain scholarly status as outsiders often find themselves implicated in their research on Pagans, as Pike found. In retrospect, she regards herself as being as much a "Pagan" as anyone she studied.[24] Sylvie Shaw responds to criticisms of insider research positions by embracing a partisan stance. She finds that to be partisan is to be accountable, and responsible to informants. Shaw notes that all approaches have drawbacks and that researchers just need to be aware of what they are.[25]

Scholars of Pagan studies are very much aware of the issue of "going native" in conducting their research. Some scholar practitioners see criticisms of insider research as delegitimizing of theology as an academic discipline. In theology, it is assumed that scholars are "native" or insiders in the traditions they study.[26] Graham Harvey explains that those who continue to participate deeply in the communities they study after completing fieldwork are accused of becoming "advocates" and of being incapable of reflecting critically on the religion they study. The perception in religious studies when it was created as a discipline, he says, was that religious studies aims to describe religion phenomenologically as "'lived realities,' 'as they are' rather than 'as they ought to be,'" while theology describes the ideals of the religion according to sources regarded as authentic within the religion.[27] Pike notes that religious studies has distinguished itself from theology through claims to undertake the objective study of religion, in contrast to research motivated by faith. She remarks, "Perhaps my more critical readings of festival experience came out of the need to distance myself from that world and from the changes the festivals wrought in me."[28]

While Harvey feels that religious studies should not become theological, he objects to the "pervasive view of many of our academic colleagues that we have in fact gone native and lost our ability to think and talk critically."[29] Marina Warner criticized Ronald Hutton for "going native" in her review of *Triumph of the Moon*, published in *The Times*, suggesting that scholars should not participate in the religions they study.[30] The idea of "going native" is colonialist, a remnant of the idea that religion is something that "other" people *do* and that Westerners *study*. Hutton remarks that anthropologists have been participating in the cultures they study since at least the 1930s, beginning with Evans-Pritchard's study of the Nuer in Sudan. Until the advent of experiential ethnography, the assumption was that researchers should immerse themselves in the culture studied during fieldwork, but not *"stay* native."[31] Hutton suggests that participation is crucial in studying Wicca, since "only somebody who has got inside it can write about it with authority."[32] Hutton is not a convert to Paganism; he was raised Pagan,[33] and was known before the publication of *The Triumph of the Moon* for rejecting the "traditional historiography of pagan witchcraft." He wanted to write an accurate history that would not abuse the dignity of the religion or violate any initiatory oaths. Despite Warner's review, Hutton suggests that accusations of "going native" are more often imagined than substantive, and he indicates that critics such as Warner are likely to construe any sympathetic presentation as conversion and advocacy.[34] Perhaps critical views are more often expressed through the teasing of colleagues than in print, similar to petty workplace harassment of Pagans in some office settings.

Salomonsen developed what she calls a "method of compassion" to deal with the fear of "going native." She was dissatisfied with the scholarly assumption that "anthropologists are permitted to 'go native' behaviorally ('participant observation'), even emotionally ('empathy'), but not cognitively."[35] She felt that if it is not acceptable to believe what informants say, then it is not possible to take their beliefs seriously. Salomonsen stresses the need to engage with practice, not just to pretend to participate, but also the need to maintain enough distance to make observations about rituals and participants' social interactions.[36] This is similar to the methodology of scholar practitioners, but Salomonsen expresses a need to return to the perspective of an outsider as an academic researcher upon completion of study to maintain her scholarly integrity. She says that her "'method of compassion' demands that we never forget that we are scholars," and that one should "not end up as scholarly converts and proselytizers."[37] However, one might suppose that taking beliefs seriously in terms of cognition should entail the possibility (not necessity) of conversion. Study of religious beliefs should entail a certain willingness to change, as Salomonsen says,[38] which might entail taking the risk that one could change one's religious perspective.

Scholar practitioners take the risk of becoming disillusioned in studying their own religious tradition. Andy Letcher experienced a process of "straightening out," in a reverse procedure of "going native" into the academy.[39] During graduate studies, he cut his hair, shaved his beard, stopped wearing outlandish clothing, and found that his studies prevented him from staying up playing music all night as he had previously done as part of his involvement with hippy/protest culture. Letcher found that his understanding of Druidry was challenged by his readings in religious studies and the general academic assumption that religious belief needs explanation.[40]

Figure 22a & b.   Andy Letcher, before and after entering academia (photos provided by Andy Letcher; latter is by Chris Holland)

Douglas Ezzy refers to the assumption that religious belief needs explanation in terms of the "methodological atheism" of sociological and anthropological studies of religion. However, as Ezzy says, it is "bad social science to assume prima facie that spiritual experiences are not genuine or real." To explain magical experiences in terms that attempt to demystify them is to misunderstand them. The phenomenological method in religious studies tries not to make prior assumptions about the truth of religious beliefs and experiences, and to accept the reality of religious experiences for practitioners. A hermeneutical approach recognizes the importance of language in interpretation and that all experience is already interpretive. Ezzy explains that extraordinary experiences do not need special treatment in interpretation, because all experiences are shaped through language and social context. The focus of research on extraordinary experience, he says, should be on how people make sense of them, not the accuracy of their accounts.[41]

Academic study of Paganism by scholar practitioners can undermine the beliefs of other practitioners. Hutton's work presents a challenge to some practitioners' beliefs about the history of their traditions, as might this text. Publishing research about Pagans commonly influences how they understand themselves and their religion. In the social sciences, this is called "reactivity," "the effect produced on a social group by the scholar who is studying it."[42] It can have effects other than directly challenging practitioners' beliefs. Even superficial participation of a researcher changes how practitioners behave. Wendy Griffin worried about "data contamination" in her experiences with participant observation, finding that the questions one asks have an impact on practitioners, and one's reactions in interviews influence outcomes.[43] Letcher suggests that he may have inadvertently created the categories he intended to study.[44] Robert Wallis indicates that research on Paganism often influences Pagan practice. He finds that neoshamanic practitioners are quite familiar with academic writings on various forms of shamanism and have addressed criticisms of cultural appropriation and developed political awareness of the issue.[45]

A lasting issue in methodology in Pagan studies is that of the ethics of the relationships between researchers and the communities researched. Participant observation research always entails issues of informed consent, and more recently, researchers have been dealing with the issue of ownership of the knowledge generated by research. There can be additional issues to consider in researching communities that maintain secret traditions, or when practitioners become scholars subsequent to their involvement with Paganism. Reid chose not to engage in participant observation, and to be open and honest with interviewees about her identity as a researcher and practitioner, because of her experience as a research subject in a previous study. The events discussed in the work resulting from that research project took place as much as three years before the person started to identify as a researcher in the community. In addition, the results of the study were not made available to participants until after submission and evaluation of the study. Consequently, the participants felt "exploited and betrayed" by the researcher's perceived violations of personal confidences. They were dissatisfied with how they were represented in the work, and resented strategic omissions in the data to make them fit the researcher's interpretative paradigm.[46]

Participants in Tanya Luhrmann's 1989 study also expressed anger and feelings of betrayal at her representation of them. Pagans were incensed by what they saw as Luhrmann's infiltration of their groups under false pretenses. Luhrmann felt it necessary to misrepresent herself to her research subjects in participant observation to maintain her academic credibility, but practitioners felt harmed by her discussions of the secrets of their traditions in her published work. Her research methods would probably not be acceptable under current ethics review processes, due to changes in methodology in anthropology since the 1980s. At that time, it was commonplace to immerse oneself in the culture one studied but to reaffirm a distanced and neutral academic stance upon completion of the research.[47]

Hutton relates that he had to deal with the "legacy of distrust" in historians of Witchcraft in conducting his research.[48] This experience led him to conclude,

> I believe firmly that a scholar should enter into an area of research not merely with the ambition of extracting as much as possible from it, for the benefit of oneself, one's colleagues and one's public, but with that of leaving it in the best possible condition for the next researcher: much as a good guest leaves a bedroom or hotel room as tidy as possible on departing. This means dealing with documents as delicately as is practicable, providing all references as clearly as may be done so that they can be followed up, and treating people who are the subjects of research or custodians of archives in such a manner as to encourage them to take a good view of scholars and inclined to welcome the next to come their way.[49]

In a similar attitude, Harvey advocates "guesthood" as a responsible alternative to the insider/outsider dichotomy. He indicates that scholars of religion are guests and should treat their hosts with respect. The goal of interaction should be to develop responsible relationships between researchers and practitioners. The researcher should not be afraid of changing the religion by participating in it (although s/he should not tell practitioners what their religious practice should be) but should engage in responsible dialogue. Harvey suggests a metaphor not of trying to "'walk in the shoes' of the 'other,'" but to sit across the campfire and converse.[50]

Robert Wallis espouses a similar view, seeing himself as a culture broker between practitioners and academics, and the work of research as a collaborative construction of meaning between researcher and informants. He suggests that insider research is not better but can be at least as good as standard participant observation. In his position as a "double insider," Wallis does not "go native" but retains a critical academic stance. Wallis concludes, "It does not matter how close researchers get to their 'subjects' so long as their findings express the level of insight and constructive, critical evaluation which one's academic peers require for acceptable scholarship."[51]

Research in Pagan studies is at the leading edge of methodologies in participant observation, developing methods that respect practitioners beliefs and that are politically aware. The emergence of Pagan studies as a new field of study has resulted in the newly formed Pagan studies research group in the American Academy of Religion. The academic community is coming to recognize Paganism as a full-fledged religion among the world's religions. After sixty years, contemporary Paganism is no longer a new religious movement, but a world religion.

FURTHER READING

Blain, Jenny, Douglas Ezzy, and Graham Harvey. *Researching Paganisms: Religious Experiences and Academic Methodologies.* Walnut Creek, CA: AltaMira Press, 2004.

NOTES

1. This historical information is drawn from Chas S. Clifton, *Her Hidden Children* (Lanham, MD: AltaMira, 2006), 103–5.

2. Kevin Marron, *Witches, Pagans & Magic in the New Age* (Toronto: Seal Books [McClelland-Bantam], 1989), 4, 71.

3. Referenced in Clifton, *Her Hidden Children*, 104.

4. Margot Adler, *Drawing Down the Moon: Witches, Druids, Goddess-Worshippers, and Other Pagans in America Today*, revised and expanded ed. (Boston: Beacon Press, 1986), xii–xiii.

5. This is less true of some reconstructionist and revivalist Pagan traditions in Eastern Europe. Pagans in Ukraine, for example, regard the *Book of Veles* as holy scripture (see Adrian Ivakhiv, "In Search of Deeper Identities: Neopaganism and Native Faith in Contemporary Ukraine," *Nova Religio: The Journal of Alternative and Emergent Religions* 8, no. 3 [March 2005]: 7–38).

6. Naomi R. Goldenberg, *Changing of the Gods* (Boston: Beacon Press, 1979), 113.

7. Aiden Kelly first aired his ideas about Gardnerian history in the Llewellyn magazine *Gnostica* and in Chas Clifton's journal *Iron Mountain: A Journal of Magical Religion* in the mid-1980s.

8. Jenny Gibbons, "Recent Developments in the Study of the Great European Witch Hunt," *The Pomegranate: A New Journal of Neopagan Thought* 5 (1998): 16.

9. Jone Salomonsen, "Methods of Compassion or Pretension? The Challenges of Conducting Fieldwork in Modern Magical Communities," in *Researching Paganisms: Religious Experiences and Academic Methodologies*, ed. Jenny Blain, Douglas Ezzy, and Graham Harvey (Walnut Creek, CA: AltaMira Press, 2004), 43.

10. Graham Harvey, "Pagan Studies or the Study of Paganisms? A Case Study in the Study of Religions," in *Researching Paganisms: Religious Experiences and Academic Methodologies*, ed. Jenny Blain, Douglas Ezzy, and Graham Harvey (Walnut Creek, CA: AltaMira Press, 2004), 243.

11. Graham Harvey, *Contemporary Paganism: Listening People, Speaking Earth* (New York: New York University Press, 1997), vii.

12. This is surely evident to me because it is the problem that is most likely to be found in my own research and writings in Pagan studies. As a practitioner, it is deeply tempting to describe one's religion as one would like it to be. It is also difficult not to overcompensate for this desire by becoming overly critical of one's fellow practitioners.

13. Kathryn Rountree, *Embracing the Witch and the Goddess: Feminist Ritual-Makers in New Zealand* (London: Routledge, 2004), 11.

14. Sabina Magliocco, *Witching Culture: Folklore and Neo-Paganism in America* (Philadelphia: University of Pennsylvania Press, 2004), 15.

15. Sarah M. Pike, "Gleanings from the Field: Leftover Tales of Grief and Desire," in *Researching Paganisms: Religious Experiences and Academic Methodologies*, ed. Jenny Blain, Douglas Ezzy, and Graham Harvey (Walnut Creek, CA: AltaMira Press, 2004), 111.

16. Magliocco, *Witching Culture*, 10.

17. Pike "Gleanings from the Field," 105.

18. Síân Lee MacDonald Reid, "Disorganized Religion: An Exploration of the Neopagan Craft in Canada" (Doctoral thesis, Carleton University, Ottawa, 2001), 37–38. Sylvie Shaw also notes this point, "At the Water's Edge: An Ecologically Inspired Methodology," in *Researching Paganisms: Religious Experiences and Academic Methodologies*, ed. Jenny Blain, Douglas Ezzy, and Graham Harvey (Walnut Creek, CA: AltaMira Press, 2004), 136.

19. Reid, "Disorganized Religion," 36, 39–40.

20. Jenny Blain, "Tracing the In/Authentic Seeress: From Seid-Magic to Stone Circles," in *Researching Paganisms: Religious Experiences and Academic Methodologies*, ed. Jenny Blain, Douglas Ezzy, and Graham Harvey (Walnut Creek, CA: AltaMira Press, 2004), 219–20.

21. Blain, "Tracing the In/Authentic Seeress," 230.

22. Blain, "Tracing the In/Authentic Seeress," 233–34.

23. Jenny Blain, Douglas Ezzy, and Graham Harvey, introduction to *Researching Paganisms: Religious Experiences and Academic Methodologies*, ed. Jenny Blain, Douglas Ezzy, and Graham Harvey (Walnut Creek, CA: AltaMira Press, 2004), 4.

24. Blain, Ezzy, and Harvey, "introduction," 9.

25. Shaw, "At the Water's Edge," 136.

26. Salomonsen, "Methods of Compassion or Pretension?" 48.

27. Harvey, "Pagan Studies or the Study of Paganisms?" 241.

28. Pike in Blain et al. 2004, 136.

29. Harvey, "Pagan Studies or the Study of Paganisms?" 252, 247.

30. Ronald Hutton, "Living with Witchcraft," in *Researching Paganisms: Religious Experiences and Academic Methodologies*, ed. Jenny Blain, Douglas Ezzy, and Graham Harvey (Walnut Creek, CA: AltaMira Press, 2004), 176–77.

31. Hutton, "Living with Witchcraft," 177, 178.

32. Hutton, "Living with Witchcraft," 176.

33. Hutton, "Living with Witchcraft," 173.

34. Hutton, "Living with Witchcraft," 183.

35. Salomonsen, "Methods of Compassion or Pretension?" 47.

36. Salomonsen, "Methods of Compassion or Pretension?" 51.

37. Salomonsen, "Methods of Compassion or Pretension?" 52–53.

38. Salomonsen, "Methods of Compassion or Pretension?" 53.

39. Andy Letcher, "Bardism and the Performance of Paganism: Implications for the Performance of Research," in *Researching Paganisms: Religious Experiences and Academic Methodologies*, ed. Jenny Blain, Douglas Ezzy, and Graham Harvey (Walnut Creek, CA: AltaMira Press, 2004), 33. Jo Pearson has also written about the process of "Going Native in Reverse" in Jo Pearson, "'Going Native in Reverse': The Insider as Research in British Wicca," in *Theorizing Faith: The Insider/Outsider Problem in the Study of Ritual*, ed. E. Arweck and M. D. Stringer (Birmingham, UK: University of Birmingham Press, 2002).

40. Letcher, "Bardism and the Performance of Paganism," 28.

41. Douglas Ezzy, "Religious Ethnography: Practicing the Witch's Craft," in *Researching Paganisms: Religious Experiences and Academic Methodologies*, ed. Jenny Blain, Douglas Ezzy, and Graham Harvey (Walnut Creek, CA: AltaMira Press, 2004), 113, 116, 121, 123.

42. Hutton, "Living with Witchcraft," 171.

43. Wendy Griffin, "The Deosil Dance," in *Researching Paganisms: Religious Experiences and Academic Methodologies*, ed. Jenny Blain, Douglas Ezzy, and Graham Harvey (Walnut Creek, CA: AltaMira Press, 2004), 65–66.

44. Letcher, "Bardism and the Performance of Paganism," 33.

45. Robert J. Wallis "Between the Worlds: Autoarchaeology and Neo-Shamans," in *Researching Paganisms: Religious Experiences and Academic Methodologies*, ed. Jenny Blain, Douglas Ezzy, and Graham Harvey (Walnut Creek, CA: AltaMira Press, 2004), 201–2.

46. Reid, "Disorganized Religion," 38–39.

47. Hutton, "Living with Witchcraft," 178.

48. Hutton, "Living with Witchcraft," 173.

49. Hutton, "Living with Witchcraft," 185–86.

50. Harvey, "Living with Witchcraft," 252–54.

51. Wallis, "Between the Worlds," 207, 196–97, 206–7.

Glossary

ADF. Short for Ár nDraíocht Féin, or A Druid Fellowship (more literally, "our own Druidism," from Gaelic). A contemporary Druid organization founded in the United States by Isaac Bonewits.

altar. An altar is a structure for ritual use, usually with a flat surface on which are placed ritual items such as candles and incense, and possibly images of a deity or deities. Pagans often have a permanent altar somewhere in or around their house, such as a shelf or small table, and may also construct temporary altars for specific rituals.

anarchist. A supporter of the political orientation of anarchism. Rather than believing that all forms of social control should be eliminated, anarchists usually support the idea of direct democracy and consensus decision making and hold to the ideal of living harmoniously in relatively small groups.

animism/animistic. The belief that all things in the world are alive, or that all things might be or become persons. Animism was initially a category developed by scholars for the study of what they saw as "primitive" religion that was less evolved than monotheism and modern secularism, but "animist" has been adopted as a self-descriptive term.

antidefamation. To defame is to say inflammatory and untrue things about a person or group of people. Antidefamation work counters such mean statements through public education and media relations. People doing such work provide support for those who have been maligned, and present a public face of the group as they counter stereotypes.

archetype/archetypal. "Archetypal" means of or relating to an archetype or archetypes. "Archetype" is a term introduced to psychology by Carl Jung, for persistent figures or structures in what he called the collective unconscious, such as the Mother, the Father, the Child, the Hero, and the Trickster. These figures occur cross-culturally and are sometimes regarded as deities or mythic figures in various cultures.

Asatru/Asatruar. Asatru is a denomination of Paganism that draws on the culture and mythology of northern Europe, particularly Iceland and Norse or Nordic mythology. Practitioners are known as Asatruar, although some prefer the term Heathen and refer to their tradition as Heathenry.

barrows. Artificial hills found in Britain and northwestern Europe, which are burial mounds. According to English folklore, the faeries live in these mounds.

BDSM (bondage, discipline/domination, and sadomasochism). Consensual sexual practices that involve bondage or the use of restraints, in which the participants enjoy inflicting/receiving pain.

bitheism/bitheistic. Refers to belief in two divinities. This is sometimes called duotheism. In the context of Paganism, the two divinities are generally the Goddess and the God.

ceremonial magic. A tradition based on Western esoteric practices derived from Jewish mysticism and a number of Neoplatonic sources such as Hermes Trismegistus. Originally these traditions were practiced within the context of Christianity and Judaism, but practitioners began to move outside these traditions in the late nineteenth century. Ceremonial magicians tend to conduct rituals in strict accordance with set recipes and scripts.

chant. A short song used in ritual.

clergy. A class of religious professionals, such as priestesses and priests, variously called rabbis, imams, pastors, reverends, and ministers in other religions.

Co-Mason. See Freemasonry.

cosmology. Worldview, what someone or a group of people thinks about how the world is structured and how humans and divinity fit into it.

countercultural. Alternative to mainstream culture. The term "countercultural" came into use in the 1960s to describe the rebellion of youth against social conventions and authorities that they found overly restrictive. It also describes political activity against established institutions, such as antiwar and global justice demonstrations.

coven. A group of Witches or other Pagans who regularly conduct ritual together.

Craft. This is a term used by some practitioners in preference to calling what they do religion. Some use it in place of the terms "Witchcraft" or "Wicca." Initially "Craft" referred to the practices of the Masons, and practitioners derive their use of the term from the influence of Masonry and Co-Masonry on early Wicca.

Craft lineage. Line of descent of who initiated whom in Witchcraft traditions, which forms something like a family tree.

creed. An institutionally sanctioned statement of belief, which often unifies members of a denomination and differentiates them from other denominations. Pagan denominations generally do not have standardized creeds.

crone/croning. "Crone" is a term of respect in Paganism and indicates a woman valued for her age and experience. A croning is a ritual that recognizes the passage of a woman from her fertile years into menopause, and celebrates her new status as a crone.

cultural borrowing/appropriation. Borrowing or stealing ideas, symbols, and practices from a culture to which one does not belong; sometimes discussed in nonjudgmental terms as globalism or bricolage.

dedicant. A term used in the Druid group Ár nDraíocht Féin for those who are beginning study in their clergy training program. More generally, a dedicant is one who has expressed an interest in learning about a tradition and has made an oath dedicating her/himself to growing in a particular tradition.

deity. A generic term for goddesses and gods, God and/or Goddess. Practitioners of other religions might refer to these beings as "supernatural," but Pagans often do not think of deities in this way.

divination. The practice of trying to gain insight into the past, present, or future by means of consulting a seemingly random system, such as dice or cards. Practitioners believe that the results of such castings are not random but reveal hidden knowledge, and they have developed elaborate systems such as Tarot card readings.

divinity. A generic term for goddesses and gods, God and/or Goddess, and any other form of deity; whatever is considered sacred or holy.

dogma. Religious teaching, especially teachings that have been passed down through the ages and are regarded as unquestionable.

eclectic. Inspired by diverse sources; drawing together different ideas, symbols, and practices into new forms, sometimes insensitive to charges of cultural appropriation.

ecofeminism. Combines the politics of the ecological movement and feminism. Ecofeminists note that the subordination of women and of the natural world often go hand in hand, using similar metaphors and symbols.

Enlightenment. "The Enlightenment" refers to what is often thought of as the dawning of the age of reason in Western culture, which entailed a critique of the established institutions of the Roman Catholic Church and rule by monarchy. In the Enlightenment, individual capacity for rational thought came to be valued more than loyalty to received traditions. The Enlightenment also coincided with the industrial revolution, urbanization, colonial expansion, and the erosion of peasant and indigenous cultures.

ethnography/ethnographers. An ethnography is a focused study of a specific group of people in their cultural context, usually conducted through the method of participant observation. Ethnographic studies often produce more qualitative than statistical data, reporting on what people say and do in narrative terms rather than collecting data through counting and numbering. People who conduct ethnographic studies are known as ethnographers.

folklore. Culturally specific beliefs and practices that may or may not be perceived as part of the religion with which people identify.

Freemasonry/Freemason. Freemasons are members of an international secret society. Membership is exclusive to those who have been initiated and know the secret signs of the organization. Initially membership in the Masons was restricted to men, but women have been allowed to join, at least in some groups, which are called Freemasonry groups, or sometimes Co-Masonry. Freemasonry is characterized by certain metaphysical beliefs, rituals, and a hierarchical organization. Originally the Masons were actual masons, builders in stone, but current members are upper-middle-class professionals in a variety of fields.

Gaia/Gaea. The Greek goddess of nature; a name given to the Earth in some pantheist cosmologies.

Gardnerian. A denomination of Wicca based on the teachings of Gerald Gardner, the British civil servant who first popularized Witchcraft as a religious tradition in Britain in the 1940s and 1950s.

globalism. See cultural borrowing/appropriation.

gnostic. This term sometimes refers to occult or esoteric knowledge. It is a label applied to the belief that the world was created by God but left in the care of a demiurge or lesser being, who controls matter and is opposed to spiritual concerns. When capitalized, Gnostic refers to Christian heretics of the first to third centuries who held this and similar views.

handfasting. A Pagan ritual solemnizing a loving commitment, similar in social function to marriage, but not necessarily legally recognized as such.

Heathen/Heathenry. See Asatru.

hereditary witch. Someone who learned magic from older members of her/his family. Often these magical practices are not identified with Witchcraft until later-generation practitioners cease to identify with mainstream religious practices. Usually the magical practices are part of a folklore tradition that may have some pre-Christian content but that has been long incorporated in the folk practices of people who identify as Christian.

immanent/immanence. "Immanent" means within or inside. Belief in immanence refers to belief that divinity is inherent to or dwells within the material or natural world.

laity. Nonprofessional members of religious groups, or practitioners of religious traditions.

landwights. A general term for local nature spirits used by some Asatru and Heathen practitioners.

late modernity. A term describing contemporary mainstream Western culture in contrast to postmodern and traditional culture. It indicates that most people in Western culture live in a culture that is no longer bound by tradition and that has aspects of postmodernity but has not entirely rejected the modern values of the Enlightenment. Late modernity is characterized by modern values such as democracy, equality, and individualism; social trends of ethnic diversity; and cultural trends toward cultural mixing. Postmodernity embraces relativism more fully, moving from tolerance of diversity to doubts about the reality of truth.

lifeways. The things people do in their daily lives that distinguish them as belonging to a particular cultural or religious tradition, such as asking permission and/or giving thanks before harvesting and consuming plants.

liturgy. Ritual script. Sometimes formulaic words said during religious functions. Liturgies can be in poetry or prose and can be repeated from traditional sources or created for specific events.

Masonry. See Freemasonry

mystery religion. A religion that is structured through initiation into "the mysteries," often through a series of degrees. After prolonged instruction, initiates receive knowledge of the mysteries of the tradition. These mysteries might include things such as secret names of the deities or hidden meanings in ritual practices.

occult. Esoteric or little-known knowledge and/or practices. "Occult" is often used synonymously with "New Age" but means "hidden," and often implies secret knowledge.

pantheism. Belief that everything is God or part of God, or the belief that God or divinity is immanent in the world, sometimes in conjunction with the belief that the world is the body of the Goddess or God.

participant observation. A common anthropological method in the study of religion in which the researcher does not merely observe research subjects but does what they do in an effort to more fully understand what the people are doing, why, and what it means for them.

polyamorist/polyamory. A polyamorist is one who maintains multiple loving relationships and is committed to more than one other person. Polyamory describes the practice in general. Polyamorous relationships take a variety of forms, including group marriage, marriage with additional partners who do not cohabit with the married partners but maintain relationships with one or both of the married partners, as well as various configurations of cohabitation and affiliation.

polytheism/polytheistic. Refers to belief in multiple divinities or deities.

reconstructionist. Religious practices that are based on historical or archaeological evidence and are designed to re-create past practices in a historically accurate fashion. The term also refers to denominations that favor such practices.

reincarnation. The rebirth of one's essential being or soul in another earthly life after one's body dies.

romanticism. A nostalgic idealization of the past. Cultural trends that idealize the past are identified as German Romanticism or English Romanticism, for example.

routinization. The process of creating institutions and standardized religious practices. This process is often associated with the second generation of a new religious movement, as adherents harmonize the statements and practices of early leaders of the movement and teach these practices to children and new members of the religion.

sabbat. Any of the eight major seasonal festivals in the Wiccan wheel of the year. They are called "sabbats" following the name used for secret witchcraft meetings in accusations during the medieval witch hunts. The term "sabbat" is derived from the Jewish sabbath, which is celebrated weekly on Saturdays. Heretics were accused of also holding secret religious meetings on days other than Sunday, which is regarded as the proper Christian day to hold religious service.

scrying. Scrying is a form of divination in which a practitioner looks into a pan of water, a polished stone, or some other reflective surface to see the future, events happening at a distance, or images answering a question about the past, present, or future.

seidr. A Heathen ritual practice derived from a passage from the Saga of Erik the Red. In *seidr*, the practitioner goes into trance with the help of other ritual participants and answers questions from the other participants.

shamanism/shamanistic. A type of religious practice or beliefs that entail communication with a nonempirical realm or aspect of reality, sometimes conceived as interaction with spirits. Shamanism was initially a category developed by anthropologists and scholars of religion for the study of "shamans" or religious specialists in indigenous cultures who contacted nonhuman entities on behalf of their communities or, in some cases, to do harm to certain individuals. It has subsequently been adopted as a self-descriptive term in contexts outside of indigenous culture and in reconstructionist traditions.

shrine. Technically, a shrine is dedicated to a specific deity, but many Pagans use the term interchangeably with altar.

solitaries. Solitary practitioners of Paganism; those who do ritual work alone rather than in a group setting.

spell casting. Using magic to effect change or bring about a desired state of events. Spell casting can be a simple practice of something like making a hand gesture for luck, or it can be integrated into a more elaborate ritual, such as one designed to heal a friend, family member, or oneself.

spiritualism. A religious movement beginning in the latter part of the nineteenth century, which prominently featured communication with the dead.

Tarot cards. The Tarot is a special deck of seventy-eight cards used for divination. They are similar to playing cards in having four suits, but these are called cups, wands, swords, and pentacles. In addition to these suited cards, called the minor arcana, the Tarot includes twenty-two other cards called the major arcana.

teleological. Oriented toward, or proceeding toward, a final end.

thealogy. A parallel term to theology, which means study of God or the gods; this term refers to study of female deity, the Goddess or goddesses.

theoilogy. Study of deity in a polytheistic sense, including goddesses and gods. Some people prefer the term polytheology, although neither of these terms is in common use.

theodicy. A theological explanation of why suffering and death exist.

trance work. The use of altered states of consciousness to pursue ritual work. Practitioners may conceive of this as journeying to the dream world, or alternate realms such as the underworld, the astral plane, or the land of the dead.

transcendence. Going beyond. In some religious traditions, this is envisioned as an ascension beyond the mundane world into the supernatural, but Pagans are more likely to speak of transcending their own limits than the limits of nature, or to speak of the transcendence of divinity in terms of a transcendence of the ordinary. See also immanent/immanence.

Umbanda. An Afro-Amerindian initiatory tradition that developed in Brazil beginning in the late nineteenth or early twentieth century, which combines elements of indigenous culture, African traditions, and Catholicism.

Wiccaning. A ritual celebration for welcoming children into Wicca, usually done when the child is an infant.

world religion. One of the religions typically studied in introductory courses on religion. These traditionally include Christianity, Judaism, Islam, Buddhism, and Hinduism, which are globally dominant or have been perceived to be so, but sometimes include traditions such as Bahai, Sikhism, and indigenous religion. There is no accepted rationale for what religions should be regarded as world religions.

Bibliography

Abram, David. *The Spell of the Sensuous: Perception and Language in a More-Than-Human World*. New York: Vintage (Random House), 1996.

Abrams, M. H., ed. "John Keats," "William Butler Yeats," and "Robert Graves." In *Norton Anthology of English Literature*, 5th ed., edited by M. H. Abrams, 2:826–44, 1927–34, 2244–52. New York: W. W. Norton, 1986.

ADF. *Ár nDraíocht Féin/A Druid Fellowship*. 2004. www.adf.org/core (accessed May 14, 2004).

Adler, Margot. *Drawing Down the Moon: Witches, Druids, Goddess-Worshippers, and Other Pagans in America Today*. Revised and expanded ed. Boston: Beacon Press, 1986.

Albanese, Catherine L. *Reconsidering Nature Religion*. Harrisburg, PA: Trinity Press International, 2002.

Amethyst. "The Charge of the Crone." *Amethyst's Wicca*, 2004. www.angelfire.com/realm2/amethystbt/chargeofthecrone.html (accessed June 24, 2004).

Andrews, Lynn W. *Medicine Woman*. New York: HarperSanFrancisco, 1981.

Apuleius, Lucius. *The Golden Ass*. Trans. Robert Graves. London: Penguin Books, 1990.

Archer. "Bumps along the Pagan Path." *PanGaia* 39 (2004): 22–28.

Aswynn, Freya. *Northern Mysteries & Magick: Runes & Feminine Powers*. St. Paul, MN: Llewellyn Publications, 1998.

Barstow, Anne Llewellyn. *Witchcraze: A New History of the European Witch Hunts*. San Francisco: HarperSanFrancisco, 1994.

BBC Online Network. "UK Pagans Celebrate as Numbers Soar." *BBC Online Network*, October 31, 1999, 16:06 GMT. http://news.bbc.co.uk/1/hi/uk/500484.stm (accessed March 1, 2004).

Beattie, Antonia. *The Girl's Handbook of Spells: Charm Your Way to Popularity and Power*. Sydney: Lansdowne, 2000.

Berger, Helen. *A Community of Witches*. Columbia: University of South Carolina Press, 1999.

Berger, Helen, Evan A. Leach, and Leigh S. Shaffer. *Voices from the Pagan Census: A National Survey of Witches and Neo-Pagans in the United States*. Columbia: University of South Carolina Press, 2003.

Bibby, Reginald W. *Unknown Gods: The Ongoing Story of Religion in Canada*. Toronto: Stoddart, 1993.

Blain, Jenny. "Contested Meanings: Earth Religion Practitioners and the Everyday." *The Pomegranate: A New Journal of Neopagan Thought* 12 (2000): 15–25.

———. *Nine Worlds of Seid-Magic: Ecstasy and Neo-Shamanism in North European Paganism.* London: Routledge, 2002.

———. "Tracing the In/Authentic Seeress: From Seid-Magic to Stone Circles." In *Researching Paganisms: Religious Experiences and Academic Methodologies,* edited by Jenny Blain, Douglas Ezzy, and Graham Harvey. Walnut Creek, CA: AltaMira Press, 2004.

Blain, Jenny, Douglas Ezzy, and Graham Harvey. *Researching Paganisms: Religious Experiences and Academic Methodologies.* Walnut Creek, CA: AltaMira Press, 2004.

Bonewits, Isaac. "Defining Paganism: Paleo-, Meso-, and Neo- 2.5." *Isaac Bonewits' Homepage,* 2001 [1979]. www.neopagan.net/PaganDefs.html (accessed August 6, 2004).

———. "The Second Epistle of Isaac." The Druid Chronicles (Evolved). Berkeley, CA: Drunemeton Press, 1974.

Bonewits, P. E. I. *Real Magic.* Berkeley, CA: Creative Arts Book, 1971.

Bowman, Marion. "Cardiac Celts: Images of the Celts in Paganism." In *Paganism Today,* edited by Charlotte Hardman and Graham Harvey, 242–51. London: Thorsons (HarperCollins), 1996.

———. "Nature, the Natural, and Pagan Identity." *Diskus* 6 (2000), Web edition. http://web.uni-marburg.de/religionswissenschaft/journal/diskus (accessed May 16, 2001).

Bradley, Marion Zimmer. *The Mists of Avalon.* New York: Del Rey (Ballantine), 1982.

Brucato, Phil. "Chalice & Keyboard." *New Witch* 7 (2004): 29–30.

Buckland, Raymond. *Buckland's Complete Book of Witchcraft.* St. Paul, MN: Llewellyn Publications, 1986.

Budapest, Zsuzsanna. *The Holy Book of Women's Mysteries.* Oakland, CA: Wingbow Press, 1989.

Budapest, Zsuzsanna E. *The Holy Book of Women's Mysteries, Part 1.* Oakland, CA: Susan B. Anthony Coven No. 1, 1979.

Campanelli, Pauline. *Wheel of the Year: Living the Magical Life.* St. Paul, MN: Llewellyn Publications, 1989.

Chapple, Christopher Key, ed. *Jainism and Ecology: Nonviolence in the Web of Life.* Cambridge, MA: Harvard University Press, 2002.

Christ, Carol. *Rebirth of the Goddess: Finding Meaning in Feminist Spirituality.* Reading, MA: Addison-Wesley, 1997.

———. "Why Women Need the Goddess: Phenomenological, Psychological, and Political Reflections." In *The Politics of Women's Spirituality: Essays on the Rise of Spiritual Power within the Feminist Movement,* edited by Charlene Spretnak. Garden City, NY: Anchor Books, 1982.

Christ, Carol P. *She Who Changes: Re-imagining the Divine in the World.* New York: Palgrave Macmillan, 2004.

Circle Magazine. "Lady Liberty League Report." *Circle Magazine* 88, 89 (2003). www.circlesanctuary.org/liberty/report (accessed September 24, 2004).

Circle Magazine. "Lady Liberty League Report." *Circle Magazine* 90 (2003). www.circlesanctuary.org/liberty/report (accessed September 24, 2004).

Clifton, Chas S. "Fort Hood's Wiccans and the Problem of Pacifism." Paper presented at the annual meeting of the American Academy of Religion, Nashville, Tennessee, November 20, 2000.

———. *Her Hidden Children: The Rise of Wicca and Contemporary Paganism in America.* Lanham, MD: AltaMira, 2006.

———. "Tents, Not Cathedrals: An Argument against Paid Clergy." *The View from Hardscrabble Creek* 2 (March 1993).

———. "Witches and the Earth." In *Witchcraft Today, Book One: The Modern Craft Movement*, edited by Chas S. Clifton, 123–32. St. Paul, MN: Llewellyn Publications, 1992.

Clifton, Chas S., and Graham Harvey. *The Paganism Reader*. New York: Routledge, 2004.

CNN (Time Warner). "Supreme Court: Prisons Must Accommodate Religions." May 31, 2005. www.cnn.com/2005/LAW/05/31/scotus.prison.religion (accessed September 5, 2005).

Cohn, Norman Rufus Colin. *Europe's Inner Demons: An Enquiry Inspired by the Great Witch-hunt*. New York: New American Library, 1975.

Corcoran, Kevin. "Judge: Parents Can't Teach Pagan Beliefs." *Indystar.com*: the online edition of the *Indianapolis Star*, May 26, 2005.

Corrigan, Ian, et al. ADF Dedicant Program. Document produced by Ár nDraíocht Féin: A Druid Fellowship, 1997.

Coughlin, John J. *Out of the Shadows: An Exploration of Dark Paganism and Magick*. Blooming-ton, IN: Authorhouse, 2002.

Council for a Parliament of the World's Religions. 2002. www.cpwr.org (accessed September 28, 2004).

Coyne, Brendan. "Court Approves Wicca for Kids, Dodges Constitutional Issue." *New Stan-dard*, August 19, 2005. http://newstandardnews.net/content/?action=show_item& itemid=2250&= (accessed August 31, 2005.)

Crossley-Holland, Kevin. *The Penguin Book of Norse Myths: Gods of the Vikings*. London: Pen-guin Books, 1980.

Crowley, Aleister. *The Book of the Law*. York Beach, ME: Samuel Weiser, 1976.

———. "Hymn to Pan." In *Liber Aba*. 2nd rev. ed., 4:121–22. York Beach, ME: Samuel Weiser, 1997.

Crowley, Vivianne. *Wicca: The Old Religion in the New Age*. London: Aquarian, 1989. Reprinted as *Wicca: The Old Religion in the New Millennium*. London: Thorsons, 1996.

Cuhulain, Kerr. *Law Enforcement Guide to Wicca*. Victoria, British Columbia: Horned Owl Publishing, 1989.

Cunningham, Scott. *Living Wicca: A Further Guide for the Solitary Practitioner*. St. Paul, MN: Llewellyn Publications, 1993.

———. *Wicca: A Guide for the Solitary Practitioner*. St. Paul, MN: Llewellyn Publications, 1988.

Cunningham, Scott, and David Harrington. *The Magical Household: Spells & Rituals for the Home*. St. Paul, MN: Llewellyn Publications, 2003.

D'Apremont, Anne-Laure Ferlat, et al. "The Nature of the Divine: Transcendence and Im-manence in Contemporary Pagan Theology." *The Pomegranate: The Journal of Pagan Studies* 16 (2001): 4–16.

Davy, Barbara Jane. "Nature" In *The Encyclopedia of Modern Witchcraft and Neo-Paganism*, edited by Shelly Rabinovitch and James Lewis, 165–66. New York: Citadel, 2002.

———. "Nature Religion." In *The Encyclopedia of Religion and Nature*, edited by Bron Taylor, 2:1173–75. London: Continuum International, 2005.

de Angeles, Ly. *When I See the Wild God: Encountering Urban Celtic Witchcraft*. St. Paul, MN: Llewellyn Publications, 2004.

de Lint, Charles. *The Ivory and the Horn*. New York: Tor (Tom Doherty Associates), 1995.

Dewr, Dagonet. "The Vibe" (editorial). *New Witch* 7 (2004): 1.

diZerega, Gus. *Pagans & Christians: The Personal Spiritual Experience*. St. Paul, MN: Llewellyn Publications, 2001.

Doyle, Tom, Jr. "More from Pagans in Prison." Letter to the editor published in *PanGaia* 39 (2004): 9.

Drew, A. J. *Wicca for Men: A Handbook for Male Pagans Seeking a Spiritual Path*. New York: Citadel Press, 1998.

Durkheim, Emile. *The Elementary Forms of Religious Life*. New York: Free Press, 1965.

Ehrenreich, Barbara, and Deidre English. *Witches, Midwives, and Nurses: A History of Women Healers.* Oyster Bay, NY: Glass Mountain Pamphlets, 1973.

Eilers, Dana D. *Pagans and the Law: Understand Your Rights.* Franklin Lakes, NJ: New Page Books, 2003.

Eller, Cynthia. *Living in the Lap of the Goddess: The Feminist Spirituality Movement in America.* Boston: Beacon Press, 1995.

———. *The Myth of Matriarchal Prehistory: Why an Invented Past Won't Give Women a Future.* Boston: Beacon Press, 2000.

Ellwood, Robert S. *Religious and Spiritual Groups in Modern America.* Englewood Cliffs, NJ: Prentice Hall, 1973.

Enstrom-Waters, Jacqueline, and Jason Pitzl-Waters. "When Goth and Pagan Collide." *New Witch* 3 (2003). www.newwitch.com/archives/03spring/index.html (accessed September 23, 2004).

Epistates. Hellenion website. 2004. www.hellenion.org (accessed August 16, 2004).

Ezzy, Douglas. "The Commodification of Witchcraft." *Australian Religion Studies Review* 14 (2001): 31–44.

———. "New Age Witchcraft? Popular Spell Books and the Re-enchantment of Everyday Life." *Culture and Religion* 4 (2003): 47–65.

———. "Religious Ethnography: Practicing the Witch's Craft." In *Researching Paganisms: Religious Experiences and Academic Methodologies*, edited by Jenny Blain, Douglas Ezzy, and Graham Harvey. Walnut Creek, CA: AltaMira Press, 2004.

Farrar, Stewart, and Janet Farrar. *A Witches' Bible: The Complete Witches' Handbook.* Custer, WA: Phoenix Publishing, 1996.

Foucault, Michel. "On Popular Justice: A Discussion with Maoists." In *Power/Knowledge: Selected Interviews and Other Writings 1972–1977*, 1–36. New York: Pantheon Books, 1980.

Fox, Selena. "Bridges: Pagans at the Parliament." *Circle Magazine* 91 (2004): 34–35.

Frazer, James George. *The Golden Bough.* 2 Vols. 3rd ed. London: Macmillan, 1911.

———. *The New Golden Bough: A New Abridgment of the Classic Work.* Edited by Theodor H. Gaster. New York: Criterion Books, 1959.

Frew, Donald. "Methodological Flaws in Recent Studies of Historical and Modern Witchcraft." *Ethnologies* 20 (1998): 33–63.

Frost, Gavin, and Yvonne Frost. *Good Witch's Bible.* New Bern, NC: Godolphin House, 1999.

Gadon, Elinor W. "Gaia Consciousness: Ecological Wisdom for the Renewal of Life on Our Planet." In *The Once and Future Goddess: A Symbol for Our Time*, 341–68. San Francisco: Harper & Row, 1989.

Gardner, Gerald. *Witchcraft Today.* 1954. Secaucus, NJ: Citadel, 1973.

Gardner, Gerald Brosseau. *The Meaning of Witchcraft.* New York: Magical Childe Publishing, 1959.

Gibbons, Jenny. "Recent Developments in the Study of the Great European Witch Hunt." *The Pomegranate: A New Journal of Neopagan Thought* 5 (1998): 2–16.

Gimbutas, Marija. *The Civilization of the Goddess.* San Francisco: Harper & Row, 1991.

———. *The Language of the Goddess.* New York: HarperSanFrancisco, 1991.

Ginzburg, Carlo. *Ecstasies: Deciphering the Witches' Sabbath.* Translated by Raymond Rosenthal. New York: Penguin, 1991.

Goldenberg, Naomi R. *Changing of the Gods.* Boston: Beacon Press, 1979.

Grahame, Kenneth. *The Wind in the Willows.* London: Puffin Books, 1994.

Graves, Robert. *The White Goddess: A Historical Grammar of Poetic Myth.* London: Faber & Faber, 1948.

Griffin, Wendy. "The Deosil Dance." In *Researching Paganisms: Religious Experiences and Academic Methodologies*, edited by Jenny Blain, Douglas Ezzy, and Graham Harvey. Walnut Creek, CA: AltaMira Press, 2004.

———. "The Embodied Goddess: Feminist Witchcraft and Female Divinity." *Sociology of Religion* 56 (1995): 35–49.

———. "Goddess Spirituality and Wicca." In *Her Voice, Her Faith: Women Speak on World Religions,* edited by Arvind Sharma and Katherine K. Young, 243–81. Boulder, CO: Westview Press, 2004.

———, ed. *Daughters of the Goddess: Studies of Healing, Identity, and Empowerment.* Walnut Creek: AltaMira, 2000.

Guédon, Marie-Françoise. *Le Rêve et la Forêt : Histoires de Chamanes chez les Nabesnas et Leurs Voisins.* Quebec: Presses de l'Université Laval, 2004.

Gypsy. "The Charge of the Crone." Tryskelion, edited by Lady Shayra, 2000. www.Tryskelion.com (accessed June 24, 2004).

G'Zell, Otter, and Morning Glory. "Who on Earth Is the Goddess?" In *Magical Religion and Modern Witchcraft,* edited by James R. Lewis. Albany: State University of New York Press, 1996.

Hallowell, A. Irving. "Ojibwa Ontology Behaviour and World View." In *Primitive Views of the World,* edited by Stanley Diamond, 49–82. New York: Columbia University Press, 1969.

Hanegraaff, Wouter J. *New Age Religion and Western Culture.* Leiden, The Netherlands: Brill, 1997.

Hardie, T. *Hocus Pocus: Titania's Book of Spells.* London: Quadrille, 1996.

Hardman, Charlotte, and Graham Harvey, eds. *Paganism Today.* London: Thorsons (HarperCollins), 1996.

Harner, Michael. *The Way of the Shaman.* New York: HarperSanFrancisco, 1990.

Harris, Adrian. "Sacred Ecology." In *Paganism Today,* edited by Charlotte Hardman and Graham Harvey, 149–56. London: Thorsons (HarperCollins), 1996.

Harvey, Graham. *Contemporary Paganism: Listening People, Speaking Earth.* New York: New York University Press, 1997.

———. "Fantasy in the Study of Religions: Paganism as Observed and Enhanced by Terry Pratchett." *Diskus* 6 (2000), Web edition. http://web.uni-marburg.de/religionswissenschaft/journal/diskus (accessed June 8, 2003).

———. "Pagan Studies or the Study of Paganisms? A Case Study in the Study of Religions." In *Researching Paganisms: Religious Experiences and Academic Methodologies,* edited by Jenny Blain, Douglas Ezzy, and Graham Harvey. Walnut Creek, CA: AltaMira Press, 2004.

———, ed. *Shamanism: A Reader.* London: Routledge, 2003.

Heelas, Paul. *The New Age Movement.* Oxford: Blackwell, 1996.

Heinlein, Robert. *Stranger in a Strange Land.* New York: G. P. Putnam's Sons (Penguin), 1991.

Heselton, Philip. *Gerald Gardner and the Cauldron of Inspiration.* Milverton, UK: Capall Bann, 2003.

———. *Wiccan Roots: Gerald Gardner and the Modern Witchcraft Revival.* Freshfields, UK: Capall Bann, 2000.

Hesiod. *Theogony and Works and Days.* Translated by M. L. West. Oxford: Oxford University Press, 1988.

House of Netjer. "What Is Kemetic Orthodoxy?" Kemetic Orthodoxy website, July 8, 2001. www.kemet.org/kemexp1.html (accessed August 16, 2004).

Hughes, Philip, and Sharon Bond. "The Status and Increased Following of Nature Religions in Australia." *On Line Opinion: Australia's E-Journal of Social and Political Debate,* September 29, 2003. www.onlineopinion.com.au/view.asp?article=756 (accessed March 1, 2004). Edited version of an article first published in the Christian Research Association bulletin, *Pointers* 13, no. 2 (June 2003).

Hume, Lynne. *Witchcraft and Paganism in Australia.* Melbourne, Australia: Melbourne University Press, 1997.

Hutton, Ronald. "Living with Witchcraft." In *Researching Paganisms: Religious Experiences and Academic Methodologies,* edited by Jenny Blain, Douglas Ezzy, and Graham Harvey. Walnut Creek, CA: AltaMira Press, 2004.

——. *Stations of the Sun: A History of the Ritual Year in Britain*. Oxford: Oxford University Press, 1996.

——. *The Triumph of the Moon: A History of Modern Pagan Witchcraft*. Oxford: Oxford University Press, 1999.

Ivakhiv, Adrian. "In Search of Deeper Identities: Neopaganism and Native Faith in Contemporary Ukraine." *Nova Religio: The Journal of Alternative and Emergent Religions* 8, no. 3 (March 2005): 7–38.

——. "Whose Nature? The Transcendental Signified of an Emerging Field." *The Pomegranate: A New Journal of Neopagan Thought* 8 (1999): 14–20.

Ivakhiv, Adrian J. *Claiming Sacred Ground: Pilgrims and Politics at Glastonbury and Sedona*. Bloomington: Indiana University Press, 2001.

James, William Closson. *Locations of the Sacred: Essays on Religion, Literature, and Canadian Culture*. Waterloo, ON: Wilfrid Laurier Press, 1998.

Jayran, Shan. "Thealogy." Wikipedia: The Free Encyclopedia, 2004. http://en.wikipedia.org/wiki/Thealogy (accessed November 15, 2004).

Johnston, Jennifer. "Jedi, Our Fourth Religion . . . Thanks to the Pagans." *Sunday Herald Online*, March 28, 2004. www.sundayherald.com (accessed March 30, 2004).

Jones, Prudence, and Nigel Pennick. *A History of Pagan Europe*. London: Routledge, 1995.

Jorgensen, Danny L., Lin Jorgensen, and Scott Russell. "American Neopaganism: The Participants' Social Identities." *Journal for the Scientific Study of Religion* 38 (1999): 325–38.

Jung, Fritz. "What Is a Witch War?" *The Witches' Voice*, January 4, 1998. www.witchvox.com/wars/ww_whatis.html (accessed September 20, 2004).

Kaplan, Jeffrey. "The Reconstruction of the Ásatrú and Odinist Traditions." In *Magical Religion and Modern Witchcraft*, edited by James R. Lewis, 193–236. Albany: State University of New York Press, 1996.

Kelly, Aiden. *Crafting the Art of Magic: A History of Modern Witchcraft, 1939–1964*. St. Paul, MN: Llewellyn Publications, 1991.

——. *Hippie Commie Beatnik Witches: A History of the Craft in California, 1967–1977*. Canoga Park, CA: Art Magical Publications, 1993.

Klassen, Chris. "Storied Selves: Technologies of Identity in Feminist Witchcraft's Thealogy and Fiction." Doctoral thesis, York University, Toronto, 2006.

Lammond, Federic. "Memories of Gerald Gardner." In *Celebrating the Pagan Soul: Our Own Stories of Inspiration and Community*, edited by Laura A. Wildman. New York: Citadel Press, 2005.

Larner, Christina. *Enemies of God: The Witch-hunt in Scotland*. Baltimore, MD: Johns Hopkins University Press, 1981.

Le Guin, Ursula. *A Wizard of Earthsea*. London: Puffin Books, 1968.

Leland, Charles G. *Aradia: Or the Gospel of the Witches*. New York: Samuel Weiser, 1974.

Letcher, Andy. "Bardism and the Performance of Paganism: Implications for the Performance of Research." In *Researching Paganisms: Religious Experiences and Academic Methodologies*, edited by Jenny Blain, Douglas Ezzy, and Graham Harvey. Walnut Creek, CA: AltaMira Press, 2004.

——. "'Virtual Paganism' or Direct Action? The Implications of Road Protesting for Modern Paganism." *Diskus* 6 (2000), Web edition. http://web.uni-marburg.de/religionswissenschaft/journal/diskus (accessed May 16, 2001).

Levack, Brian. *The Witch Hunt in Early Modern Europe*. London: Longman, 1987.

Lewis, James R. "Appendix: Numbering Neo-Pagans." In *The Encyclopedia of Modern Witchcraft and Neo-Paganism*, edited by Shelly Rabinovitch and James Lewis, 303–11. New York: Citadel, 2002.

——, ed. *Magical Religion and Modern Witchcraft*. Albany: State University of New York Press, 1996.

Lovelock, James E. *Gaia: A New Look at Life on Earth*. Oxford: Oxford University Press, 1982.

Luhrmann, Tanya M. *Persuasions of the Witch's Craft*. Cambridge, MA: Harvard University Press, 1989.

MacKillop, James, ed. "Ceridwen," "Taliesin." In *Dictionary of Celtic Mythology*, 76, 353–54. Oxford: Oxford University Press, 1998.

Magliocco, Sabina. *Witching Culture: Folklore and Neo-Paganism in America*. Philadelphia: University of Pennsylvania Press, 2004.

Malinowski, Bronislaw. *Magic, Science, and Religion, and Other Essays*. Garden City, NY: Dover, 1954.

Marron, Kevin. *Witches, Pagans & Magic in the New Age*. Toronto: Seal Books (McClelland-Bantam), 1989.

McKennitt, Loreena. "Stolen Child." *Elemental*, 1985. Stratford: Warner Music Canada, 1994.

Melton, Gordon. *Encyclopedia of American Religions*. Detroit, MI: Gale Research, 2002.

———. *Encyclopedic Handbook of Cults in America*. New York: Garland Publishing, 1984.

Melton, Gordon J. *An Iona Anthology*. Isle of Iona, Argyll: New Iona Press, 1990.

Miyazaki, Hayao. *Princess Mononoke*. VHS. Directed by Hayao Miyazaki. Miramax Films, 2000.

Moondrip, Lady Pixie. "Lady Pixie Moondrip's Guide to Craft Names." *Widdershins*, 2004. www.widdershins.org/vol3iss4/m9710.htm (accessed June 24, 2004).

Murray, Margaret. *The God of the Witches*. London: Samson Low, 1933. Reissued, Oxford: Oxford University Press, 1970.

Murray, Margaret Alice. *The Witch-Cult in Western Europe: A Study in Anthropology*. Oxford: Clarendon (Oxford University Press), 1921.

NatRel. Electronic discussion group of the Nature Religions Scholars Network. September 2004.

New Witch. "Rant and Rave." *New Witch* 7 (2004): 5–13.

Nova Roma. "Declaratio Religionis Romanae." *Nova Roma*. 2004. www.novaroma.org/religio_romana/declaration_religio.html (accessed August 16, 2004).

Pagan Alliance. *Pagan Alliance, Inc.* 2001. http://paganalliance.lasielle.net/index.html (accessed May 14, 2004).

Pagan Federation. *The Pagan Federation*. 2003–2004. www.paganfed.org (accessed May 14, 2004).

Pagan Unity Campaign. 2004. www.paganunitycampaign.org (accessed September 28, 2004).

PanGaia. "Toe-to-Toe: A Forum for Controversy and Opinion." *PanGaia* 39 (2004): 13–16.

Paxson, Diana. "The Matronæ." Hrafnar website. www.hrafnar.org/goddesses/matronae.html (accessed April 22, 2004). Originally published in *Sage Woman*, Fall 1999.

Paxson, Diana L. "The Religion of the North." Hrafnar website, 1996. www.hrafnar.org/norse/tract.html (accessed April 22, 2004).

———. "Worshipping the Gods." Hrafnar website. www.hrafnar.org/norse/worship.html (accessed April 22, 2004). Originally published in *Idunna* 20 (1993).

Pearson, Joanne, ed. *Belief Beyond Boundaries: Wicca, Celtic Spirituality and the New Age*. Aldershot, UK: Ashgate, 2002.

Pearson, Joanne, Richard H. Roberts, and Geoffrey Samuel. *Nature Religion Today: Paganism in the Modern World*. Edinburgh, UK: Edinburgh University Press, 1998.

Pearson, Jo E. "'Going Native in Reverse': The Insider as Research in British Wicca." In *Theorizing Faith: The Insider/Outsider Problem in the Study of Ritual*, edited by E. Arweck and M. D. Stringer. Birmingham, UK: University of Birmingham Press, 2002.

PFPC. *Pagan Federation/Fédération Païenne Canada*. 2004. www.pfpc.ca (accessed May 14, 2004).

Pike, Sarah M. *Earthly Bodies, Magical Selves: Contemporary Pagans and the Search for Community*. Berkeley: University of California Press, 2001.

———. "Forging Magical Selves: Gendered Bodies and Ritual Fires at Neo-Pagan Festivals." In *Magical Religion and Modern Witchcraft*, edited by James R. Lewis, 121–39. Albany: State University of New York Press, 1996.

———. "Gleanings from the Field: Leftover Tales of Grief and Desire." In *Researching Paganisms: Religious Experiences and Academic Methodologies*, edited by Jenny Blain, Douglas Ezzy, and Graham Harvey. Walnut Creek, CA: AltaMira Press, 2004.

Pitzl-Waters, Jason, and Jacqueline Enstrom-Waters. "Dark Paganism with John Coughlin." *New Witch* 6 (2004). www.newwitch.com/archives/06/read/dark.html (accessed September 29, 2004).

Pratchett, Terry. *Small Gods*. London: Corgi Books, 1992.

Purkiss, Diane. *The Witch in History: Early Modern and Twentieth-Century Representations*. London: Routledge, 1996.

Rabinovitch, Shelly. "'An' Ye Harm None, Do What Ye Will': Neo-Pagans and Witches in Canada." Master's thesis, Carleton University, Ottawa, 1992.

Rabinovitch, Shelly, and James Lewis, eds. *Encyclopedia of Modern Witchcraft and Neo-Paganism*. New York: Citadel, 2002.

Rabinovitch, Shelly, and Meredith MacDonald. *An Ye Harm None: Magical Morality and Modern Ethics*. New York: Citadel, 2004.

Raphael, Melissa. *Thealogy and Embodiment*. Sheffield, UK: Sheffield Academic Press, 1997.

Read, Donna. *The Burning Times*. VHS. Directed by Donna Read. National Film Board of Canada, 1990.

Rees, Alwyn, and Brinley Rees. *Celtic Heritage: Ancient Tradition in Ireland and Wales*. London: Thames & Hudson, 1961.

Rees, Kenneth. "The Tangled Skein: The Role of Myth in Paganism." In *Paganism Today*, edited by Charlotte Hardman and Graham Harvey, 16–31. London: Thorsons (HarperCollins), 1996.

Reid, Lee MacDonald Síân. "Disorganized Religion: An Exploration of the Neopagan Craft in Canada." Doctoral thesis, Carleton University, Ottawa, 2001.

Reid, Síân. "Witch Wars: Factors Contributing to Conflict in Canadian Neopagan Communities." *The Pomegranate: A New Journal of Neopagan Thought* 11 (2000): 10–20.

Rose, Elliot. *A Razor for a Goat: A Discussion of Certain Problems in the History of Witchcraft and Diabolism*. Toronto: University of Toronto Press, 1962.

Rountree, Kathryn. *Embracing the Witch and the Goddess: Feminist Ritual-Makers in New Zealand*. London: Routledge, 2004.

Sage Woman. "The Rattle." *Sage Woman* 65 (2004): 83–90.

Salomonsen, Jone. *Enchanted Feminism: The Reclaiming Witches of San Francisco*. London: Routledge, 2002.

———. "Methods of Compassion or Pretension? The Challenges of Conducting Fieldwork in Modern Magical Communities." In *Researching Paganisms: Religious Experiences and Academic Methodologies*, edited by Jenny Blain, Douglas Ezzy, and Graham Harvey. Walnut Creek, CA: AltaMira Press, 2004.

Samhain, Michael. "Defending the Craft." *New Witch* 6 (2004). www.newwitch.com/archives/06/read/defending.html (accessed September 24, 2004).

Schlegel, Friedrich. *Lucinde and the Fragments*. Translated by Peter Firchow. Minneapolis: University of Minnesota Press, 1971.

Schnoebelen, William. *Wicca: Satan's Little White Lie*. Ontario, CA: Chick Publications, 1990.

Shaw, Sylvie. "At the Water's Edge: An Ecologically Inspired Methodology." In *Researching Paganisms: Religious Experiences and Academic Methodologies*, edited by Jenny Blain, Douglas Ezzy, and Graham Harvey. Walnut Creek, CA: AltaMira Press, 2004.

Shelley, Percy Bysshe. *The Oxford Book of English Verse: 1250–1900*. Edited by Arthur Quiller-Couch. Oxford: Clarendon Press, 1919. www.bartleby.com/101/605.html (accessed June 8, 2003).

Smith, Andy. "For All Those Who Were Indian in a Former Life." In *Ecofeminism and the Sacred*, edited by Carol J. Adams, 168–71. New York: Continuum, 1993.

Spretnak, Charlene. "Toward an Ecofeminist Spirituality." In *Healing the Wounds: The Promise of Ecofeminism*, edited by Judith Plant, 127–32. Toronto: Between the Lines, 1989.

———. "Ecofeminism: Our Roots and Flowering." In *Reweaving the World: The Emergence of Ecofeminism*, edited by Irene Diamond and Gloria Feman Orenstein, 3–14. San Francisco: Sierra Club Books, 1990.

———, ed. *The Politics of Women's Spirituality: Essays on the Rise of Spiritual Power within the Feminist Movement*. Garden City, NY: Anchor Books (Doubleday), 1982.

Starhawk. *Dreaming the Dark: Magic, Sex and Politics*. New edition. London: Mandala (Unwin Paperbacks), 1990.

———. "Ethics and Justice in Goddess Religion." In *The Politics of Women's Spirituality: Essays on the Rise of Spiritual Power within the Feminist Movement*, edited by Charlene Spretnak, 415–22. Garden City, NY: Anchor Books (Doubleday), 1982.

———. *The Fifth Sacred Thing*. New York: Bantam, 1993.

———. *The Spiral Dance: A Rebirth of the Ancient Religion of the Great Goddess*. 10th anniversary ed. 1979. New York: HarperSanFrancisco, 1989.

———. *Truth or Dare: Encounters with Power, Authority, and Mystery*. New York: HarperSanFrancisco, 1987.

———. *Webs of Power: Notes from the Global Uprising*. Gabriola Island, British Columbia: New Society Publishers, 2002.

Starhawk, Diane Baker, and Anne Hill. *Circle Round: Raising Children in Goddess Traditions*. New York: Bantam, 1998.

Starhawk, M. Macha Nightmare, and the Reclaiming Collective. *The Pagan Book of Living and Dying: Practical Rituals, Prayers, Blessings, and Meditations on Crossing Over*. San Francisco: HarperSanFrancisco, 1997.

Starwoman, Athena, and Deborah Gray. *How to Turn your Ex-Boyfriend into a Toad and Other Spells for Love, Wealth, Beauty and Revenge*. Sydney: HarperCollins, 1996.

Statistics Canada. *2001 Census*. Statistics Canada website, 2001. http://www12.statcan.ca/english/census01/products/highlight/Religion/PR_Menu1.cfm?Lang=E (accessed March 1, 2004).

Stone, Lauryl. "Rant and Rave." *New Witch* 5 (2004): 5.

Strmiska, Michael. "Asatru in Iceland: Ásatrúarfélagid." In *The Encyclopedia of Modern Witchcraft and Neo-Paganism*, edited by Shelley Rabinovitch and James Lewis, 16. New York: Citadel, 2002.

———. "The Music of the Past in Modern Baltic Paganism." *Nova Religio: The Journal of Alternative and Emergent Religions* 8 (2005).

Teish, Luisah. *Jambalaya: The Natural Woman's Book of Personal Charms and Practical Rituals*. New York: HarperSanFrancisco, 1985.

Tolkien, J. R. R. *The Lord of the Rings*. London: HarperCollins, 1995.

Torgerson, Drowynn Forrest. "Elder Ritual for Men." *PanGaia* 39 (2004): 57–59.

Troth. *The Ring of Troth Official Home Page*. 1995–2004. www.thetroth.org (accessed May 14, 2004).

Valiente, Doreen. *The Rebirth of Witchcraft*. Custer, WA: Phoenix Publishing, 1989.

Wallis, Robert J. "Between the Worlds: Autoarchaeology and Neo-Shamans." In *Researching Paganisms: Religious Experiences and Academic Methodologies*, edited by Jenny Blain, Douglas Ezzy, and Graham Harvey. Walnut Creek, CA: Alta-Mira Press, 2004.

———. *Shamans/Neo-Shamans: Ecstasy, Alternative Archaeologies and Contemporary Pagans*. London: Routledge, 2003.

Willow, Vibra. "A Brief History of Reclaiming." Reclaiming website. www.reclaiming.org (accessed May 14, 2004). Earlier version published in *Reclaiming Quarterly* 76 (Fall 1999).

Windling, Terri. *The Wood Wife*. New York: Tor (Tom Doherty Associates), 1996.

Windwalker. "Lady Liberty League Report." *Circle Magazine* 91 (2004): 53–55.

Wittig, Monique. *Les Guérillières*. Boston: Beacon Press, 1985.

York, Michael. "Defining Paganism." *The Pomegranate: A New Journal of Neopagan Thought* 11 (2000): 4–9.

———. *The Emerging Network: A Sociology of the New Age and Neo-Pagan Movements*. Lanham, MD: Rowman & Littlefield, 1995.

———. *Pagan Theology: Paganism as a World Religion*. New York: New York University Press, 2003.

Young, D. E., and J. G. Goulet, eds. *Being Changed: The Anthropology of Extraordinary Experience*. Peterborough, ON: Broadview Press, 1994.

Index

About the Author

Barbara Jane Davy holds a Ph.D. in religion from Concordia University, Montreal. She has been engaged in the academic study of Paganism for more than ten years, and has written articles on Paganism, shamanism, and nature religion that have been published in refereed journals and encyclopedias. She has taught in the area of religion and ecology at Concordia University and Carleton University.